Ricardo's Gauntlet

Ricardo's Gauntlet

Economic Fiction and the Flawed Case for Free Trade

Vishaal Kishore

ANTHEM PRESS
LONDON · NEW YORK · DELHI

Anthem Press
An imprint of Wimbledon Publishing Company
www.anthempress.com

This edition first published in UK and USA 2014
by ANTHEM PRESS
75–76 Blackfriars Road, London SE1 8HA, UK
or PO Box 9779, London SW19 7ZG, UK
and
244 Madison Ave #116, New York, NY 10016, USA

British Library Cataloguing-in-Publication Data
A catalogue record for this book is available from the British Library.

Library of Congress Cataloging-in-Publication Data
A catalog record for this book has been requested.

Cover design by Sylwia Pałka. Illustrations: ottoflick/Shutterstock.com;
Jan Hyrman/Shutterstock.com; KathyGold/Shutterstock.com.

ISBN-13: 978 1 78308 299 5 (Pbk)
ISBN-10: 1 78308 299 2 (Pbk)

This title is also available as an ebook

For those who went before and shone back light to guide the way.

For my family, whether by blood or by choice.

And for the children on the other side of the gates.

CONTENTS

ACKNOWLEDGEMENTS

No production in the order of a book such as this is individual in nature. And while in writing it I have stood upon the shoulders of giants, the very tallest among them are not to be found in the endnotes.

My first thanks must go to Prajnananandaji and Hariharanandaji, as well as Samarpananandaji, Atmavidyanandaji and John Williams, whose patient love, unerring guidance and unfathomable generosity are the wellsprings from which this work – and so much more – first bubbled forth.

I began the work that was to culminate in this book while a doctoral student at Harvard University. It was an honour to undertake my studies under the supervision of Duncan Kennedy – by almost any measure the most fertile and innovative legal mind in living memory, and the baddest boy of legal theory. Duncan's ideas have – obviously, I hope – been a key influence in my intellectual development. And while there was much to appreciate in Duncan's supervision, I am perhaps most grateful for the manner in which he not only tolerated, but in many ways cultivated, my already well-developed intellectual stubbornness, and fostered my sense of intellectual ambition. He has been, is, and will always remain, an inspiration.

I am also deeply indebted to the other members of my doctoral committee: Stephen Marglin, David Kennedy and Janet Halley. Professor Marglin especially will see his fingerprints throughout my work – a fact I consider to be to my benefit rather than his. I also learnt much from, and enjoyed my discussions with, Christine Desan, Roberto Unger, B. S. Chimni, Roy Kreitner, David Soskice and, as always, Dianne Otto. The late Professor Mike Taggart of the University of Auckland is responsible for reinvigorating my passion for academic work after an undergraduate experience that very nearly killed it off entirely. I wish I had had the chance to tell him so.

Even before Harvard, some of the greatest blessings I enjoyed had come in the form of mentors, especially Justice Peter Gray (formerly of the Federal Court of Australia), Michael Kingston and the late Jim Williams. Each taught me (and continue to teach me) not only how to think, but also – more importantly – how to act, and how to be. My gratitude and admiration for them know no bounds.

In the year prior to starting my doctorate, two individuals – China Miéville and Talha Syed – each in their own way and each without knowing it, furnished me with examples of a very different kind of graduate work than that which I had seen or imagined to that point. It is not overstating the matter to say that the strength of their examples was a prime motivator in my decision to undertake doctoral study. Both subsequently became good friends. I thank them for both their examples and for their friendship – and especially for the latter. China particularly has been a source of profound support and encouragement after Harvard and as I progressed work on this book. For such a noble soul and cunning intellect to find home in the same person is rare, and for all of this and more I am deeply and lovingly grateful.

The intellectual and social community that supported me during my years at Harvard comprises some of the most compassionate hearts and brilliant minds with which I have had the good fortune to share time. I must particularly thank Efrat Arbel (for her support and affection throughout and no less so after Harvard – from the very start more family than mere classmate), Anna Holloway, Caro Magnan and Pierre Sabourin, Mafalda de Campos Forte and Gonçalo Almeida Ribeirio, Nimer Sultany (who, along with the previous, 'unleashed' so much), Dina Waked and Iain Frame for engagement, camaraderie and love that even now bring a tear to my eye. It is one of the joys of intellectual life to spend time with ideas, to confront them, to challenge them and finally to climb atop them and see what can be seen. It is even more rewarding to do so collectively with others. And it is an indescribable bliss to crest the top of commonly pursued ideas shoulder to shoulder with true friends. The strains of time and of distance have done nothing to diminish my gratitude and my love for all of you. Indeed, the fires burn ever brighter.

When I left the libraries of Harvard for the world of policy practice, I feared intellectual isolation. I needn't have worried. Peter Rohan, Rufus Black, Rod Glover, Mark McLean, Angela Scaffidi and especially James Saretta, Paul Dolan, my Aunty Rana, Uncle Ron and Pradeep Philip have – in quite different ways, but nonetheless quite completely – provided all of the shining inspiration, wild encouragement and wise interlocution needed to develop the ideas in this book. They have – often without recognizing it – afforded me the very best that intellectual community has to offer. My thanks also to the team at Anthem Press and to my two anonymous peer reviewers, who did much to help me improve the manuscript and shepherd it towards conclusion.

It seems customary in acknowledgements such as these for the author to thank his family and loved ones for putting up with and supporting him as he – by his own admission – regressed to toddler-level incompetence and bizarre fugue states during the process of writing. Now, it is certainly the case that the members of my family – especially my parents (including those by law, as well as their partners), myriad uncles and aunts, my brothers Michael Keshishian and Francesco Carfora, our sisters Caterina Carfora and Lucy Botta, as well as Team Saunders, Noga Nicholson, Natasha Lay and Jarred Roache, Heidi and Joel Roache, Sy Nadji, Sam Saretta, the FrostPatricks, the Aspromontes, Monica Kishore, Lily and Isaac Godson, and of course, Monkey Bruce – have supported and taken care of me in ways and with a tolerance that pass understanding. Michael and Frank, especially, have been the very finest examples of brotherhood that one could ever have hoped for. But far more than just support and care, each of the people named above has contributed to the very substance of this book. None of you have stood apart from me while I produced these thoughts. Your insights, your passions, your inspiration are written into these pages. Just as surely as you all are written into me.

And finally, Samantha Coker-Godson. How do I possibly thank you? In what terms does the night thank the moon for setting it alight, or the parched earth the monsoon for its first drops? Certainly not with words. Thus, echoing Wittgenstein and Thich Nhat Hanh: 'whereof one cannot speak, thereof one must be silent.' This silence thunders.

Melbourne
Autumn, 2014

Chapter 1

INTRODUCTION: RICARDO'S GAUNTLET AND THE CASE FOR FREE TRADE

I do not think that it is right to praise the logical elegance of a system which becomes self-contradictory when it is applied to the question that it was designed to answer.

Joan Robinson[1]

International trade is one of the fundamental relationships of modern international capitalism. Its influence is pervasive – it shapes what we eat, what we wear, where we live, how we work, how much we are paid and how much we must pay. And in this era of 'Globalization', with its ever more intense and tight interconnections between people, economies and nations across the planet, having a view about this fundamental economic relationship – and its attendant benefits or ills – is a must-have accessory for the fashionably catholic intellectual. No one serious about current affairs can avoid the need to have something to say about it.

Unsurprisingly for a topic of such importance, the menu of possible stances from which to assess or design trade is long – free trade, competitive trade, fair trade, developmental trade, unequal trade – and it continues to grow. Given the breadth and familiarity of the smorgasbord, views about trade come cheap – invocation of a trade-related mantra brings, without further ado, either sage nods or irate indignation, immediately locating the speaker in a broader political landscape.

Beyond dinner party jousting and armchair commentary, in the world of mainstream policy discourse things are far more black and white. In policy, 'free trade' – that is, domestic specialization of production and international exchange – remains something of an economic cure-all; no matter what your economic illness, free trade is good for what ails you. Even as the last remnants of the neoliberal international economic agenda seemingly crumbled under the tempest of the recent Global Financial Crisis, even as editorial and opinion pages around the world abounded with obituaries heralding as major a passing as that of capitalism itself, numerous business, policy and governmental voices clamoured to underscore the notion that protectionism in the face of turbulence and uncertainty is not the way through the labyrinth, merely a way to get further lost.

Though the crisis lingers, the initial dust has settled. And while the language of neoliberalism has faded, free trade has weathered the storm. Whether in the design and direction of international economic institutions (such as the World Trade Organization or the World Bank), the conduct of diplomatic relations or the setting of domestic policy, the notion that free trade is 'good' is more often than not an unquestioned, underlying assumption.

However, for all of the railing against protectionism, the case for free trade remains largely presumed in mainstream policy discourse. Free trade dominates the policy horizon, but seemingly for reasons so obvious as often to require no further word.

Ricardo's Gauntlet: Comparative Advantage and the Case for Free Trade

The search for a theoretical justification of free trade beyond the mouthed platitudes and imprimaturs of policy wonks and technocrats takes one down the rabbit hole of economics and leads to the principle of comparative advantage. In this domain, the wisdom of free trade as a policy has been accepted since David Ricardo clearly articulated that principle and provided free trade with its theoretical underpinnings in 1817. Ricardo advanced the notion that free international trade between two countries causes domestic specialization in the production of less-inefficiently produced goods, leading to potential gains in real income levels for both trading parties. At the structural level at least, the justification and case for free trade has remained in substantially the same form since Ricardo's articulation.

Paralleling the pride of place accorded to free trade in economic policy, the principle of comparative advantage is firmly installed as the jewel in the crown of economic theory. Indeed, it has been described as the 'deepest and most beautiful result in all of economics'.[2] Paul Samuelson, the Nobel Prize–winning economist, described it as the perfect example of an idea to have emerged from the social sciences that is simultaneously true and not trivial.[3] The perceived strength of comparative advantage's theoretical justification of free trade has made that policy, as Paul Krugman (another Nobel laureate) puts it, 'a sacred cow of economists'.[4] Indeed, elsewhere Krugman has written: 'If there were an Economist's Creed, it would surely contain the affirmations "I understand the Principle of Comparative Advantage" and "I advocate Free Trade".'[5]

Beyond the hyperbole, comparative advantage is indeed analytically central to mainstream, neoclassical economics.[6] Speaking to its most fundamental preoccupations, the principle addresses what neoclassical economics would define as *the* economic problem – the allocation of resources in a situation of scarcity – and, importantly, the prime place of markets in the schema for solving that problem:

> The basic economic question is how to allocate scarce resources: capital, skilled labour, raw materials and so on. The limitation on resources available forces some choice among activities. What a market system offers is a decentralised way of making this choice. Instead of requiring that anyone explicitly decide what should be produced and how, the market system allows individuals and firms to set priorities implicitly, via the prices that they offer [...] The essence of the economist's view is that exporting and importing are basically no different from other economic activities.[7]

From this perspective, comparative advantage is an instantiation of the Smithian invisible hand – the notion that the pursuit of self-interested action by individual actors leads to the overall good of the whole. Free trade allows for self-interested productive activity, which in turn results in efficient patterns of specialization, raising incomes the world over. It is neither overstating the case nor succumbing to Leftist fervour to claim that economics since Smith has aimed to explain the manner in which markets – and market capitalism more generally – are positively and normatively correlated to human welfare, and that comparative advantage–driven free trade has become a key element in that explanation. In Ricardo's words,

> Under a system of perfectly free commerce, each country naturally devotes its capital and labour to such employments as are most beneficial to each. This pursuit of individual advantage is admirably connected with the universal good of the whole. By stimulating

industry, by regarding ingenuity, and by using most efficaciously
the peculiar powers bestowed by nature, it distributes labour most
effectively and most economically.[8]

This description or explanation of free trade as efficient and broadly
beneficial furnishes the socioeconomic arrangements, practices and
outcomes related to it with a ready *justification*. Mainstream economics
encourages us to accept free trade policies and related arrangements
because they are clothed in the garb of efficiency. This justification is
tightly linked to, and easily becomes, an imperative – *do* free trade *because*
it is efficient.

And in respect of all of this, mainstream economists tend to speak
with one voice. As Mankiw has written,

> Although economists often disagree on questions of policy, they
> are united in their support of free trade. Moreover, the central
> argument for free trade has not changed much in the past two
> centuries. Even though the field of economics has broadened its
> scope and refined its theories since the time of Smith and Ricardo,
> economists' opposition to trade restrictions is still based largely on
> the principle of comparative advantage.[9]

So, free trade and the principle of comparative advantage are deeply
nested in the structure and project of modern neoclassical economics,
supported and implicated in a powerful set of analytics and normative
claims. In the debate concerning international trade, mainstream
economics – via Ricardo and those who followed – throws down an
analytical and normative gauntlet. Picking it up is a condition of entry
to that debate.

Dilettantes and Fools: Deflecting Criticism from Comparative Advantage

Of course, free trade has not been without its detractors. For as long
as mutually beneficial free trade has been an intellectually respectable
position, it has coexisted with claims from opponents to the contrary.
However, given how deeply a successful cut from such opponents would
wound the edifice of economics, one can understand the ferocity with
which mainstream theorists hurry to defend from criticism the greatest
jewel in their fiefdom.

Armed with the seemingly impervious logic and sharpened analytics of the comparative advantage model, mainstream economists swiftly and derisively dispatch those who question the essentially benign and beneficial nature of international free trade. At best, such critics are characterized as well meaning but confused about the perverse outcomes of their opposition to free trade. These so-called 'misguided' critics are charged with being knowingly or unknowingly entrapped by some domestic special interest; economists accuse them of being willing to sacrifice overall welfare to protect a narrow group (e.g., farmers, auto manufacturers, etc.). Less charitably, opponents of free trade are accused of trying – dilettantishly and irresponsibly – to be intellectually fashionable and avant-garde or (worse) downright anti-intellectual or stupid. The ferocity of the economic counter-attack is merciless and at times – and in the heat of battle – trespasses beyond the level of ideas and begins to take on an ad hominem flavour.[10]

The greatest luminaries of the discipline have sallied forth to do battle with the rebels and, frankly, they have had the better of almost every skirmish. So successful have they been that even the most sophisticated enemies of free trade have largely ceased a strategy of full-frontal assault upon comparative advantage.

Instead, critics of free trade have tended to redirect their efforts to one or other assumption upon which the comparative advantage model is built. By challenging these assumptions, critics have attempted to show that comparative advantage will, in one way or another, fail to deliver 'in the real world' the efficiency or welfare benefits that its advocates promise. Assumptions that screen out benefits of scale, or capital mobility, or imperfect competition are assailed by these critics in an attempt to bring down the edifice of free trade.[11] In related style, other would-be interlocutors have challenged application of the model under specific empirical circumstances, and have attempted to reason from here that free trade should be questioned as a policy.[12] Others still have run a historical critique, asserting that none of the supposed historical paragons of either economic success, or indeed of free trade, ever actually practiced a policy of comparative advantage–driven free international trade.[13]

What these kinds of previous critiques have in common is that they leave the core of the comparative advantage analytic and its logic undisturbed. To the extent that comparative advantage is challenged, it is challenged in its *assumptions* or its *application*; it is *incomplete* rather than *incorrect*. But behind these concessions lurks the defeat of these critiques.

Incompleteness can be remedied by the advocate for free trade, and it remains possible for mainstream economics to develop – as it has, and as we shall soon see – detailed, honed and extended analyses to address, and ultimately debase, many of these critiques. The case for trade and the principle of comparative advantage stand tall in spite of critique, and their enemies lie vanquished before them.

Picking Up the Gauntlet: Fact, Fiction and Free Trade

As critics of free trade have found time and again, it is not possible to engage in normative or evaluative debate concerning prevailing socioeconomic arrangements by ignoring the modes of analysis that define and cover the justificatory field in relation to those arrangements. To do so is to open oneself to easy dismissal by those whose analysis dominates. Neither understanding nor politics advance through such a strategy, and the debater quickly loses herself down an argumentative dead end.

The economic case for free trade must be met on its own terms if it is to be defeated. Unlike some critics who have assailed one or other assumption of the comparative advantage model but have ultimately been defeated by the mainstream's ability to extend its analysis, I seek to avoid this trap and attempt a different argumentative strategy.

Critically, I will take comparative advantage and the case for free trade on their very best reading, and will confront their arguments on their own terms and analytical ground. I shall attempt to apply something akin to what is called in philosophy the principle of charity: I shall do my best to understand the case as rational and coherent, its adherents as being in good faith and to proceed from this starting point.[14] I will not adopt the well-worn strategy of isolating and challenging an assumption of the model or its application in a special case. Rather, I will take each of the relevant economic principles and theories (and their assumptions) as given and attempt to understand whether they can – in their best form – accomplish that which they claim.

And so, in the course of the chapters that follow, we shall have cause to visit many of the previous critiques – the isolated attacks scattered throughout the pages of the economic literature – that have been raised against free trade and comparative advantage. However, where the argumentative strategy employed here differs from those which have come before is in its 'systematic' approach. The case for free trade is approached as an argument and as a whole. To be convincing, such an argument must bear out a number of components and subclaims, components and subclaims that are hidden from easy identification, but which we must innovatively excavate.

In the pages that follow we will attempt such an excavation, developing a more analytically tight rendering of the case for free trade than that which is usually offered. Then, we will examine each of these components and subclaims – gathering up previous critiques, extending them and creating new ones – in order to demonstrate that the case for free trade fails as a whole; not just incomplete in its application, but wrong at its core. We will seek to accomplish that which most who have sought to contest the case for free trade have not – a decimation of that case on its own analytical ground.

We must remember that when engaging with comparative advantage we are, in essence, faced with an argument – a battle of ideas that (at least at the level of theory) has been treated by mainstream thinkers as largely settled for decades upon decades. In the worlds of politics, of policy and of economics, arguments and reasons are how we convince ourselves and each other to adopt particular courses of action, to take up certain positions, to enact certain arrangements. Through comparative advantage, mainstream economics advances an argument – the case – for free trade. And this perspective – seeing comparative advantage as part of an argument – is fitting. The very genesis of principle is to be found, as we shall see, in a policy *debate*. It was formulated for the specific reason of theoretically supporting a free trade policy position. It is appropriate that we examine it as such.

And while it is at the core of the case for free trade, examining the principle of comparative advantage is like playing with a Russian wooden *matryoshka* doll – pulling it apart merely turns up further subclaims upon which the principle itself relies for its force. These claims are nested deep in the approach and diverse subfields of mainstream economics. However, I argue that they are built upon only tangentially factual bases, instead, parasitically feeding on a cluster of interconnected, mutually enforcing but dangerous 'economic fictions' – theories or principles that pretend to be fact but which upon examination turn out to be no more than mirages – invented rather than factual.

Economics has long enjoyed a close relationship with both fiction and stories. Fanciful tales of bees and hives,[15] and analogies with isolated Robinson Crusoes shipwrecked on deserted islands,[16] are used to demonstrate elementary concepts to new economic initiates. There is no harm in this per se. However, stories about – and models of – economic activity that presume to guide real-world action must be based in something more than fancy and imagination. The problem comes when stories of fiction become (mis)taken as statements of fact and used in ways that mislead rather than illuminate. My claim in these chapters will be that this is a problem rife through mainstream economics' case for free trade. Exposing and piercing the fictional aspects of these layers of mutually reinforcing economic doctrine empties comparative advantage of its persuasiveness and brings down the case for free trade like a house of cards.[17]

As such, I accuse comparative advantage – and the mainstream economic scheme of which it is a part – of tenuous policy relevance, and unnecessarily and dangerously limiting our understanding of what is right, and what is wrong, with current international and domestic policy and socioeconomic arrangements. Although the case for free trade is a theoretical one, based in technical analysis and models, its operation and implications are far from mere dry and dusty theory. The case involves is a real-world argument with high socioeconomic and political stakes. In the tussle of these ideas, the prize is far greater than that of technical squabbles over trade policies. As we shall see, this tussle involves nothing less than authorship of the terms of economic and social life themselves.

The path that we will tread together in the coming chapters can be understood as falling within a broadly critical tradition of challenging particular social practices by interrogating their purported explanation or rationale.[18] It is only by demolishing the case for free trade where it is thought to be strongest that space can be made for alternatives policies and futures. But first, trade theory and policy must be freed from Ricardo's death grip.

Methodological Preliminaries

In excavating and investigating the core interlocking claims implicit in the case for free trade, I am aided by a set of analytics that are united around – and extend – the insights and techniques of institutionalism and structural institutionalism in economics, social theory, political philosophy and legal theory. While seldom appreciated as such by conventional thinkers, these rebel perspectives represent a simultaneously radical and most convincing challenge to mainstream economic thought, and hence are particularly useful allies in an assault upon mainstream comparative advantage analysis. Importantly, these analytics encourage a (methodological, explanatory and normative) focus on the 'rules of the game' (broadly understood) according to which the field of economic and social interactions are governed. This focus will be the lens through which the abstract logic of the economic case for free trade will be tested.

A long, discursive recitation of the key literatures and figures in this tradition would add little here – rather than abstract discussion, I hope that the approach, its detail and its value will become clear to my reader as we walk together through the chapters of my argument. However, it is helpful to bear in mind three key aspects of the case for free trade that will be continually forced upon us by the perspective of this tradition, and that help to structure the methodological approach I will take here.

The case is a theoretical one

The case for free trade is an unashamedly theoretical one. As I will discuss in more detail in the coming chapter, the argument for free trade is one that is attractive and appealing to economists and policy-makers more than anything else because it is thought to be *theoretically* robust.

This helps us to define the field of combat – it is the perceived theoretical robustness of comparative advantage that is said to ground its strength and prestige, and hence it is in theory that we must launch our attack. I will try to show that comparative advantage is wrong in theory, not just in assumption or in application.

The case is one with real-world relevance

The discussion here is not confined to dealing with esoteric puzzles within economic theory. Rather, it takes a social theoretical perspective and grapples with the case for free trade and its associated economic fictions as ideas with social currency, social validity and social effects. Crucially, these ideas are said to ground a case for particular economic policies and justify their real-world outcomes. The comparative advantage-driven case for free trade bridges the gap between economic theory and policy practice. People – policy-makers in particular, but also politicians, voters, academics and advocates – do things differently because of the perceived strength of comparative advantage.

This real-world relevance is a point to which we will return time and again during our investigation together. In examining the case for free trade we must be ever mindful that the case has *work* to do – it aims to convince us to act in the world in a certain way – and is not just a matter of interesting theoretical bubbles floating in thin air.

As a corollary, this relevance provides the critic of free trade with further detail concerning the theatre of war, which starts with but reaches beyond pure theory. Thus, while my investigation here will lead me to engage in economic debates concerning, for example, exchange rates, capital theory or welfare economics, I do so with a particular purpose in mind: demonstrating to a broad and cross-disciplinary church of believers the fragility of mainstream economic ideology and the flaw that lurks at the heart of its justification of free trade.

To do this, and to grasp hold of this aspect of the case for free trade, our investigation is undergirded by a clear social theoretical perspective and utilizes an approach that might be termed 'ideology critique'.[19] Implicit in this perspective and this methodology are particular ideas about the nature and use of knowledge, and it is these that will structure our discussion, helping to frame and guide the kinds of questions that need to be asked and answered in the course of my argument. For much of the discussion, this perspective sits in the background. However, in the concluding chapter – where my discussion reaches its crescendo – I will bring together the strands of argument advanced earlier, and will bring this perspective clearly to the fore.

The case operates as a whole

As I will discuss further in due course, there is a tendency in mainstream economic and policy discourse to treat the various component analyses that give force to the case for free trade in a fragmentary fashion. Logical claims are separated from predicative claims, the theory of trade is delinked from international finance, normative or welfare economics is divorced from positive economics. Radical or heterodox perspectives are similarly forced to conform to this disjointed model. However, the separation and disjointedness are artificial – the argument that comparative advantage grounds operates as a whole and something is lost in disarticulating its various parts.

Rather than fall into this pattern, I attempt to maintain focus on the argument for free trade as a whole. As Hegel wrote, 'The truth is the whole' and, in a sense, the novelty of this project lies less in its individual parts and more in the putting together and relating of its various pieces.[20]

Thus, though beginning with international trade economics and policy (conventionally understood), we shall follow the enquiry wherever it leads, and this often requires traversing seldom-crossed disciplinary and subdisciplinary boundaries. The discussion and analysis in these chapters move between social theory and economic philosophy, between legal theory and international finance, between political theory and the history of economic thought, between welfare economics and economic history. The argument engages with the case for free trade at its various analytical and normative levels, providing a sustained heterodox-radical perspective in relation to each of those levels and in relation to the case and its operation as a whole. By juxtaposing arguments, errors and fallacies from each of these fields as they relate to comparative advantage, insights that evade balkanized analysis will become visible.

This strategy is, however, attended by its own difficulties. Challenging a well-established orthodoxy with a broad congregation of believers using tools that cross disciplinary boundaries enlivens the complexity of a wide audience and the related difficulty of pitch. Economists may find some of the legal and social theoretical conceptual tools that I use alien. Legal scholars and social theorists who read these chapters may be less familiar with some of the technical economic debates into which I wade. And so on. In light of these issues, I have, at times, erred on the side of inclusion and explanation when discussing certain debates and areas of theory so as to make my approach and analysis as accessible as possible. I would ask that my reader grant me some leeway in this regard if it feels as though I am digressing or labouring elementary concepts. By the end of the argument, it is my hope that the importance of each strand of investigation and analysis will be rendered clear.

Some Comments Concerning Motivation

As mentioned above, critics of free trade or comparative advantage are often painted by economists as being motivated by the intellectual egoist's desire to 'score one against economics' by slaughtering one of that discipline's sacred cows. As I hope will be clear, this is not the case here. However, the ubiquity of the accusation makes prudent a few more words concerning motivation. In summary form, I would describe the nature of my engagement in this debate as based in intellectual honesty and political strategy.

As I hinted above, this book is an attempt to understand current international economic relations and arrangements through engagement with dominant analyses and ideas – in this case, comparative advantage and mainstream economics. One cannot transcend current ideas without first confronting them on their own terms, making them one's own and importantly, telling their adherents why and where they are wrong. And if these *are* wrong, in part or in whole, I am committed to the notion that – solely at the level of understanding and intellectual honesty – there is value in pointing this out: 'To leave error unrefuted is to encourage intellectual immorality.'[21]

At a more strategic level, this book aims to support a cluster of related commitments, concerns and intuitions concerning, broadly, the explanation and evaluation of international socioeconomic arrangements and practices. International specialization and free trade constitute a form of international interdependence, cooperation and coordination. However, contrary to what is often presumed in mainstream policy and indeed, academic discourse, interdependence does not necessarily equate to mutual benefit, nor are cooperation and coordination unqualified goods.[22] The Wilsonian idealistic rhetoric of world peace based upon free trade and mutual dependence glosses over the fundamental fact that socioeconomic arrangements differ in their substance and effects, and should be evaluated as such.

Moreover, I will claim that these arrangements are – knowingly or unknowingly – collectively and socially authored; in large part we make and are responsible for our social world and arrangements. And if, upon clear examination, we find these arrangements in substance or effect bad, wrong or unjust, we can and should ask whether and how we may reauthor them.

Finally, I will claim that mainstream, neoclassical economics holds dominant sway in the most important policy and intellectual circles, and holds it in a way that obscures from view – and from the scope of legitimate remedial action – aspects of contemporary international economic relations that we might very much wish to change, were we to see them clearly. At base, I will argue that both this sway and these instances of obscuration are unwarranted and should be rejected. Indeed, I will argue that the scope for innovative thinking concerning how to evaluate and renovate our collectively created socioeconomic institutions so as to pursue more effectively more diverse and fitting normative goals is far broader than neoclassical economics might admit.

The Structure of the Investigation

To assist my reader in navigating my argument, a short summary of what is to come may be useful.

The following five substantive chapters of this book are organized as follows: chapter 2 sets the terms of the enquiry by introducing the conventional presentation of the comparative advantage–based case for free trade. The chapter then goes beyond and complicates this presentation to distil and identify the component claims upon which the case is constructed and reliant. Specifically, the comparative advantage's logical claims will be distinguished from its predictive/descriptive claims, and its analytical and normative elements will be isolated. An innovative rearticulation of the case for free trade's component claims is presented and defended. I will also take the opportunity to defend the importance of the principle of comparative advantage in relation to the economist's support of free trade.

Chapters 3, 4 and 5 each examine in more detail a particular component claim of the case for free trade, delving into the theoretical apparatus and literature that is argued to support and flesh out the case. In each instance, it is argued that the critical stories upon which each component claim is based are more fictional than factual. Through these chapters an increasingly complex understanding of the socioeconomic processes relevant to international trade and specialization is developed. With each level of complexity, our insight into the systemic failures of the neoclassical economic scheme becomes similarly more nuanced.

Chapter 3 interrogates the importance and robustness of the claim that free trade 'follows' comparative advantage, and that patterns of specialization generated by free trade will be 'efficient'. Mainstream economics' analytical basis for making this predictive claim is based upon the assertion of an 'invisible hand' that coordinates international trade and specialization towards an efficient outcome. The chapter seeks to understand whether – and if so, by what mechanism – free trade undertaken by profit-seeking actors will cause specialization to converge on comparative advantage.

Chapter 4 looks beyond the logic of efficient specialization and confronts instead the peculiar abstract, mechanical and 'clockwork' tale of production that undergirds the mainstream case for free trade. The mainstream case for free trade tends to make production, costs and trade specializations a function of scarcity of inputs and a given level of technology. This can (and does) create the impression that patterns of trade and specialization are 'exogenous', or at least less sociopolitically malleable, than they are in fact. Using a somewhat neglected set of debates in the theory of capital as a starting point, the chapter pierces the mainstream fiction concerning patterns of specialization and trade. Offered instead is a social, relational and state sponsored – specifically, an institutional – account of those patterns and the sources of advantages in trade.[23] This account importantly sets the stage for the normative enquiry undertaken in the chapter that follows.

Chapter 5 takes up and examines the normative element of the case for free trade. Specifically, this chapter asks the following question: 'Does mainstream analysis provide a compelling case for countries to adopt free trade policies, as is strongly claimed by conventional discourse?' Here, the mainstream account of the sharing of gains between trading parties, of the 'nation', and of what it might mean for it to be 'better off', are each explored and interrogated.

Finally, chapter 6 brings together the preceding arguments and conclusions to present a picture of the whole. Specifically, comparative advantage itself – and as such, the entire case for free trade – is argued, on the basis of the previous chapters, to be nothing other than an economic fiction, built as it is upon a cluster of related fictions. In this chapter I offer an interpretation of the operation, failures and stakes involved in the economic justification of free trade. Specifically, I claim that the cluster of economic fictions upon which the case for free trade relies operates as an ideology – they both comprise, and are related to, a set of interconnected categories, concepts and tools that aim to make sense of particular socioeconomic arrangements and practices. More specifically, these concepts, categories and tools rationalize – in the sense of providing a reason or explanation for – those arrangements and practices.

Fundamentally, I critique this ideology and the rationalization that it provides as mistaken and based upon telling a partial (i.e., incomplete) analytical and normative tale that incorrectly casts as a matter of efficiency that which is primarily determined by social relations of power and distributional struggle. I claim that this mistaken rationalization – and the approach and view of economics that sits behind it – have high sociopolitical stakes, not least of all the fettering of collective imagination concerning the evaluation, design and justification of alternative arrangements for international economic organization. The fairy-tale nature of the case for free trade is laid bare and we are forced to conclude that this case and its underlying economic premises – though perhaps comforting – should be rejected in favour of devising more appropriate, less fictional modes of economic and social life.

* * *

So much for background and preliminaries. Taking up arms against a discipline's most broadly accepted truths will inevitably draw a combination of knee-jerk disbelief and haughty rejection. At the very least, it is likely that my argument will be seen by many as counterintuitive. To stave off potential doubts, I will move without further ado to demonstrate that which I claim.

In order to make sense of the explanation and justification of international free trade and specialization that is offered by comparative advantage's case for free trade, what is necessary now is a clear presentation of that case, its core claims and their operation. To this presentation I now immediately turn.

Chapter 2

EXPLORING THE CASE FOR FREE TRADE: UNEXPECTED TWISTS IN A SIMPLE STORY

> When you get the dragon out of his cave on to the plain and in the daylight, you can count his teeth and claws, and see just what is his strength.
>
> Oliver Wendell Holmes Jr.[1]

Let us begin by sketching the outline of the case for free trade. As we have discussed, this forces us to confront the principle of comparative advantage, which sits at the core of that case. Though in some sense a simple concept, comparative advantage is quite counterintuitive, and a clear presentation at the outset of the principle may be helpful.[2]

The purpose of this discussion is to strip the case for free trade and its operation back to its elemental claims and – by being as clear as possible about those claims – ensure that the investigation and interrogation of the theory that follows proceeds on the correct basis.

Though seldom (if ever) clearly presented as such by mainstream economic discourse, I will argue that the comparative advantage-driven case for free trade involves a string of interrelated claims. However, before articulating these, let us begin with the 'textbook' story of comparative advantage told by economists to their fledgling students and economic illiterates.

Once upon a Time: The Textbook Story

To understand the analytical kick of comparative advantage, it is helpful to take a step back and to briefly consider the alternative that the principle was designed to rebut – that of absolute advantage.[3] Absolute advantage (usually associated with the political economist Adam Smith) is possessed when a country requires a smaller quantity of inputs than another country in order to produce a particular amount of a particular good. This might also be termed having superiority in productivity. Taking the simplest two-country, two-commodity model, absolute advantage focuses us on the question of which country can produce a particular good with fewer inputs (more 'cheaply'). Prior to Ricardo,[4] conventional thinking supposed that international trade would be mutually beneficial only in situations where one country had an absolute advantage in one good, and the other had an absolute advantage in the other good.

The question is then raised – what if one country is more productive in relation to both commodities (i.e., if one country has an absolute advantage in the production of both goods)? Can trade still be mutually beneficial in such circumstances? Should the more productive country fear a policy of free trade?[5]

David Ricardo, writing in part to demonstrate what he saw as the perverse economic outcome generated by England's protectionist Corn Laws,[6] argued that free trade could hold benefits for all countries *irrespective of absolute productivity differences*. Protection – the restriction of trade – on the other hand, would reduce the welfare of average citizens in all countries. This is because, so Ricardo claimed, in a situation of free trade it will be *comparative* rather than *absolute* advantage that drives the pattern of international trade and specialization.

Comparative advantage in its modern form starts from the notion that scarcity and full employment of resources requires that trade-offs be made in the production of commodities.[7] These trade-offs are neatly encapsulated in the concept of 'opportunity cost'[8] – in this context, the amount of one good that must be forgone if resources are to be directed towards producing another good. Ricardo's brilliance was to focus attention on these opportunity costs rather than absolute productivity differences. As long as opportunity costs in production differ between two countries, free trade offers the possibility of gains from specialization and trade.

The fundamental idea behind the principle of comparative advantage is that in the context of free trade, a country will focus on producing the good that it can produce least inefficiently (i.e., the good in relation to which it has the lowest relative or 'comparative' opportunity cost), and trade to acquire the good that it is relatively more inefficient in producing. By doing so, each country essentially transfers the production of its relatively less efficiently produced good to a location where it can be less inefficiently produced.

Put another way, if domestically, a country needs to give up a certain amount of good A to produce good B, but can, through trade, sacrifice less of good A to get the same amount of good B, then there are gains to be had through trade. Each country takes advantage of the ability to exchange overseas at a better rate than it can 'exchange' at home through reorganization of domestic production.

It is easier to see the operation of comparative advantage with the aid of an illustrative example. Imagine, for simplicity's sake, a two-nation, two-commodity world – for nostalgic reasons[9] – England and Portugal, wine and cloth. Now suppose that in a given time period, say one month, the following production levels are possible, given resources and technology in each country:[10]

Table 2.1. Production possibilities for one month

	Cloth	Wine	Opportunity cost of 1 bottle of wine in terms of cloth	Opportunity cost of 1 bolt of cloth in terms of wine
England	1 bolt	1 bottle	1 bolt	1 bottle
Portugal	2 bolts	4 bottles	0.5 bolts	2 bottles

Notice that Portugal is more productive in relation to each good (and therefore has an 'absolute advantage' in each). The opportunity costs for the production of the goods, however, differ as between two countries. This is the genius of the comparative advantage model. Unlike absolute advantage, within the confines of the (two-nation, two-commodity) model, it is impossible for the same country to have a comparative advantage in more than one good, given the inverse relationship between the *relative* production costs for the two goods – if one has a high opportunity cost in relation to one good, it must have a low one in relation to the other. Therefore, no country need fear free trade, only to prepare for the gains that it brings.

Consider first, wine. In a situation of no trade (or 'autarky'), the opportunity cost of a bottle of wine for Portugal (in terms of the amount of cloth that must be given up to produce it) is 0.5 bolt, while in England it is one bolt. If Portugal uses domestic resources to produce a bottle of wine, and then trades it for more cloth than its opportunity cost for producing wine (0.5 bolt), it will be better off – it will have more cloth – than if it redeploys its productive resources towards domestic cloth production. Portugal gets its cloth cheaper (in terms of wine sacrificed) through trade than through domestic production. And if the trading ratio is lower than England's opportunity cost for producing wine (one bolt), that country too will be better off and will have an incentive to trade rather than produce wine at home.

The same is true in respect of cloth. Without trade, each bolt of England's cloth comes at the 'cost' of one bottle of wine, while Portugal's comes at a cost of two bottles. If England produces cloth and trades a bolt of it for more than one bottle of wine and less than two bottles, it ends up with more wine and Portugal more cloth than either could secure by redirecting the same resources domestically.

What is most important about this result is that, as long as

1. there are differences in opportunity costs for production as between the two countries,
2. each country specializes in the production of the good in relation to which it has a comparative advantage, and
3. goods trade at some intermediate exchange ratio between the autarky opportunity costs for each country (the 'feasible range'), mutual benefits will result.[11]

To illustrate these benefits clearly, assume that in the absence of trade, England and Portugal each dedicated their productive resources to produce a mix of both cloth and wine in the manner set out in Table 2.2.

Now, suppose instead that the two countries specialize in the production of the good in relation to which they have a comparative advantage. The production that results would be as is detailed in Table 2.3.

As is made clear by Tables 2.2 and 2.3, while international production of cloth has remained constant, through specialization of production,

Table 2.2. Autarky production – unspecialized

	Cloth	Wine
England	0.5 bolt	0.5 bottles
Portugal	1 bolt	2 bottles
TOTAL	1.5 bolts	2.5 bottles

Table 2.3. Autarky production – specialized

	Cloth	Wine
England	1 bolt	0 bottles
Portugal	0.5 bolt[12]	3 bottles
TOTAL	1.5 bolts	3 bottles

'global' or aggregate production of wine has actually increased. That is, specialization has increased total productive output, enabled by the more efficient use of resources in production.

Let us now build trade into the picture. As mentioned above, in order for trade to be beneficial, the exchange ratio (or terms of trade) must sit at some intermediate point between the countries' opportunity costs for the production of each good.[13] Assume for the purposes of this exercise that the exchange ratio of one bottle of wine for two-thirds bolt of cloth. Given these terms of trade, imagine that England trades 0.5 bolt of cloth for 0.75 bottle of wine. Table 2.4 contrasts the resulting consumption possibilities for each nation with those possible without trade.

Table 2.4. Consumption possibilities

	Autarky		With trade	
	Cloth	Wine	Cloth	Wine
England	0.5 bolt	0.5 bottle	0.5 bolt	0.75 bottle
Portugal	1 bolt	2 bottles	1.0 bolt	2.25 bottles

Notice that consumption of wine in both countries has increased; both England and Portugal can – happily – consume more wine than without trade, with no diminution in the amount of cloth available. In Ricardo's words, after specialization and trade, the 'mass of commodities' has increased in each country, and 'therefore the sum of enjoyments'.[14]

The result of the model is clear – relative opportunity costs, not absolute productivity differences, are the source of advantages in free international trade and as such, that trade can be mutually beneficial, irrespective of absolute advantage.

Assumptions and Complications of the Model

The role of assumptions in relation to the principle of comparative advantage is well acknowledged by economists. For our present purposes, it is not necessary to exhaustively identify and classify these here. However, these assumptions would include

1. atomic assumptions of the general model:
   a. two nations constituted by:
      i. a factor (resource) endowment; and
      ii. a level of technology (giving rise to a particular level of productivity of labour in terms of the two commodities); and
   b. 2 homogenous commodities;

2. the full and costless mobility of productive resources between industries within each country, and complete immobility between countries;

3. full employment both before and after trade;

4. competitive markets and no increasing returns to scale;

5. proper operation of the price mechanism such that prices reflected social costs;[15]

6. a country's external trade opportunities are independent of its own trade policies;[16]

7. trade within feasible terms of trade; and

8. costless transportation of goods between countries.

As I have hinted in the previous chapter, it is a usual technique of both orthodox and radical critics (from both inside and outside the academy of economics) to focus upon and challenge the robustness of one or other of these assumptions and then, on that basis, to either modify or reject the basic comparative advantage model or its conclusions.[17]

Growing in part out of responses to such critique and modification, but also from the 'natural' process of honing and extending the comparative advantage-related analysis to address questions with which Ricardo and other early theorists did not deal directly,[18] economics has developed a sophisticated set of associated technical literatures that develop the basic comparative advantage analytic. Economics, through this gradual – and mind you, utterly appropriate – working out of its model, has been able to isolate and defend comparative advantage from many of its critics. As such, the case for free trade has become somewhat hydra-like – ever developing in response to successful cuts from its opponents.

While I will engage with certain of these more detailed literatures in the pages that follow, as an initial step, I want to put these aside and focus attention on the principle of comparative advantage in its most basic form. Unpacking this basic form of the principle will invariably lead into more contentious and complicated territory. However, at its base, the principle of comparative advantage is claimed to capture a relatively simple idea.[19] My goal will be to identify and examine that idea as clearly as possible, and on its own terms. However, in order to do this I must now advance to isolate the key claims of comparative advantage with more precision.

Distilling the Claims

Comparative advantage is one of economics' sweetest and most subtle truths, and free trade represents – for the economist – one of the most basic and fundamental policy must-haves. Even critical voices (both heterodox and radical) within economics laud and praise the principle for its undeniable logic and analytical elegance,[20] redirecting their critical endeavours less against the principle itself but rather, its completeness in certain circumstances.

What these critical economists tend to have in mind when they speak about comparative advantage is the same idea that is encapsulated in the basic textbook presentation. This is the claim that

> specialization on the basis of comparative advantage (lower opportunity costs), and exchange (within the feasible range), will lead to gains.

Chang is correct to remark that 'One cannot argue with that.'[21] Hahnel is right to describe this logic as sound,[22] making disputing it strategically hopeless.

However, is this all there is to the principle of comparative advantage? I claim that it is not. This fragment of logic is not the full story but rather a partial telling of the tale of comparative advantage. Specifically, this understanding of comparative advantage moves too quickly between different components of what comparative advantage is said to show.

The claim set out above essentially constitutes a logical claim about the supposed gains from trade that can be realized when countries specialize in producing and trading their relatively less-inefficiently produced good (i.e., the good in relation to which a comparative advantage is held). Recall, however, that comparative advantage involves more than merely this logical claim. The reason that comparative advantage is so important is because it has policy legs – it grounds a case for international free trade. To do so, the principle must somehow *link* free trade to specialization on the basis of comparative advantage. It must also presume some normative or evaluative criteria by which the situation of free trade can be judged 'better' than a situation without free trade.

Bearing this in mind, the core claims of comparative advantage can be rearticulated as consisting of a prediction, the usual logical claim and a normative assertion. Taken together, these claims ground a dependent normative conclusion concerning free trade:

1. In a situation of free trade,[23] the direction and pattern of trade and specialization will be driven by comparative advantage.
2. Specialization on the basis of comparative advantage and trade will lead to gains.
3. Gains from trade can potentially make each country better off as a whole.
4. Therefore, a policy of free trade should be adopted.

There is much at stake in this clarification.[24] Usual presentations and renditions of the principle of comparative advantage tend to focus on the logical claim, dropping from view the predictive element and shortcutting the normative assertion, while simultaneously suggesting that the principle justifies a policy of free trade. This move tends to create a misleading and incomplete impression of the logical unassailability of the principle. However, comparative advantage's logical claim is only one – alone incomplete – element of what the principle claims. Importantly, the logical element of comparative advantage alone says *nothing at all* about free trade. Hence, for comparative advantage to do any work at all as a justification for letting the market, through free trade, direct productive activity towards the potential good of all, each of these three necessary claims of the principle of comparative advantage need to be properly established. Only then can it be argued, as Ricardo did, that

> under a system of perfectly free commerce, each country naturally devotes its capital and labour to such employments as are most beneficial to each. This pursuit of individual advantage is admirably connected with the universal good of the whole.[25]

In the following three chapters I will explore each of these linked claims of comparative advantage, claims upon which the case for free trade depends. As we will see, however, each relies on an account of trade, or of economic activity more broadly, that bends credulity beyond its breaking point.

Before moving on to this exploration, however, a few more words concerning the nature of the economic case for free trade are warranted.

Economics and the Advocacy of Free Trade: Optimal Policy, Rebuttable Presumption or Something Else?

It might be thought at this stage – notwithstanding the prevalence of comparative advantage in academic and broader public debate as a justification for free trade, notwithstanding clear statements in standard textbooks, notwithstanding the dedication of all but a small part of trade-relevant sections in leading international economic textbooks to comparative advantage and its related models and notwithstanding explicit statements by leading international economists – that I am somehow misrepresenting the manner in which sophisticated mainstream international economists think about comparative advantage and its relationship to free trade. I shall therefore take a moment to allay any such fears on the part of my reader.

It is important to be exceedingly clear about what it is that the principle of comparative advantage is actually said to show in respect of free trade. It is sometimes suggested that the principle was at one time – and perhaps remains – an airtight argument for a policy of free trade. Another perspective is that comparative advantage provides justification for a rebuttable presumption in favour of free trade. One could imagine that the latter may take different forms, with variations concerning the strength of the presumption and the kinds of arguments that would qualify as 'rebutting' it. It might even be suggested that comparative advantage is 'old hat' and that sophisticated economists no longer ground their advocacy of free trade in comparative advantage terms.

Just to be clear, economists tend to be rather unambiguous on this point. It is worth repeating Mankiw:

> Although economists often disagree on questions of policy, they are united in their support of free trade. Moreover, the central argument for free trade has not changed much in the past two centuries. Even though the field of economics has broadened its scope and refined its theories since the time of Smith and Ricardo, economists' opposition to trade restrictions is still based largely on the principle of comparative advantage.[26]

Now, I acknowledge that the most sophisticated of economists may seem to have had a somewhat more complicated relationship to comparative advantage and free trade than some – more ham-fisted – economic proponents. However, I think the position of the most sophisticated of mainstream economists can be relatively easily identified, and the core movements of that complicated relationship simply charted.

Specifically, I contend that the sophisticated mainstream position concerning comparative advantage is that, although there may be situations in which certain of its (well recognized) assumptions are breached, the theoretical strength of the principle licences an almost practically indefeasible presumption in favour of free trade policies. The strength of the presumption is clearly and unambiguously traceable to the perceived theoretical strength of the comparative advantage analytic.

When it comes to international economists, they do not come much more sophisticated than Nobel Prize-winner Paul Krugman. His intellectual path vis-à-vis comparative advantage and free trade is quite representative of the movement of the most sophisticated element of mainstream international economists in respect of free trade. In 1987, in an article entitled *Is Free Trade Passé?*, Krugman suggested that

> free trade is not passé, but it is an idea that has irretrievably lost its innocence. It has shifted from optimum to reasonable rule of thumb. There is still a case for free trade as a good policy, and as a useful target in the practical world of politics, but it can never again be asserted as the policy that economic theory tells us is always right.[27]

However, it would be possible to over-read this seeming concession. This 1987 article was published just as the New International Economics/Strategic Trade Theory school was gaining ground.[28] This was a time at which Krugman and others were arguing that because of external industries and increasing returns to scale (i.e., because of real-world departures from standard comparative advantage assumptions), trade between certain countries might not be explicable solely by reference to comparative advantage–relevant considerations of differing opportunity costs in production. But we must be clear, the issue for that school was not that comparative advantage is *wrong*, just that in certain circumstances other factors and dynamics might become important. The theorists of the New International Economics school were interested in debasing the 'perfect markets' assumption of the comparative advantage model, and in looking for alternative explanations for trade in the face of imperfect markets. Krugman is pointing to comparative advantage's *incompleteness* as a description of all trade, not its *incorrectness*. It remains, for Krugman, an important analytic that justifies free trade in situations absent of market failure.

In the remainder of that article, Krugman advanced a range of arguments suggesting that the presence of imperfect markets should not, however, lead to a submission to calls for trade interventionism. His basic claim was that the gains from interventionist policies can be shown to be limited and the risks of interventionism high, and therefore, free trade remains the 'right policy.'[29] It is important here to notice that Krugman is asserting that while there may be a 'theoretical' possibility that free trade might not be the best policy, that possibility remains *theoretical* – the space for actually rebutting the presumption for free trade is so limited as to be *practically* nonexistent. To the extent that free trade is a rebuttable rule of thumb, it is rebuttable in theory and on the basis of the failure of one of the model's assumptions, rather than replaceable in practice.

Moreover, in later writings Krugman seemed even to question the *theoretical* robustness of certain of the New International Economics/ Strategic Trade Theory arguments for interventionist trade policies.[30] Indeed, as time has moved on, Krugman has been even clearer about his defence of comparative advantage and its grounding of free trade policies. In a 1993 piece he argued that the essential things to teach students about international trade were the ideas of Hume (to which we will come later) and Ricardo, and that 'international trade is not about competition, it is about mutually beneficial exchange.'[31] In 1991 he claimed that 'trade follows comparative rather than absolute advantage', and while it was possible to work up a respectable academic argument for government intervention in the market based upon arguments such as external industries, he insisted that the 'fact that an argument is intellectually respectable does not mean that it is right'.[32]

Then, in 1996, Krugman wrote a piece entitled *Ricardo's Difficult Idea* in which he defended comparative advantage against its critics as 'extremely relevant to the modern world', notwithstanding the need to extend the basic model in situations highlighted by the New International Economics literature. Again, Krugman's point is not that there is something wrong with comparative advantage, just with its *assumptions* in a limited domain of cases. Krugman argued that the work of the New International Economics should be seen as a supplement to – rather than a wholesale rejection of – traditional comparative advantage–based free trade. International economists can and should accept *both* comparative advantage *and* its supplements where the model's assumptions are disturbed.[33]

It is worth noting that even before Krugman and the New International Economics school, mainstream (and indeed classical) economists acknowledged that there were some 'theoretical' reasons that the case for free trade might not be absolute. Generation after generation of economists understood the point that market failures of one form or another can make the analysis of international trade more complicated. This is, as noted, the basis of the economic insistence upon the assumptions mentioned above; the bulk of these assumptions aim to specify the absence of market failures. And as I mentioned above, there have developed voluminous literatures concerning the qualifications necessary to the base comparative advantage model.

So again, the question for us is how sophisticated economists imagine the scope of the qualification vis-à-vis the scope of the rule, and what this means for setting policy. I think that Jagdish Bhagwati had it right when he wrote that, in spite of a flirtation with the opposite in the 1980s and perhaps very early 1990s, since then

> the economist defectors from the doctrine of free trade have returned to the fold; indeed today, there is harmony of agreement among the major economists on this policy position.[34]

Bhagwati attributes this move to a perspectival shift at the theoretical level: economists accept the theoretical coherence of comparative advantage which grounds a policy for free trade and accept the (narrow) theoretical scope for market failures, perhaps advocating remedy of those failures through appropriate policies where possible. The key is to accept that a single policy solution cannot solve both problems:

> A simple intuitive way to understand all this is also to recall the wisdom of our forefathers in virtually every culture: you cannot kill two birds with one stone (leaving out fluke success, of course). So, if you seek to do that, you will likely miss both birds.[35]

Now, in respect of market failures that may require trade-inhibiting policies for correction, the theoretical case for free trade is buttressed by pragmatic arguments against protectionism (e.g., political reasons to avoid intervention, the gains from intervention are not that great or are fraught by the risk of retaliatory protectionism by other countries).

Thus, intervention will still be a bad move. Bhagwati, I think, presents the dominant economic view at present:

> The latest revolt, of the 1980s, has died down. Only Neanderthals among the economists now militate against free trade: unfortunately, they will never lack an audience but fortunately, they have little effect presently.[36]

The basic deficiency of arguments for protection is that they, in the view of mainstream economists, remain unable to match comparative advantage for theoretical completeness and coherence. The strength of comparative advantage narrows the theoretical scope for arguments for protection to such an extent that they are easily overawed by the exigencies of prudence. They remain based upon frail assumptions that are easily debased and, with them, the arguments themselves.[37] Moreover, the general absence of empirically based argument in the area means that theoretical or conceptual frailties tend to spell the end of debate.[38] As the leading mainstream intellectual historian of free trade Douglas Irwin has stated that

> one should recognize that free trade commands respect among economists largely because of its continuing theoretical attractiveness.[39]

All of this is to say that the theoretical case for free trade remains very much based upon the principle of comparative advantage. Even sophisticated economists who understand that the case for free trade provided by comparative advantage is a qualified one, nonetheless accept the case both as strongly persuasive in all but an extremely limited set of policy situations. Critically, they also hold that, in its proper domain of operation, comparative advantage has not been undermined on its own terms. It is the analytical starting point and default position.

To be clear, this debate among sophisticated international economists is nothing other than the mainstream's attempt to grapple with the fact that – sometimes – the clear assumptions of the comparative advantage model do not hold. As such, their disenchantment with comparative advantage is as fleeting as the critiques of those who argue that the principle can be debased by troubling one or other assumption of the model.

Even if I were wrong about this, and the most sophisticated of mainstream economists *did* think that there was something flawed about the connection between free trade policies and comparative advantage on its own terms (and not merely where its assumptions have been debased), a further point should be raised. As I mentioned in chapter 1 and as will be discussed in more detail in chapter 6, we are here engaged in a project of critiquing the ideological effect generated by comparative advantage – of the rationalization that it provides for certain kinds of policies and socioeconomic arrangements. The views of the most sophisticated of academic economists are one – although not the only – part of this, particularly when a less sophisticated version of their ideas predominate outside of the halls of economics departments. The manner in which the ideas of intellectuals permeate education, the media and public debate are often more important to the practices of actual agents, policy-makers, and so on, than the most sophisticated renderings of those ideas that emerge from the academy. It matters little if the most sophisticated of economists doubt the connection between free trade and comparative advantage if politicians, commentators, policy-makers or indeed, the public at large, buy the connection between the two and therefore support free trade policies. Indeed, my point – and this enquiry as a whole – is lent it sharpness by its relevance to the world of action, to policy, to normative concerns, to what people do – and think is right to do – because of the ideas that are peddled by intellectuals.

*   *   *

Comparative advantage thus remains the Atlas upon whose shoulders stands the weight of free international trade – for both sophisticated economists and others alike. It is precisely because of its centrality to the case for free trade that we must be exceedingly clear in articulating its various subcomponents and necessary subarguments. Having done so, we are now in a position to take to the argumentative battlefield, to meet our opponents and to test their claims. We begin with the prediction that free trade drives specialization to follow comparative advantage.

Chapter 3

THE TALE OF INTERNATIONAL TRADE'S INVISIBLE HAND

It does not follow from the fact that a statement cannot be demonstrated that it is not true [...] Which is true, but could equally be used to defend claims about unicorns and witches.

Alasdair MacIntyre[1]

In the previous chapter I disaggregated and specified the core claims of the case for free trade. Let us now consider in more detail the first of these:

1. *In a situation of free trade, the direction and pattern of trade and specialization will be driven by comparative advantage.*
2. Specialization on the basis of comparative advantage and trade will lead to gains.
3. Gains from trade can potentially make each country better off as a whole.
4. Therefore, a policy of free trade should be adopted.

This claim is critical to the case's policy relevance, providing the bridge between free trade on the one hand, and specialization on the basis of comparative advantage on the other. As such, testing the efficiency and welfare promises of comparative advantage-based trade theory requires first grappling with this claim.

The importance of this investigation cannot be overstated: if it cannot be established that free trade and specialization will follow the predicted pattern, the case for free trade is dealt a serious blow. If free trade does not result in countries specializing in their comparative advantages, the unambiguous statements of economists and economic rationalists in favour of free trade on the grounds of comparative advantage become difficult to justify.

There are two ways in which the claim that trade and specialization follow comparative advantage might be established. First, it might be demonstrated *empirically* on the basis of careful examination of real-world patterns of trade. The alternative is to show that as a matter of *analysis* it can be shown that this result will obtain. Mainstream international trade theory predominantly (if not exclusively) has followed the second route.[2] Specifically, mainstream theory asserts that an automatic, market-based adjustment mechanism exists in international trade that causes free trade and specialization to follow comparative advantage.

And herein lies the first fiction that lurks behind the case for free trade. Mainstream economics asserts that trade will follow comparative advantage. But the story that it tells about how and why this will happen is weak, unconvincing and ultimately make-believe.

Before proceeding to consider how this claim has been sought to be established by the mainstream, it is worth spending a moment to consider the nature of the claim itself.

Invisible Hands and Mechanisms

As touched upon in earlier chapters, the principle of comparative advantage is an instance of what Adam Smith called the 'invisible hand':[3] the notion that individual pursuit of individual ends leads to a positive unintended outcome for society as a whole.

However, in order for claims such as these to be compelling, further information is required. Specifically, we need to be told *how* the activity in question will bring about the specified result. That is, some kind of 'mechanism' needs to be specified connecting the individual pursuit of individual ends to the common good. The archetypical economic invisible hand, identified by Smith, did precisely this. His argument was that the pursuit of individual interest in a situation of market competition would force producers to offer goods more cheaply than their rivals. However, the effect of this is also to utilize available economic resources as efficiently as possible and make goods cheaper for consumers, effectively raising real incomes across the board.

The key point here is not empirical testing or testability, but rather analytical closure – without a mechanism, invisible hand claims and predictions become merely assertions without clear foundations. Importantly, assertions of this kind cannot, alone, create the basis for a normative preference in favour of one policy or another – in the context of our current exploration, in favour of free trade policies – on the basis of their supposedly beneficial effects.

Mechanisms – and the need to supply them – have been a significant focus of certain branches of (particularly analytical) social theory and explanation. The work of Jon Elster in particular stands out.[4] In order to avoid terminological confusion, a few clarificatory words about mechanisms are in order. Elster uses the notion of the supplying of mechanisms in the context of explaining observed social phenomena *ex post* or after the fact. Providing a mechanism involves specifying the 'microfoundational' basis for social phenomena, that is, the explanation of complex phenomena in terms of their individual components (the opposite of doing so being the creation of a 'black box').[5]

For our present purposes, however, the notion of supplying a mechanism is helpful less as a way of explaining observed phenomena that have already occurred[6], but more as part of evaluating and assessing the strength, coherence and analytic closure provided in respect of a 'law-like', general and conditional predictive claim that has been analytically – rather than empirically – generated.[7]

To put it in more abstract terms, what I am calling a law-like conditional prediction conforms to the following form:

If conditions $C_1, C_2 \ldots C_n$ obtain, then outcome O will result.

My claim is that, in order for a prediction in this form to be acceptable as a matter of social analysis, some plausible causal story must be told (i.e., some mechanism specified) that links the fulfilment of the conditions $(C_1, C_2 \ldots C_n)$ to the relevant outcome (O). Mechanistic claims such as this by their very nature require causal mechanisms to be supplied in order to be convincing.

Although I have resisted the temptation to do so in these pages, comparative advantage is often styled by economists and others as the '*law* of comparative advantage.'[8] This bears a resemblance to a trend in philosophy – birthed in Europe's seventeenth-century scientific revolution but with lingering currency – of seeing the natural world (and indeed the broader universe and individual beings) as mechanical or 'clockwork' in character, governed by a certain set of discernible natural laws.

It is often tempting to decry such usage on the part of economists as a rhetorical recourse to the language of the natural sciences, attempting to put economic principles on the same footing as natural 'laws', such as the law of gravity or those of thermodynamics. However, it is important not to overclaim, and to be clear about what precisely is wrong with economists so doing, if this is in fact what they are doing. We must defer the answer to this question for the moment, though it will be one to which we will return. For now it is enough to note that while some economists caught in the thrall of natural scientism might claim that comparative advantage is a law in this sense, my discussion here does not rely upon them doing so.

What is important here is that – whether or not 'like gravity' – the relevant claim of comparative advantage with which we are concerned in this chapter does follow the exact form of a law-like generalization mentioned above: 'If (condition) free trade obtains, then (outcome) specialization on the basis of comparative advantage will result.' The question is: How? By what mechanism?

The importance of this point might usefully be illustrated by means of an example. Recall the two-country (England and Portugal), two-commodity (wine and cloth) model presented in the previous chapter. Remember that in autarky, Portugal is absolutely more productive in relation to both goods than England, and that England has a comparative advantage in cloth and Portugal in wine. Now imagine a move from autarky to free trade. There are two options: Either trade will not occur at all, England having no goods for which Portugal would be willing to trade. Alternatively, assuming that England has reserves of money or currency of some kind that Portugal will accept by way of payment for goods, Portuguese goods (being cheaper in relative terms than English goods) will flood the English market, conceivably decimating English industry. English goods – whether wine or cloth – being more expensive, will not compete successfully with Portuguese goods, either domestically or, importantly, in Portugal. England will suffer a trade deficit until the money runs out, and then trade ceases altogether.

Ricardo predicts that neither of these scenarios will occur. The fundamental question must therefore be answered: How is this predicament – in which trade either does not occur or follows absolute advantage – converted into a situation where trade follows comparative advantage?

Two (flawed) objections

Though to the social theoretically minded reader the import of this question may seem obvious, bitter experience of discussing comparative advantage with neoclassically trained economists tends to suggest that this obviousness is perhaps controversial. Accordingly, I will take a moment to impress upon my reader the significance of the point here, and particularly to defend it against two related objections:

1. The objection that I am misdescribing the principle of comparative advantage, specifically by identifying as one of its component claims the predictive claim concerning the direction of trade.
2. Even if the principle of comparative advantage is properly associated with a prediction concerning the direction of trade, it may be objected that providing a mechanism to bring about that prediction is not a 'claim' that the principle seeks to establish, but rather an 'assumption' of the model.

In relation to the first objection, two points must be made. First and foremost, it seems that this objection simply does not resonate with the clear and explicit statements of leading academic and international economists. Economists are clearly of the view that comparative advantage says something about a policy of free trade and its effects. That is, as we have discussed, they are clearly of the view that comparative advantage grounds the case for *free trade policies*, not just the wisdom of specialization and trade according to lower opportunity costs. At the risk of repeating what has been set out above, Ricardo was unambiguous about what he was doing in formulating the principle of comparative advantage – specifically, generating an argument against protectionism and for a system of 'free commerce'.

Further, Paul Krugman – a leading and truly sophisticated advocate of comparative advantage – in a merciless defence of the principle, was abundantly clear that comparative advantage speaks directly to the actual pattern of free trade and specialization in the real world of trucking and bartering, and to the benefits of the more efficient patterns that result. He expressly states this:

> The idea of comparative advantage – with its implication that *trade between two nations normally raises the real incomes of both* – is, like evolution via natural selection, a concept that seems simple and compelling to those who understand it.[9]

Even more unambiguously, in their leading international economics textbook, Krugman and Obstfeld identify the 'basic prediction' of the Ricardian model in respect of 'actual international trade flows' is that countries 'tend to export those goods in which their productivity is relatively high'.[10]

Mankiw, as is standard, also describes comparative advantage as the 'driving force of trade'.[11] And, as a logical matter, he – and free trade–favouring economists generally – must so describe it. It simply makes no sense to speak about comparative advantage justifying international trade unless a connection can be drawn between free trade and comparative advantage. That is, there *must* be a prediction about the direction of trade implicit in the principle of comparative advantage and in the case for free trade that it grounds.

Related to this, there is another reason that economists must assert this connection between free trade and comparative advantage. Economics is a social science. Indeed it is the self-styled 'Queen of the Social Sciences'. Leaving aside perennial debates about the proper scope, epistemology or methodology of social science, its analogies and disanalogies to the physical sciences and so on, it is, and must be, the case that any (even appropriately modest) social science must aim to say something about social phenomena, and perhaps their causes and effects. Economics must, if it is to fairly answer the definition of social science, be relevant in some way to the social world.

Comparative advantage's logical claim (that specialization on the basis of comparative advantage yields gains from trade) says nothing at all about the social world. It is, in itself, nothing other than a claim of mathematical logic. However, it would be very peculiar if the Queen of the Social Sciences confined herself to claims entirely within the realm of mathematics and logic. And nor does she so confine herself – her putative kingdom is much broader.

Economics is neither a matter of arid logic, nor of pure mathematics.[12] To the extent that the latter is used in modern economics, economists claim (not unreasonably) that the use of mathematics is to aid in precision and clarity in economic analysis.[13] This is not necessarily a problem. But, as economists realize, the mathematical element in economics must be *applied* to social phenomena. Mathematics for the sake of mathematics, or logic for the sake of logic, is not the economic analysis of anything.

In the current context, then, for comparative advantage to go any distance towards establishing the case for free trade, it must actually link comparative advantage to free trade. Economists know this, and assert that it does. The first potential objection – that comparative advantage is not properly associated with a prediction concerning the direction of free trade – therefore lacks foundation.

Let us turn to the second objection: that a mechanism to cause comparative advantage to dominate the pattern of trade is properly seen as an assumption – rather than a claim – of the comparative advantage model. It is useful to begin by noting that the usual formulations of comparative advantage tend not to expressly assume either a mechanism to guarantee comparative advantage-driven trade (or balanced trade) in the long list of well-acknowledged assumptions that accompany the articulation of the model.[14]

More importantly, however, it is helpful to point out a difficulty concerning the use of the term 'assumption' in economics. The difficulty is, as Alan Musgrave asserted in his notable 1981 piece,[15] the fact that 'assumption' in the English language can refer to three very different kinds of propositions (at least as it concerns economic models):

1. *Negligibility assumptions* – that assert the absence of a factor on the basis that the factor is irrelevant to the object of study.
2. *Domain assumptions* – that specify the domain of applicability of a theory or analysis, the falsity of which makes invalid that theory or analysis.
3. *Heuristic assumptions* – that are neither (1) nor (2) above, but are made to simplify the relevant analysis or theory and which, at a later stage of investigation, will be relaxed in order to further develop that theory or analysis.

The majority of the usually understood assumptions concerning the comparative advantage model fall (or are claimed by economists to fall) into the last of these three categories. These assumptions – it is argued – aim to simplify the analysis such that key dynamics can be isolated, and then the model is revisited and complicated at a second round of analysis, at which point the assumptions may be relaxed.

The provision of a mechanism by which trade will follow comparative rather than absolute advantage is not a heuristic assumption. In the absence of a clear and expressed decision on the part of the economic analyst to designate it as such, it seems somewhat peculiar to impute such classification. This is especially the case given the definitionally 'interim' nature of heuristic assumptions. Neither is it a negligibility assumption – free trade following comparative advantage is not irrelevant to the comparative advantage analysis.

Rather, the mechanism that generates specialization on the basis of comparative advantage is a domain assumption: if no mechanism can be shown, then the principle of comparative advantage cannot promise (as it must and does) that free trade leads to such specialization.

Thus, the objection leads to nothing. Even if a mechanism that ensures that trade and specialization follow comparative advantage is an 'assumption' of the comparative advantage model, it is a domain assumption – one that must be *established* if comparative advantage is to do the work that is required of it. Sophisticated economists know this. And they do claim that they can bear out the mechanism. Thus, as we will see, Ricardo provided a mechanism.[16] Sophisticated mainstream international economists assert one.[17] And they must if comparative advantage is to have any relevance as a technique of social or policy analysis.

Proposed Mechanisms

In order to force trade and specialization into the pattern of comparative advantage, what needs to be supplied is a mechanism that causes prices for goods in the deficit country (in our example, England) – and particularly the good in relation to which that country has a comparative advantage – to become competitive with those of the surplus country (Portugal). Relative cost differences in production (comparative advantages) must somehow become reflected in price differences in trade.

It is worth noting by way of preliminary clarification that comparative advantage models of international trade are balanced trade models or – from an accounting point of view – models in which there operates an automatic adjustment in the balance of payments account. That is, where trade between two countries is following comparative advantage, that trade will balance. Thus, establishing that trade balances is often seen as equivalent to establishing that comparative advantage dominates specialization and trade, and vice versa.

To the extent a mechanism to guarantee balanced or comparative advantage-driven trade is provided by mainstream economic theory, it is the market's price mechanism that is relied upon automatically to cause trade to follow relative opportunity costs and to correct for trade imbalances. The search for such a mechanism takes us into the economics of international payments and finance. For reasons that I will discuss further, in most presentations this area is separated from exploration of issues concerning international trade. However, given my framing of our enquiry – and how deeply this issue is intertwined with the justification of free trade – confronting this area of theory is a necessary step in our investigation. The economics of international payments is vital to the coherence of the case for free trade.

Ricardo's mechanism

Again, Ricardo was himself well aware of the importance of articulating a mechanism that would push specialization and trade towards comparative advantage. Ricardo's solution[18] was to import into his conceptual scheme David Hume's specie-flow mechanism[19] and quantity-of-money theory of prices, which together provided an automatic adjustment in gold prices of commodities in each trading country so as to correct for trade imbalances.[20]

According to the quantity-of-money theory of prices, Ricardo (and Hume before him) believed that – in the context of a 100 per cent specie-reserve money standard – an increase in the specie stock of a country would lead to a directly proportionate rise in its price level (i.e., more money chasing a constant supply of goods). From the international perspective, then, an increase in a country's domestic specie stock would cause a rise in domestic prices, and (other things being equal) an increase in that country's price level relative to the price level in other countries.[21]

Returning to the example of England and Portugal to illustrate the point, the steps of the mechanism are as follows:

1. Starting from the (contemporaneously unexceptional) assumption that precious metals such as gold and silver are the primary medium for exchange in international trade, the effect of England's trade deficit would be the outflow of specie (for ease of reference, let us say gold) from England to Portugal.[22]
2. Following the quantity-of-money theory of prices, gold prices in England will decrease, and gold prices in Portugal will increase.
3. The flow of gold will continue from England to Portugal until relative prices adjust to such an extent so as to make English cloth competitive with Portuguese cloth
4. English cloth, now being cheaper in Portugal than Portuguese cloth, would become favoured by Portuguese consumers while Portuguese wine, having become more expensive in England would be consumed less.
5. The effect of all of this is a rise in England's exports and a fall in imports, and the inverse moves for Portugal, until the trade imbalance is eliminated.

Thus, Ricardo provides a mechanism that explains how free trade follows comparative advantage and that guarantees that trade will balance.

At the analytical level at least, Ricardo links free trade to comparative advantage in a way that provides justificatory closure to comparative advantage's predictive claim.

Modern mechanisms and the importance of exchange rates

Today, international economists recognize that the Humean–Ricardian specie-flow mechanism tends not to be sufficiently explanatory in the context of contemporary international trade.[23] The modern mechanism that is argued by economists to cause comparative rather than absolute advantage to determine patterns of international trade and specialization is seen by economists as somewhat more complex.

There are three primary candidates for performing that adjustment in respect of nongold standard, modern economies – exchange rates, wages and prices. As Krugman has noted, in modern times, governments tend to be unwilling to allow wages or prices to fall, concentrating monetary policy on stabilizing these and instead allowing exchange rates to adjust in the face of trade imbalances.[24] As such, exchange rates have tended to be the focus of the literature.[25] And while the story has changed somewhat from the time of Hume and Ricardo, its moral remains the same – the takeaway point remains that 'trade deficits are self-correcting.'[26]

As we will see, there are a number of discernible mainstream positions concerning the determination of exchange rates. This is a complicated and technical area of international economics. However, for present purposes (and at a general level), most traditional open economy macroeconomic models embody 'simple-minded stories of exchange rate determination' that focus on the importance and role of trade flows in determining exchange rates.[27] The result common to the majority of these models is that exchange rates move in a way that balances trade, at least in the long run.[28]

One can discern the hint of closure here. Comparative advantage-driven trade requires the existence of an adjustment mechanism that causes trade to balance. The movement of exchange rates is driven by trade flows, and driven in a way that balances trade, providing the adjustment mechanism required. This neat closure is vitally important to the analytical coherence of the case for free trade. Now let us now consider the efficacy of this closure in more detail.

Will the Exchange Rate Mechanism Balance Trade?

The complexity of the theoretical and analytical literature concerning international payments can be helpfully navigated by confronting it with two questions relevant to our present investigation. Specifically:

1. Will exchange rates adjust in the face of unbalanced trade (i.e., in the presence of a trade deficit, will the foreign exchange market react by causing a devaluation in the deficit country's currency)?
2. Will exchange rate–driven changes in relative price levels correct for trade imbalances?

As should be clear, for mainstream economic theory to bear out the claim that exchange rates ensure that comparative advantage guides international trade, both of these questions must be analytically answered in the affirmative. I will consider each question in turn.

Do exchange rates adjust in the face of unbalanced trade?

Exchange rates are a crucial piece of the global economic picture. In an open international economy, they importantly mediate the relationships between national economies in a way that has far-reaching consequences at both domestic and, of course, global levels. Our current enquiry provides a pointed example of the importance of exchange rates in practical relief. Here, exchange rates bear the burden of directing specialization of domestic production towards efficient locations by pricing these goods appropriately on international markets.

There is, however, a problem. Notwithstanding the importance of exchange rates to international economic relations and domestic economies, mainstream economic *theories* of exchange rate determination are in a state of disarray. Many models exist but none has managed to garner universal support from economists, and no common economic explanation of the behaviour of exchange rates has emerged.

While there is much disagreement at the level of theory and analysis, the mainstream tends to agree on the following breakdown:

1. In the short term, movements in exchange rates are driven by asset market forces and therefore might display significant (nonfundamental or nontrade connected) volatility.
2. In the long run, exchange rates are determined by 'fundamentals', which implies that trade imbalances will be corrected.

As Harvey notes, 'there appears to be little interest in modelling the former and little agreement on the specifics of the latter.'[29]

Even more problematically, as we shall see, the mainstream models in this area are startlingly fictitious, with complex and convoluted storylines wildly disconnected from anything that might fairly answer the description of fact or reality. This has special significance in the context of the case for free trade. Let us look at the most important of these models in more detail to demonstrate the point.

Mainstream exchange rate determination models

Much can be and has been written about the field of exchange rate economics, but the discussion here will be tightly marshalled towards the questions relevant to our current enquiry. Specifically, I will focus on four of the dominant models of exchange rate determination: the monetary, Mundell–Fleming, portfolio balance and Dornbusch approaches.[30] To be clear, my purpose in sketching the contours of these models is to highlight the aspects of these that speak directly to the issue under consideration here – whether orthodox economic theory can provide an analytical answer to the question of whether exchange rates will shift in the face of trade imbalances.

The monetary model. The monetary model tends to be the most empirically tested (and, as we shall see, failure-riddled) of neoclassical exchange rate models.[31] In the most basic rendering, the model assumes purchasing power parity (the idea that once exchange rates are taken into account, the average price of goods and services worldwide should be equal) and flexible prices. Although interest rates figure into such models, their role is limited and, importantly, they do not directly influence the determination of exchange rates, effectively reading international capital movements out of the exchange rate story.[32] This is a particularly peculiar model for a world of open financial markets.[33]

Returning to our England–Portugal example, the basic rendering of the monetary mechanism is something like this:

1. The effect of England's trade deficit is that there is an increased supply of English currency (pound), and an increased demand for Portuguese currency (escudo) on the international foreign exchange

market as English purchasers seek to trade pounds for escudo to pay for Portuguese imports.

2. The effect of a trade surplus on Portugal's part is that there is a decreased supply of escudo, and a decreased demand for pounds on the international foreign exchange market.

3. The rate of exchange of pounds for escudo will fall in response to these movements in supply and demand, the effect of which is to cause English goods to cheapen relative to Portuguese goods, and Portuguese goods to become more expensive relative to English goods.

4. This shift in exchange rate will continue until relative prices adjust to such an extent so as to make English cloth competitive with Portuguese cloth.

5. English cloth, now being cheaper in Portugal than Portuguese cloth, would become favoured by Portuguese consumers while Portuguese wine, having become more expensive in England would be consumed less.

6. The effect of all of this is a rise in England's exports and a fall in imports, and the inverse move for Portugal's, until the trade imbalance is eliminated.

The monetary approach comes closest of modern approaches to something like the Humean–Ricardian specie-flow mechanism. It sees the exchange rate as directly linked to the relative price of goods and services, and only tangentially related to prices and flows of international financial assets. The exchange rate mediates the price levels between countries, drawing them into equilibrium and balancing trade.

But in our current context, the problem is that the model itself is predicated on the conclusion that we need it to prove – the model is designed around the hardwired assumption that exchange rates are fundamentally driven by and balance trade flows and imbalances.[34] It assumes rather than proves the assertion we need it to substantiate.

The Mundell–Fleming approach. A number of exchange rate models exist that focus on the role of floating exchange rates in 'clearing' macrolevel markets or balances. Such balances include the trade balance, but also investor portfolio balances and so on. Importantly, many of these models tend to bring capital flows and finance variables more clearly into the picture than does the monetarist model – a critical improvement. However, we shall see that although they do bring in the financial side of the economy, these models tend to do so myopically, making these variables 'white noise' that does not disturb – and merely reflects – more 'fundamental' trade flows.

The Mundell–Fleming model, which is of Keynesian inspiration, was an early model that integrated international capital flows into macroeconomic analysis.[35] The model ties together the domestic interest rate, output and the exchange rate, seeking to determine the value of each through their equilibrium interaction. Specifically, levels of output change in response to excess demand, interest rates adjust in the face of asset market imbalances and exchange rates shift where the balance of payments does not clear. The model establishes equations in respect of each and solves them simultaneously.[36]

Though there is a great deal of quite complex accounting and algebraic infrastructure undergirding this approach – and while for a time the model captured policy analysis in its domain – our present purposes allow us to quickly see its flaw. Specifically, within the model's complex web of algebra lurks a balance-of-payments equation. This equation is posited as both independent of and determinative of exchange rates, driving them to an equilibrium trade balancing level.[37] In this model too, then, the existence of equilibrium balanced trade is essentially assumed – built into the model as a precursor to the analysis.[38] Given that what we seek in our current enquiry is a robust *reason* or mechanism – rather than just an assertion – that causes exchange rates to behave in this way, we must again find the Mundell–Fleming model unsatisfying from the perspective of justificatory closure.

The portfolio balance approach. In a related (though distinct) direction is the 'portfolio balance' model.[39] This model also recognizes that international financial flows are important to understanding exchange rate determination. It assumes that investors are faced with three nonidentical domestic and foreign assets – domestic currency, domestic bonds and foreign bonds. The exchange rate is derived by reference to the interaction of supply and demand in respect of each asset with the equilibrium exchange rate, domestic and international interest rates being those that clear the markets in relation to each of these assets.

Notwithstanding its focus on international capital movements, however, the model ensures that it is the current account (which captures, for simplicity, trade in goods and services) rather than the capital or financial account (which records capital flows) that drives the exchange rate.[40] Changes in the desired composition of portfolios occur either through changes in government monetary policy (which shifts interest rates, and hence rates of return and demand of certain assets) or, critically – in the absence of such intervention – by the existence of a current account (trade) imbalance.

When a country experiences a deficit, it loses foreign bonds; this creates a shortage of foreign bonds on the market and leads to an appreciation in the foreign currency. Eventually, the appreciation should cause a shift in prices of internationally traded goods that will eventually clear the deficit (the opposite being true in respect of a surplus). This approach starts from and *assumes* a long-run equilibrium in which the current account is balanced, and posits an automatic correction mechanism when it is not. Capital market adjustments are only short term and occur in response to current account movements.[41] The model makes no room for independent behaviour of investors to interrupt the influence exerted by the current account. Importantly, what are framed out of the picture are all of the kinds of speculative expectations, conventions and behaviours that characterize the domain of finance.

I shall say more about this in a moment. For now what is important to note is that, like the monetary and Mundell–Fleming models, the portfolio balance approach essentially presumes rather than demonstrates that exchange rates will be driven to correct trade imbalances.

Dornbusch's hybrid model. The final contemporary model that we shall look at is the Dornbusch model, which found its genesis in the mid-1970s through an attempt to build upon insights from both the monetary approach and more Keynesian thinking.[42]

The model seems at first blush to make room not only for imports and exports in determining exchange rates, but also expectations as to future developments in the foreign exchange market. Obviously, this appears to be an advance on the ignoring of these dynamics that we witnessed in the earlier models. However, the advance is somewhat illusory. The model is again carefully constructed to cabin the effect of money, finance and expectations, and to insulate these from disrupting long-run fundamentals such as output and trade.[43] The former react to rather than influence the latter. And although market actor expectations are incorporated into the model, they are defined so as to be given a very constrained role. Specifically, in usual renditions, the assumption made about expectations is that economic actors believe that trade will balance in the long run.[44] That is, expectations are sterilized, rational and again become predictable in terms of fundamentals,[45] and thus are analytically and definitionally tied to the result in question here – that exchange rates will balance in the long term. However, for our present purposes, this is to gear the model to prove the outcome that it is set to investigate.

Piercing the fiction: Back to first principles

As I have attempted to highlight, the key mainstream exchange rate determination models basically assume – or incorporate equations or elements that ensure that – at least in the long run, exchange rates will settle on trade-balancing levels. This, of course, merely asserts without demonstrating a mechanism that causes free trade to follow comparative advantage.

Neoclassical exchange rate models, though diverse and multivariate, are essentially united in being underwritten by a peculiarly defined and sterilized view of the way that foreign exchange markets work. These mainstream models tend to answer the question of the source of supply and demand in foreign exchange markets by pointing to the 'fundamentals' – poorly defined, but ultimately trade-balancing variables – in exchange rate determination.[46] Critically, in these models import and export flows are seen as the key determinants. And as we have seen, the focus on fundamentals is often 'cunningly' accomplished by the mainstream theoretical apparatus.[47] Specifically, in the fairy-tale world of the mainstream models,

1. capital flows are passive – nothing more than either background static and white noise in the determination of exchange rates or a 'mere reflection of trade flows',[48] or
2. even where capital flows are taken into account, common speculative investor behaviour in foreign exchange markets are screened out – made predictable in artificial ways, or removed from the story altogether. [49]

However, in today's international economy the volume of daily foreign exchange transactions exceeds USD 4.0 trillion.[50] The total volume of transactions dwarfs that which would be necessary to facilitate international trade in goods and services (even assuming multiple covering (i.e., risk-shifting) transactions).[51] Indeed, total exports of merchandise and commercial services globally during the *entire* 2011 year totalled some USD 21.3 trillion.[52] In light of this fact, it becomes crucially important to the mainstream analytic scheme concerning exchange-rate determination (and specifically its role in the justification of free trade) to explain why the full and immense volume of supply and demand in the market for foreign exchange merely reflects its relatively smaller component (that portion referable to the trade in goods and services). Put another way, why should we believe that the current account drives the capital account,[53] with capital flows passively following trade flows? Indeed, in approaching the question in simple form (even assuming equilibrating foreign exchange markets) we shall see that logic would appear to take us to a different conclusion, highlighting the fictional nature of the mainstream's account.

First, however, it is worth raising one issue here. Mainstream comparative advantage models – as I have pointed to in previous chapters – tend to rely on a series of relatively well-known assumptions. Again, against the tide of many critiques that fasten on and trouble one or other of these assumptions as a means of attacking the case for free trade, the argumentative strategy that I deploy here is different – accepting as it does as many of these assumptions as possible to test the coherence of the case on its own terms.

As we have seen, one of comparative advantage's standard caveats assumes away the possibility of capital mobility. At a very basic level, if capital *were* mobile as between countries, the search for the best rate of profit would conceivably cause investment in absolutely advantaged industries around the world, rather than comparatively advantaged ones domestically.

It is interesting that the assumption of capital immobility is made for different reasons by Ricardo than it is by contemporary mainstream analysts. For the former, capital should be treated as immobile as the connections that people feel for their home countries, and the uncertainty they experience in entrusting investments to the laws and governments of unfamiliar places, act as checks on foreign investment.[54] On the other hand, mainstream analysts – confronted by a world in which Ricardo's assertion simply does not bear itself out – have converted the issue of capital immobility into a 'heuristic' or simplifying assumption: one which is made for reasons of expediency, and that can be relaxed at further stages of analysis. As is its *modus operandi* in respect of such assumptions, mainstream economics has generated a series of analyses to handle real-world departures from this assumption and to address critiques that the case for free trade is abrogated where capital is mobile.[55]

In keeping with my strategy of not unduly disturbing the base assumptions of the comparative advantage model in examining that model, I do not wish to quibble with economists on this point for the moment. However, there *is* a difficulty here. While comparative advantage models cleave to the assumption of capital immobility in the context of international trade, exchange-rate determination models do not necessarily do so in the context of international payments (though they do tend to characterize the relationship between capital flows and exchange-rate determination in a peculiar – problematic – way, as we shall see). This complicates matters, given the parasitic relationship between these two areas in the context of the case for free trade.

My strategy to address this will be the following: I will not weaken the assumption of capital immobility as it relates directly to the principle of comparative advantage. I *will*, however, interrogate the coherence of the economic treatment of capital flows in relation to exchange rates on its own terms (i.e., allowing capital mobility), and will then track back and identify the implications of that coherence (or not) for the analytical completeness of the case for free trade.

The theory of exchange-rate determination has opened the door to consider capital flows – I just seek to walk through it and examine whether the theory's stories are accurate. In this regard, I wish to merely take each branch of economics on its own – though different – terms and assumptions. At base, the problem here is thrown up by the rigid balkanization of international economics into international trade and international finance camps. I will have more to say about the reasons and results of this separation in due course.

So, back to the matter at hand and starting from the beginning – in a situation of floating exchange rates, the determination of currency prices occurs in foreign exchange asset markets, and specifically, will be determined by supply and demand for the relevant currency in those markets. Fundamentally, the question that we must ask is: What are the sources of the relevant supply and demand?

At a fundamental level (and assuming away government intervention), there are four key purposes for which foreign currency may be demanded:

1. The importation of goods and services.
2. Direct foreign investment.

3. Portfolio foreign investment.
4. In order to shift assets from one country or another for reasons of political, fiscal or business benefit, and so forth.[56]

The total demand for a given foreign currency will be the aggregate of these four elements. Imagining a two-country model, supply of foreign currency occurs when local currency is demanded by foreigners. Finding an equilibrium point (exchange rate) for supply and demand in the market follows easily from this.

But, again, total demand is a composite of demand referable to four separate elements, with supply of foreign currency similarly composite. Whether or not supply and demand referable to *trade* will be the predominant factor in determining the equilibrium exchange rate will depend upon the size of that component of demand referable to trade in goods (and services) relative to that portion of demand referable to other transactions. In a situation of no (or very small as compared to trade-related demand) capital flow-related demand, it is possible that that the equilibrium exchange rate will settle on (or very close to) a trade-balancing exchange rate.

However, in a situation where demand from capital flows significantly dwarfs trade flow-related currency demand (as is often the case in today's foreign currency markets), and where there is no reason to think that (especially portfolio) capital investors are concerned about factors that drive imports and exports, the foreign exchange market could easily be in equilibrium and trade be unbalanced. A surplus country may accrue liquid assets, but there is no reason to think that these will be converted into illiquid assets (goods and services), and especially not foreign-made illiquid assets.[57]

Moreover, when the role of market participant behaviour and expectations are acknowledged (as they are by some of the models that I have canvassed above), the question must be answered: Why would participants in foreign exchange markets behave in a way that ensures that the actual exchange rate would converge in the trade-balancing exchange rate?[58] As John Harvey notes, following Keynes, '[...] the driving factors of these massive financial flows [are] [...] fundamentally distinct from those determining trade flows – different people, different agendas, different goals and worldviews.'[59] While international traders may require currency to facilitate the flow of goods and services, currency wholesalers and portfolio investors are playing in foreign exchange markets to generate quite a different set out outcomes, and in quite different ways.

Indeed, in recent times, interesting paths of investigation have opened in exploring the role of heterogeneous and nonrational investor expectations, arbitrage and speculative behaviour, momentum and bandwagon effects, bubbles and other macroeconomic disequilibria in determining exchange rates, particularly in light of the dominance in that market of capital flow-related foreign currency trade.[60] These speculative, risk-hedging, arbitrage-based and at times irrational elements of both expectations and behaviour are driven by purely *financial* (i.e., not trade-related) considerations.[61] Just as a range of considerations will be relevant to market actor behaviour, a range of considerations will be relevant to expectation formation – from trade imbalances to assumptions about how to interpret such information, to a range of investor psychological responses in the face of uncertainty, such as availability defaulting to best available courses of action, biases towards strategies based upon past results or experience, the desire for quick results, irrational exuberance or pessimism and convention.

The effect of this behaviour on the operation and dynamics of capital markets in general, and foreign exchange markets in particular, creates intense volatility in respect of exchange rates. This volatility may – and often does – drag the exchange rate in directions bearing no connection to a level that would balance trade.[62] Movements in exchange rates represent the effects of runaway speculation, not merely trade flows or anything that might realistically answer the description of the 'fundamentals' such as the relative health of economies or demand for currency to facilitates trade flows. Speculation and profit seeking defines the path of production; funds are allocated by reference to potential for speculative gains, leading to – from a comparative advantage point of view – massive misinvestment and incorrect price signals in respect of domestic specialization and international trade.[63]

Given the possibility of non-trade-balancing equilibria in foreign exchange markets, it is difficult to imagine why short-term nonbalancing of trade will be overcome in the long run. The Keynesianesque critique of long-run analysis – the notion that the long run is nothing other than the sum of multiple short runs – must be confronted.[64] Moreover, the impediments to balanced trade are not the sorts of constraints, rigidities and transaction cost issues that are often thought to be overcome in the long run. Rather, what prevents the balancing of trade in the short run are structural and systemic issues in respect of foreign exchange markets that remain unchanged in the long run.

In light of all of this, insistence on the role of fundamentals in the construction of exchange rate determination models, on the assumed passivity of financial flows, and on the lack speculative behaviour in foreign exchange markets, take on a shrill tone. In the context of comparative advantage and balanced trade, this insistence appears to be (explicitly or implicitly) an attempt by mainstream theorists to – in a suspect and circular fashion – recite, assume or structure their way into the result that is sought to be confirmed. But the assertion is based upon a fictional picture of the efficient and smooth operation of foreign exchange markets and the dominance within these of trade flows and other 'fundamentals'. As others have convincingly argued, 'fundamentals' are defined in an ad hoc manner to ensure the efficient operation and beneficence of currency markets.[65] It is to secure the outcome (balanced trade and more broadly socially optimal and efficient market outcomes) by rigging the models, by making the result depend on variables that guarantee that result and excluding others that do not. Beyond fiction, however, and speaking analytically, there is no robust reason to expect an automatic adjustment in exchange rates in the face of a trade imbalance.

Do exchange rate variations correct for trade imbalances?

Even if exchange rates did – or could be made to – adjust so as to cause a currency deflation in the event of a trade deficit (or inflation in the case of a trade surplus), a question remains: Will such a movement have the *effect* of ameliorating unbalanced trade?

As a first step, it is important to note that an unfavourable trade balance will be corrected only if there is a net change in the monetary value of a nation's exports minus the value of its imports. Simply – for a period the deficit country must export relatively more than it imports. Returning to our example, what this means is that if England is running a trade deficit and Portugal a surplus, a decrease in the prices of England's exports *alone* says nothing about whether trade will adjust and balance. Rather, for this to happen, the volume of English exports traded must increase, and increase sufficiently such that the increase, when multiplied by the new (decreased) price, leads to a net improvement in England's trade balance.

The question of whether such a shift will in fact occur depends upon how sensitive the volumes of imports and exports demanded are to fluctuations in price (i.e., the price elasticity of demand of imports and exports). Alternatively put, much depends on the extent to which an exchange rate shift (which causes a change in the prices of foreign traded goods) will cause consumers in each country to choose to consume different goods.

Mainstream economics has developed an apparatus to address this issue. The Marshall–Lerner condition states that only when the sum of price elasticities for imports and exports is greater than one will exchange rate fluctuations cause a shift in trade balances. That is, a further condition must be fulfilled before exchange rate shifts will cause trade to balance; balancing is not automatic. Furthermore, where the condition is only just satisfied, there remains a question as to whether the fluctuation will be large enough to cause a significant enough shift to correct for the relevant trade balance.[66] Mainstream presentations of exchange rate fluctuations often assume that income and export price elasticities of demand are infinite, such that even small changes in the exchange rate correct for trade imbalances.[67] Of course, again, this is tantamount to assuming away the question of whether trade balances be ameliorated by exchange rate fluctuations, not answering it.[68]

Empirical studies appear to demonstrate that for developed countries (at the very least), the Marshall–Lerner condition tends not to be satisfied, and therefore an exchange rate fluctuation will not rectify a trade imbalance. Indeed, in the short run, a currency depreciation can actually seem to worsen a trade imbalance.[69] This is the issue of the so-called 'J-Curve' – the idea that a country's current account balance may initially deteriorate following a currency depreciation, as consumers are carried forward by a sort of consumption pattern 'inertia', notwithstanding changes in price of foreign goods (and vice versa in the case of a currency appreciation). While this deterioration is thought to be a short-run phenomenon, an often-unanswered (and indeed, unanswerable on the basis of mainstream theoretical accounts) question is: For precisely how long will the downward trend in the J-Curve persist?[70] Currency fluctuations and persistently noncorrected trade balances are neither rare nor exceptional in today's global economy.[71]

While the Marshall–Learner condition is one that is well known, acknowledged and indeed, was generated by mainstream economists, its implications (or more importantly, those of its possible nonfulfilment) for the justificatory scheme supporting free trade are perhaps less well acknowledged. The condition further highlights the inability of the mainstream to analytically demonstrate a mechanism – the easy and automatic operation of the invisible hand – that guarantees a connection between free trade and efficient domestic specialization. Indeed, the Marshall–Learner condition is an express acknowledgement that such a mechanism will not operate in all places and at all times.

Economic Theory's Double Failure – Analytical and Empirical

As I hope will be clear from the discussion above, mainstream economic theory fails to provide rigorous analytical closure in respect of the first component claim of comparative advantage–based justification for free trade. It claims – but fails to establish – that an automatic mechanism exists to ensure that free trade and specialization will follow comparative rather than absolute advantage.

In a situation where one country's absolutely advantaged goods are flooding the market of its trading partner, in order for comparative advantage rather than absolute advantage to dominate, exchange rates must adjust to trade-balancing levels. As we have seen above, there is no necessity that they will. Even if they do, will this adjustment actually lead to an equalization of the trade imbalance? Again, not necessarily.

It is therefore altogether possible that relative prices will not shift in a way that causes free trade and specialization to follow comparative advantage, allowing trade imbalances to persist and goods essentially to be incorrectly priced.[72] Goods in which a country does not have a comparative disadvantage may be domestically produced, and goods in which a comparative advantage is held may not be produced or exported. This possibility requires abandoning the 'comfortable' fantasy offered by the principle of comparative advantage that a country cannot be 'undersold all around',[73] and that free trade *necessarily* generates efficient patterns of international specialization.

It is possible to begin to make sense of the theoretical disarray found in the economics of exchange rates and international payments more generally when one considers the well-known and acknowledged fact that, empirically,[74] exchange rates do *not* obey the theoretical models that have been constructed by economists, and that – at least in the short to medium term – international trade does not balance.[75] There seems to be some assertion from mainstream economists that it may balance in the long term.[76] In addition to Keynesian-style critiques of long-run analysis (mentioned above), such arguments must also confront the fact that since the liberalization of international capital flows beginning in the mid-1970s and 1980s,[77] persistent imbalances have become commonplace,[78] and that such imbalances and currency fluctuations coexist. In addition to leaving unanswered the question of precisely how long the 'long term' actually is, it also forces us to doubt the efficiency promises of comparative advantage in the (potentially persistent) interim.

The recent history of the global economy – and particularly the recent Global Financial Crisis[79] – provides us with a stark example that highlights the incredulity of the mainstream fiction of trade flow-dominated and efficient foreign exchange markets. I quote liberally from the United Nations Conference on Trade and Development (UNCTAD) *Trade and Development Report* for 2009:

> The financial crisis has shown that the basic assumption underlying this approach to economic policymaking is wrong: financial markets do not make correct judgments on economic performance and on the quality of economic policies. They are not concerned with the proper interpretation of macroeconomic fundamentals; otherwise a number of economies with excessive private debts – including those that were destinations of carry trade operations, but also the United States – would not have attracted excessive amounts of capital. Moreover, actors in financial markets are not concerned with properly assessing the performance of corporate firms or with the long-term valuation of real estate; otherwise large bubbles would not have occurred in stock and real estate markets. And they are not concerned with a correct interpretation of real demand-supply relations in primary commodity markets; otherwise there would not have been excessive commodity price fluctuations. Rather, they are concerned with guessing how certain 'news' will influence the behaviour of other financial market participants, so as to derive maximum benefits from asset price movements triggered by 'herd behaviour', no matter whether this is justified by fundamental economic performance indicators...
>
> The most important lesson of the recent global crisis is that financial markets do not 'get the prices right'; they systematically overshoot or undershoot due to centralized information handling, which is quite different from the information collection of normal goods markets. In financial markets, nearly all participants react in a more or less uniform manner to the same set of 'information' or 'news', so that they wind or unwind their exposure to risk almost in unison.

The currency market, in particular, causes results quite different from those envisaged by theory, such as an appreciation of the nominal exchange rate in countries that have high inflation rates over considerable periods of time. In fact, high-inflation countries are the main targets for short-term capital flows, because they usually offer high interest rates. In so doing, they attract 'investors' that use interest rate arbitrage by carrying money from countries with low interest rates to those with high interest rates, thereby putting pressure on the currency of the latter to appreciate. This is just the opposite of what is required by macroeconomic fundamentals: countries with relatively high inflation need nominal devaluation to restore their competitiveness in goods markets, and those with low inflation need appreciation.[80]

In light of mainstream economics' analytical and empirical failures, we are thrown back to the problem with which we began this chapter. On what basis does mainstream economic theory claim that free trade will follow comparative advantage? Mainstream economics attempts to recite itself into the conclusion that it seeks to prove. However, the recital is weak and plagued by analytical suspiciousness and empirical contradiction. Fiction is heaped upon fiction; however, the task of specifying an automatic adjustment mechanism – and therefore justifying the beneficence of international trade – is severely hampered by the impossibility of the task. No such mechanism in fact exists.

Even where mainstream economists are forced to cognize the lack of an automatic adjustment mechanism in the balance of payments, they shirk from appreciating its logical implications for the case for free trade. For example, some economists – having first argued that trade will balance in the long term – when faced with the reality of longstanding large imbalances, then argue that the balance of payments 'is not a problem'. For instance, Krugman has written that

even persistent trade imbalances are not necessarily a problem, and certainly [...] surpluses are not a sure sign of health or deficits one of weakness [...] the trade balance is equal to the difference between savings and investment, and that a country may justifiably run persistent deficits if it is an attractive site for foreign investment.[81]

In fact, Krugman is speaking about something slightly different and seems to miss the point. A trade imbalance, while perhaps tolerable in an overall economic sense, is – as we have seen – *absolutely* a problem for the justificatory scheme that comparative advantage establishes for free trade. Without balanced trade, the model cannot establish that specialization will converge on comparative advantage.

Moreover, this fallback argument is peculiar coming from Krugman, who himself – as we saw above – has asserted that a mechanism of the sort required does in fact operate, and that a core lesson that economics students should be taught is that trade imbalances do self-correct.[82] In light of the above concession that persistent trade imbalances may exist, this starts to look like a suggestion that we should teach people what we want them to think, rather than what can be shown in theory. Even if basic and simplified models are argued to be usefully applied for the purposes of policy analysis, surely their use is rendered acceptable only if mainstream economics can 'cash out' its claims at more sophisticated levels of analysis. The problem is that economics does not appear to be able to do so.

The Linked Fiction: Trade Misimagined

There is another way of thinking about the problem here. The failure to specify a robust, nonfictional mechanism to link free trade and specialization on the basis of comparative advantage is essentially the shadow of a related – but equally fictional – understanding of international trade that undergirds the mainstream case for free trade. This one-dimensional conceptualization of trade is instantiated through several of orthodox theory's key assumptions and is the reason that mainstream international trade and economic theory struggles without success to complete the justificatory circle here.

Specifically, mainstream comparative advantage–based models of international trade essentially conceptualize that trade using what might be called 'abstract barter' models. I want to highlight both aspects of this – the barter and the abstraction. While these aspects are linked, the former in particular is useful in explaining the difficulties that were highlighted above concerning the lack of analytical or empirical closure concerning comparative advantage's predictive claim.

Let us begin with the 'barter' aspect of the model. What I mean by this is that trade is understood as involving the exchange of goods or commodities for other goods or commodities, wine for cloth, for example. According to this conception, while the use of 'money' as a means of exchange might create the impression that there is something more complicated going on, this is simply a confusion. Money is nothing more than a neutral intercommodity medium that is fundamentally irrelevant to trade itself. As John Stuart Mill remarked,

> Since all trade is in reality barter, money being a mere instrument for exchanging things against one another...international trade [is] in form, what it always is in reality, an actual trucking of one commodity against another.[83]

My characterization of international trade models as barter-based is not a controversial one – modern mainstream economists agree that this conceptualization is an appropriate understanding of trade. At a simplistic though not inaccurate level, it is because international trade is barter that trade will always balance – a country cannot suffer a trade imbalance, because in order to secure goods (imports), it must trade for other goods (exports) of the same value. The two transactions net off to zero. Again – so the argument goes – while the introduction of money as medium of exchange might make things look like something else is going on, this is merely a deception of appearances. Money is neutral. It is, to borrow Schumpeter's terminology, merely a 'veil' that is cast over trade in commodities,[84] and does not affect the real economy.

This barter model highlights – and indeed, allows – the schism in, and balkanization of, international economics into 'international trade' and 'international finance' subdisciplines. It makes possible the separate and autonomous lives of money and finance on the one hand, and 'real' issues barter and trade on the other, that we saw playing itself out in the mainstream models discussed earlier in this chapter. Trade and trade balances are about the exchange of goods. Payments and exchange rates reflect that barter, and hence, money and finance are nothing other than white noise that cannot affect trade, which *always* balances. Moreover, the effect of the balkanization of the discipline of international economics means that even where, at higher levels of sophistication, researchers in one subdiscipline develop results or models that might potentially cast doubt on those of the other, these insights tend not to cross-pollinate.[85] This allows, for example, trade theorists to continue on oblivious (wilfully or not) of developments in international finance that seriously undermine their most basic conclusions.[86]

In addition to imagining international trade as premised on barter, comparative advantage models of trade are also 'abstract' models. What I mean by this is that there is little or no regard paid to differences as between different economies, or – critically for our current purposes – different participants within economies. In fact, this is considered to be the great strength of neoclassical economic theory. Neoclassical models *abstract* from the concrete specificities of economies and economic actors and attempt to lay out rules and principles equally applicable to differentially placed economies and actors. Joan Robinson put the matter nicely when she wrote,

> The neoclassics enunciated what purported to be universal laws, based on human nature – greed, impatience and so forth [...] [they] rarely say anything about the kind of economy to which the argument is to be applied. The suggestion is that the same laws which govern the supposed behaviour of Robinson Crusoe are equally valid [...] for analysing the vagaries of Wall Street.[87]

When confronting mainstream economic models of international trade, the noneconomist is immediately struck by the conspicuous lack of people in those models. Barter of commodities occurs between England and Portugal – producers, sellers and consumers seem largely absent from the story (at least initially). A little further thought, however, reveals that it is not so much the case that there are *no* people in the story, as that the people are all the *same* – countries and economies are constituted by numerous Robinson Crusoes, or following Marglin's terminology, 'yeomen producers' – each at once producer and consumer, worker and owner – producing goods, consuming part, and trading the rest.[88] These people are identically motivated in their interaction with the market – they participate to secure goods through trade of goods they have produced. The farmhand, the factory manager, the unemployed single mother and Bill Gates remain impelled by the same basic considerations.

None of this – so the argument goes – is necessarily a problem; simplification and abstraction are utterly legitimate techniques in economic (and other) analysis. This argument is correct. The relevant question is, however, does the simplification and abstraction *here* aid analysis or divert in the wrong direction and to wrong conclusions?

And in respect of this point we have cause to worry. Our discussion of international trade and payments above shows us the dangerous fictitiousness of this abstract, barter conception of trade. Critically, this conception leads us to ignore key dynamics and elements of the modern economic environment. The contemporary capitalist economy is inherently financialized, driven by investment and production decisions of profit-seeking actors, and riddled with uncertainty. Players in the global economy are not identically situated agents. Countries are not populated by homogenously placed and motivated actors. Rather, actors are differentially empowered, constrained and characterized – involving themselves in global markets for goods, services, capital and currencies for a range of purposes. Importantly, many of these actors play in these markets for the purposes of short-term financial gain, rather than merely to facilitate the movement of goods and services, or in ways that guarantee the smooth and efficient operation of these markets.

To model behaviour, market activity, expectations or anything else without properly understanding the nature of economic activity in the global economy leads the modeller into profound error and practical irrelevance, their models tending to distort rather than harmlessly simplify. The ill effects of this fictional modelling become apparent in the context of the comparative advantage model of international trade. The abstract barter model encourages economists to see the balancing of trade as inevitable. The assumption of monetary neutrality diverts attention away from the role of finance in matters of international trade. The motivations of actors are misconceived and misunderstood by these models, confusing and mystifying the dynamics of foreign exchange markets.

We shall have cause to return to the question of neoclassicalism's faulty and fictitious simplification and abstraction in subsequent chapters. For the moment, it is sufficient to recognize that these are critical reasons that the actually existing economic phenomena of, and related to, international trade so stubbornly defy assimilation by the neoclassical models.[89]

Summary: The Imagined Hand

The case for free trade suffers from an immediate problem of justificatory insufficiency. Though necessarily called upon to analytically bear out the claim that free trade will cause countries to specialize in their comparative advantage, mainstream economics does not supply the mechanism that is needed to justify this claimed result. In fact, observable phenomena seem to fail to throw up even the necessary empirical precursors to this result. Exchange rates cannot do the work required of them in the mainstream analysis – they cannot bear the explanatory burden placed upon them.

The asserted invisible hand of international trade gently but firmly guiding trade and specialization towards efficiency has eluded our search and revealed its illusory and fairy-tale nature. It is based in a fictional understanding of the nature of international trade in the global economy. As posited, the invisible hand is imagined but absent, and our hunt devolves into the search for 'the grin of a black cat in a dark room who is not there anyway'.[90] We shall have reason to encounter more such economic searches in the coming pages.

We have already touched on the gravity of the problem created by this imagination run wild. Without a mechanism to convert relative cost differentials into price differentials, there is nothing about free international trade that will cause specialization on the basis of comparative advantage. Returning to our example, Portugal will be producing and exporting goods in relation to which it does not have a comparative advantage, while England's comparative advantage remains untapped as it imports rather than produces good in which it holds such an advantage. Free trade, that is, will not merely serve efficiency. For as long as England has foreign currency reserves so as to allow it to continue to purchase, it will do so. However, when the money runs out, England either stops buying or sinks into spirals of debt (and importantly, of interest and repayment), monetary instability and macroeconomic crisis.[91]

Importantly, our discussion in this chapter has hinted at a critical theme to which we will have cause to return. Comparative advantage involves a prediction about economic phenomena. But it must not be forgotten that what this means is a prediction about *human behaviour*. The case for free trade posits, but does not supply, a mechanism in law-like form by abstracting from that which makes and motivates that behaviour. Cause and effect are sought to be established in a way not dissimilar to the manner in which the natural sciences attempt to describe physical phenomena. Economic actors become nothing other than bodies colliding in a vacuum. But, of course, economic phenomena are not identical to natural phenomena in ways that this faulty and fictitious simplification and abstraction might have us believe. It is barely surprising that economics cannot supply a mechanism to drive international trade – as we have seen, economic actors are not driven by the same kinds of cause-and-effect relations that science posits when bodies collide in a vacuum. People do not bounce consistently.

Chapter 4

CLOCKWORK PRODUCTION AND THE ORIGIN-MYTHS OF SPECIALIZATION

> We are told that free trade would create an international division of labour, and thereby give to each country the production which is most in harmony with its natural advantages. You believe, perhaps, gentlemen, that the production of coffee or sugar is the natural destiny of the West Indies? Two centuries ago, nature, which does not trouble herself about commerce, had planted neither sugarcane nor coffee trees there.
>
> Karl Marx[1]

In the previous chapter, I identified the manner in which mainstream economic theory conceptualizes international trade through the prism of a fictional abstract barter model and posits an eerily absent invisible hand that automatically nudges trade and specialization into an efficient shape. We saw that this conceptualization fails to capture important – and indeed, driving – dynamics that are at play in international trade and in the modern global economy more broadly. What emerged from that discussion is that the mainstream theory of international trade cannot analytically and nonfictionally support the claim that free trade will cause countries to specialize in production of those goods in which they hold a comparative advantage.

In this chapter, we will examine a further and related fiction that permeates the case for free trade – specifically, the story that is told of production and the productive process. The question of production is central to the case for free trade, though it is often underemphasized by mainstream analysis (in ways that will become clear).

To begin with, recall the second component claim of the comparative advantage–driven case for free trade:

1. In a situation of free trade, the direction and pattern of trade and specialization will be driven by comparative advantage.
2. *Specialization on the basis of comparative advantage and trade will lead to gains.*
3. Gains from trade can potentially make each country better off as a whole.
4. Therefore, a policy of free trade should be adopted.

I have already discussed the coherence of this logical claim.[2] Where relative opportunity costs differ between countries, there certainly are gains (in the relevant sense) to be had in producing and trading lower opportunity cost goods. This is a matter of logic, and I do not wish to challenge that claim *qua* logic.[3] Rather, I wish to take a step back and get behind this logical claim by asking a more basic question – where do comparative advantages come from?

Now, to say that a country 'has a comparative advantage' is at base to say something about the character of the domestic production of a good. The question that we will ask in this chapter is: When will a country have a comparative advantage – and what precisely is going on in the social world when this is the case?

Taking this step back and exploring the origins of comparative advantages themselves will assist us greatly in understanding the true force of the case for free trade. The stories that are usually told about the sources of trade advantage and of specialization – and particularly the fictions that are at the core of these – tend to create the *impression* that comparative advantages are borne of simple natural and technical constraint, determinate and/or given in a quasi-naturalistic fashion, in some sense passive and beyond the scope of human action. This conceptualization in turn militates towards a presumption in favour of a hands-off or laissez-faire approach to policy setting: leave the market alone and let the invisible hand optimize and deliver the available gains. However, this framing of the issue is apt to cause confusion in respect of both the role and scope of sociopolitical forces in influencing patterns of advantage and specialization, and also the straightforwardness of discerning what precisely is meant by a policy of 'free' international trade. Delving, therefore, into the origins of trade advantage will allow us to shine new light on the very core of the case for free trade.

A quick note: for the purposes of this chapter I will assume (contrary to what was shown in the previous chapter) that trade does, or can be made to, follow comparative advantage. However, this assumption is of little moment – as will become clear, the fundamentals of the analysis here will hold in respect of the bases of absolute advantages in trade as much as for those of comparative advantage.

The Determinants of Comparative Advantage: Mainstream Tales of the Origins of Specialization

Recall that comparative advantage analysis traces gains from trade to differences in opportunity costs in the production of the relevant goods between trading partners, and that having a comparative advantage in the production of a good means that a country can produce the relevant good at a lower opportunity cost relative to its trading partner. Therefore, where trade follows comparative advantage, particular patterns of advantage and specialization – as well as the magnitude of the resultant gains from trade – will depend upon on the particular patterns of costs and opportunity costs *in production* that exist in and between trading countries.

Thus, to understand the sources of advantages in trade, the question becomes: What determines those patterns of costs and opportunity costs? Production – one would imagine – must therefore take centre stage in the analysis. I will argue that international economics in its neoclassical form tends to conceptualize the process of production in a much-stylized fashion that actually retards economics' ability to grasp and understand patterns of costs and opportunity costs. To bear out this claim, I begin by sketching mainstream perspectives concerning the sources of comparative advantages in international trade.

Ricardian half-stories

Ricardo was primarily concerned with the manner in which comparative opportunity costs (however they arise), rather than absolute productivity differences, define the pattern of international free trade. He did not have much to say about the source of comparative advantages, though it is possible to draw some conclusions from his discussion of international trade in his *Principles of Political Economy and Taxation*.

Ricardo's approach might be helpfully understood as a technology and resources-based approach to comparative advantage. The thrust of his – relatively sparse – comments about the sources of comparative advantages is that they are exogenous, given existing resources, and technology,[4] which defines the relationship between inputs and outputs of a production processes, is assumed to be fixed.[5] Fixed in the model does not imply immutable in reality, however. Ricardo was pointing to the dependency of comparative advantages on levels of technology and resultant productivity. He was *not* saying that comparative advantages are immutable, or that technology and productivity would not change over time.[6]

Modern retellings: The Heckscher–Ohlin–Samuelson approach

Although Ricardo himself was less interested in explaining particular patterns of specialization and trade, the international trade theory that has grown from his work *has* focused on trying to understand in more detail the reasons for differences in comparative opportunity costs.

Following the development of technical machinery to handle general equilibrium interactions of tastes, technology and factor endowments in the 1930s, trade theory became clearly established as a branch of neoclassical general equilibrium theory.[7] As part of this subsumation into the neoclassical camp, the basic trade model has expanded from a two-nation x two-commodity x *one*-factor model to a two-nation x two-commodity x *two*-actor model, which introduces capital as a primary factor (or input into the productive process) on the same footing as labour.

According to that model, if it were to be the case that economies have identical technology, factor endowments and consumer preferences, they would have the same autarky equilibrium and would therefore have no incentive to trade. Thus, countries must differ in relation to one of these three elements if trade is to occur. The dominant strand of neoclassical theorizing has focused on the role of relative factor endowments in defining patterns of trade and specialization.

After Ricardo, the key theoretical development in the comparative advantage analysis came through Scandinavian economists Eli Heckscher and Bertil Ohlin. Paul Samuelson also contributed to the finessing and elaboration of that approach some years later. The resulting Heckscher–Ohlin–Samuelson branch of trade theory is basically a combination of four interlocking theorems,[8] each starting from the premise of identical tastes and technology. It is fundamentally based upon the twin observations that

1. countries differ from each other in the composition of their factor endowments (i.e., capital and labour); and
2. productive activities are distinguished by the different relative intensities with which they use these factors.

The Heckscher–Ohlin–Samuelson approach basically assumes that for every commodity there is a single best or most efficient technique for the production of that good, and that technology does not differ as between countries (i.e., the most efficient technique is available to all countries). Thus, the neoclassical rendering of sources of comparative advantages diverts focus away from the technology issues that were of such importance to Ricardo, at least as an initial step.

Rather, Heckscher–Ohlin–Samuelson theory asks how intensively a production technology uses a factor in relation to which a given country is relatively well endowed. Broadly, the Heckscher–Ohlin–Samuelson approach states that a country's comparative advantage will be determined by the relative abundance of factors of production intensively used in the production of the relevant commodity.[9] For example, if England is relatively well endowed with capital, and if capital is intensively used in the production of cloth as opposed to wine, it is likely, according to the Heckscher–Ohlin–Samuelson approach, that England will have a comparative advantage in the production of cloth.

Critiques of the Heckscher–Ohlin–Samuelson Approach to the Origins of Comparative Advantage

The Heckscher–Ohlin–Samuelson approach has been assailed by both theoretical and empirical attacks. In relation to both of these, and as we shall now briefly see, the critics of the approach have had the better of the argument.

Analytical failures

The first – and often pointed to – problem for Heckscher–Ohlin–Samuelson is its dependence on a highly restrictive set of assumptions. One which has been the particular focus of criticism is the assumption of a shared level of technology across all countries. As mentioned above, the Heckscher–Ohlin–Samuelson approach relies upon this notion so as to make possible the prediction that factor abundance will make more viable the production of particular commodities. However, this assumption is, of course, patently false.[10] The predictive task that this approach sets itself becomes much more complicated (though arguably not impossible) where access to technology varies between countries.

Even assuming these difficulties can be overcome, is it the case that a single 'best' productive technique exists that it is easily tied to relative factor abundance as the Heckscher–Ohlin–Samuelson approach requires? Answering this question goes to the heart of neoclassical capital and production theory. Importantly, issues relevant to this question received profound treatment as part of a scathing analytical and theoretical assault upon neoclassical capital theory – and by implication, the Heckscher–Ohlin–Samuelson family of theorems – by a group of economists associated with the University of Cambridge (often dubbed the 'Cambridge Radicals'). This critique has become known as the Cambridge Capital Critique and represents one-half of the Cambridge–Cambridge Capital Controversy, a theoretical and mathematical debate that raged in the pages of economic journals between the mid-1950s and the mid-1970s.

The debate concerned the nature and role of capital goods in economic theory, and the dominant neoclassical accounts of aggregate production and distribution of that which is produced between economic actors.[11] The key Cambridge Radical debaters were Joan Robinson, Piero Sraffa and their followers at (though not exclusively) the University of Cambridge and Paul Samuelson, Robert Solow and others at (again, though not exclusively) the Massachusetts Institute of Technology, in Cambridge, Massachusetts. This critique – though generally seen as both important and (on balance) unanswered by the 'US' side of the Controversy[12] – has faded from memory and is now a relatively forgotten episode in the history of economic thought.[13] For these reasons, and for the fact that my argument later in this chapter involves an extension of certain aspects of that critique, I will take the time here to briefly set out its core moves.[14] I will then relate these back to the Heckscher–Ohlin–Samuelson approach and its predictions.

The Cambridge Capital Critique

The key problem to which the Cambridge Radicals point is the difficulty in specifying a metric by which to measure 'capital', or perhaps more precisely, the fictional manner in which neoclassical analysis attempts to do this.

Why is measuring capital important? Neoclassical economic theory relies on the notion of scarcity to dictate prices, including factor prices and thus the price of capital itself. If one seeks – as neoclassical economics does – to establish that markets generate efficient, fair and optimal outcomes, getting a handle on aggregate economic performance and economic returns to particular factor owners is critical.

The neoclassical aggregate production function for society suggests that the total output of society (Q) is some function of available capital (K) and labour (L) such that:

$$Q = f(K, L)$$

Under usual neoclassical assumptions, this model gives rise to three 'parables' (to use Samuelson's term[15]):

1. The real return on capital (the rate of profit[16]) is determined by the technical properties of the diminishing marginal productivity of capital.
2. A greater quantity of capital leads to a lower marginal product of additional capital, and thus lowers the rate of profit. This relation between the quantity of capital and return or price of capital is therefore an inverse monotonic one (i.e., in sequence consistently increasing and never decreasing, or consistently decreasing and never increasing).
3. The distribution of income between labourers and capitalists is explained by the relative factor supplies and their marginal products. That is, in respect of capital – the price of capital (i.e., the rate of interest or profit) is determined by the relative scarcity and marginal productivity of aggregate capital.

Factor (for neoclassical economists, labour and capital) productivity, prices and returns are thus a 'neutral' or objective matter of technical properties and relative abundance.

However, problems immediately arise when we try to grasp hold of and measure aggregate capital. First, consider precisely what is meant when we say an amount of capital.[17] The term capital can mean either capital goods (e.g., machines) or financial flows. However, financial flows are not *factors* of production in the sense that one can speak about them being used in any particular physical production process – they must first be converted into capital goods.

But, if by 'capital' we mean heterogeneous capital *goods*, there must be some way of establishing a standard measurement as to their value: either on a costs-of-production basis,[18] or on the basis of the present value of future income that they will bring. However, valuation on either of these bases requires the consideration of 'real' time, and presumes a rate of profit. But herein lies a problem of circularity. As we have seen, in mainstream theory, the rate of profit can only be ascertained – because it is a function of the scarcity of capital – by reference to the return on an *amount* of capital. The circularity is this – the amount of capital cannot be determined without presuming a profit rate, which in turn depends on specifying an amount of capital.

The interdependence of rate of profit and quantity of capital gives rise to what are called Wicksell effects – changes in the value of capital stock associated with different interest or profit rates. For example, revaluations of the same physical stock can occur due to new capital good prices (a price Wicksell effect). Alternatively, different physical stocks of capital goods can lead to changes in the value of capital stock (a real Wicksell effect). The problems that such effects create in turn are 'reswitching' and 'capital reversal'. The former occurs when the same technique (a particular physical capital to labour ratio) is preferred at both of two (or more) profit rates, with some other technique preferred at the intermediate profit rates. 'Reswitching' in turn implies the possibility of 'capital reversing', a situation in which a lower capital to labour ratio is associated with a lower rate of profit. In other words, there may be points at which capital has a lower return or price when it is relatively more scarce, or relatively more intensively used in production.

Both reswitching and capital reversal deny the monotonic relations in respect of the interest rate and capital intensity that forms the basis of neoclassical analysis. One technique (capital intensity) can be associated with more than one interest (or profit) rate – the monotonic relationship between intensive use of capital and return to capital cannot hold (which contravenes Samuelson's neoclassical parables 1 and 2). Further, prices and rates of return (such as the interest rate/profit rate) do not yield unambiguous demand effects or vice versa (denying parables 2 and 3). That is, for example, lower rates of interest may not always translate into a greater demand for capital. Samuelson's parables thus start to take on a rather fictional hue.

To illustrate, imagine two different production techniques, each involving different amounts of capital and labour.[19] Suppose that one (technique A) involves a two-stage production process which involves seven units of labour, and that all of the labour is used in the first period.

Imagine the second (technique B) involves eight units of labour, but is a three-stage process, in which two units of labour are used in the first period, none in the second, and six units in the third. A tabular presentation may aid clarity here.

Table 4.1. Production techniques

	Technique A	Technique B
Period 1	7 units of labour	2 units of labour
Period 2	0 units of labour	0 units of labour
Period 3		6 units of labour

We can then imagine the following technique selections in light of changes in the price of capital or interest rate:

1. At very high interest rates, compounding interest in relation to the expenditure on labour early in a *longer* production process (Technique B) will be high, and so the profit maximizer will prefer Technique A.
2. As the interest rate declines, there will be a point at which the compounding effect of the interest will become less significant, and early labour input will be less significant. Technique B will become preferred, and the profit-maximizing actor or firm will switch to it from Technique A.
3. If the interest rate continues to decline, labour (rather than capital) costs become the most important factor, at which point the profit maximizer will switch back to the lower labour input Technique A.[20]

What this illustration belies is that simple reliance on the scarcity or abundance of capital can be used as a clear indication of either price or rates of return or election of technically efficient production process. The difficulties and paradoxes highlighted by the Cambridge Capital Controversy decimate the coherence of the neoclassical account of capital, of its use in the production process and of distribution of that which is produced through that process. The concept of capital that sits as a building block for the neoclassical scheme is simply incoherent.

Back to comparative advantage

What then is the impact of the Cambridge Capital Critique on the neoclassical approach to international trade and comparative advantages?

Well, the Heckscher–Ohlin–Samuelson family of theorems, as is the case with neoclassical economic theory in general, requires an inverse monotonic relationship between the quantity of capital and its rate of return (i.e., the more scarce is capital, the higher is its return). Those theorems also require that the rate of return to capital is monotonically related to the capital to labour ratio in the production of each commodity (i.e., the more intensively that capital is used in production, the more expensive it is or the greater is its return). Additionally, the main Heckscher–Ohlin–Samuelson theorems must also assume that in a two-country, two-commodity, two-factor model, the price ratio between the capital-intensive good and the labour-intensive good will be monotically related to the rate of interest or profit (i.e., where capital is more expensive, goods produced relatively more intensively using capital will also be relatively more expensive). Together, these presumptions suggest that the more scarce is capital, the higher the relative price of capital-intensively produced goods, and the less likely it will be that a country will export a commodity that intensively uses that scarce capital.

The predictions of the theorems as to patterns of comparative advantage are based on these relationships holding.[21] However, in light of the Cambridge Capital Critique, these necessary relationships are thrown into disarray.[22] Factor scarcity does not unambiguously define factor rewards. Nor does it determine relative prices of commodities, the production of which intensively use those factors. It is impossible to make any general prediction about the effect on interest or profit rates of an increase in the relative price of 'capital-intensive' goods, or vice versa.[23] Without the holding of a monotonic relationship between the rate of profit or interest and capital intensity, it is not possible to make robust and unambiguous predictions about the choice of particular productive techniques, or the capital intensity of those techniques. In the absence of bald assumption to the contrary, capital reversal cannot be ruled out, and hence the 'efficient' production technology for a given commodity cannot be specified in a once-and-for-all (or at least in a 'for-all-interest-rates') fashion.

In the context of the Heckscher–Ohlin–Samuelson approach, this translates into the impossibility of making unambiguous statements concerning the production advantages that will be held by a country on the basis of differences in factor abundances. Where multiple techniques exist for the production of certain commodities, countries may be either forced or may elect to use different technologies by reason of both relative factor endowments. The easy connection between factor abundance and election of production technique is thus ripped asunder.[24] The Cambridge Capital Critique thus spells disaster for the predictive ability of the Heckscher–Ohlin–Samuelson approach in respect of patterns of comparative advantage.

Empirical failures

Given that the Heckscher–Ohlin–Samuelson approach claims to be able to explain patterns of comparative advantage by reference to relative factor abundances, it might be imagined that – in the face of theoretical assault – recourse would be had to empirical validation. However, there is an issue here of frying pans and fires: the Heckscher–Ohlin–Samuelson approach has not fared well in empirical testing.

The most famous instance of failure is the so-called Leontief Paradox, named after the (in)famous 1953 study of United States trade by Wassily Leontief. That study found that the United States (the most capital-abundant country in the world by almost any criteria) exported labour-intensive commodities and imported capital-intensive commodities, in contradiction to Heckscher–Ohlin–Samuelson predictions.[25] While theoretical refinement and further testing have proliferated since Leontief's intervention in the debate, paradoxes persist in the empirical testing of the theory.[26] Many economists have continued to support the Heckscher–Ohlin–Samuelson approach on the basis that it predicts something about patterns of comparative advantage, although this is surprising given its failure to consistently do precisely that.

Fiction, Production and Comparative Advantage Analysis

I have taken some time to set out the Cambridge Capital Critique that can and has been levelled against the Heckscher–Ohlin–Samuelson approach to understanding the sources of comparative advantages. That critique powerfully undermines, at the level of internal logic, the Heckscher–Ohlin–Samuelson approach to modelling comparative advantages. That approach attempts to derive predictions about the conduct of profit-maximizing actors in response to resources that are lying around in the economy in greater or lesser abundance. In large part, so too do more Ricardian-style models that build in a larger role for technology differences. What the Cambridge Capital Critique points towards is the fact that the economy and its processes of production and exchange cannot not be nonfictionally modelled as a simple response to scarcity in the mechanistic manner neoclassical economics attempts. For the Cambridge Radicals, scarcity alone does not define prices, distribution, election of technology or, by implication, patterns of costs and comparative advantage.

What does, then? The Cambridge Radicals gestured instead towards context – differing 'power and social relationships in production' and their implications – in determining distributional shares between economic classes.[27] However, they stopped short of explaining or articulating in any substantially clear fashion the nature or determinants of these social and power relations.[28] Theirs was a task of internal critique of neoclassical logic, and as such, their analysis was neither geared towards nor (as a result, unsurprisingly) successful in detailing the social and relational aspects of production.

What the Cambridge Radicals did was open space to better understand the workings of economic processes by undermining the coherence of mainstream economic theory. We will now take advantage of this opened space and build upon their work. My claim will be that the failure of mainstream economic theory in tackling costs, opportunity costs and comparative advantages lies – as it did in the previous chapter – in its employment of a fictional model of economic activity that ignores and obscures important aspects and dynamics at play in actually existing economies and production processes. But again, to highlight the failures of the mainstream approach, let us start with the basics.

Production possibilities, opportunity costs and the 'exogeneity' of comparative advantages

The standard analysis of international trade in a two-country x two-commodity x two-factor model starts from what is called a production possibility frontier. It is usually the case that for each country, two abstract (rather than empirically based) production functions (which indicate the rate of transformation of inputs into outputs) are assumed, one for each commodity. When these production functions are combined with given quantities of inputs,[29] a set of points can be generated in relation to which any increase in the production of one commodity implies a decrease in the production of the other. These points – if plotted on two axes – generate an optimal production possibility frontier, illustrated below.

Figure 4.1. Production possibility frontier and opportunity costs[30]

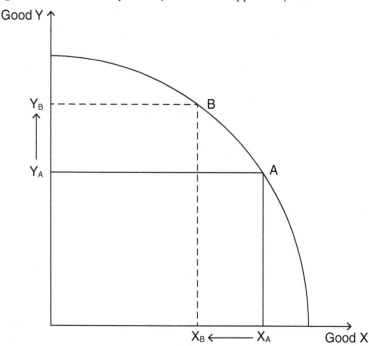

It is possible to read the opportunity costs in respect of the production of a given good from a production possibility frontier. For example, refer to Figure 4.1. Point A represents a combination of produced goods X and Y (in volumes X_A and Y_A) that can be achieved with full employment of resources. If, however, an increase in the production of good Y is desired from amount Y_A to Y_B (represented by a movement vertically along the y-axis), this necessitates that some amount of good X will have to be forgone (the difference between amounts X_A and X_B – represented by a horizontal move along the x-axis towards the origin). The resulting new combination of goods produced will be represented by point B.

It is important to note that, so far, the assumption has been that defining and constructing the production possibility frontier involves a relatively 'objective' set of exercises. One takes a production function, a particular supply of inputs that is merely given and a particular level of technology that is to be assumed – and the process of understanding the total amount of goods that can be produced is a technical matter of proper allocation of resources between production processes.[31] Irrespective of whether production possibility frontiers are constructed on the basis of assumed functions or empirical evidence, there is a tendency to treat these frontiers, and the opportunity costs associated with movements along them, as analytically but also ontologically 'given' or 'exogenous' in a sense.[32] That is, *given* the physical scarcity of resources and a level of technology, there exist limits to production and opportunity costs for the production of one rather than another good. Those opportunity costs, and their relative levels as between countries, are simply 'facts' that emerge from – and are a function of – that scarcity and that technology. They are the exogenous in the sense that the follow ineluctably from and reflect independently given parameters.[33]

The underlying fiction: Physical scarcity and clockwork production

I have already touched on the criticality of the productive process to understanding the origins of comparative advantage. So what is the conception of that process implied by the neoclassical scheme set out above?

To the extent that comparative advantage-based approaches to international trade have a conception of that process, it is a limited one. Scarce resources are brought to the production process, and outputs emerge from that process as 'commodities' at a rate defined by a particular level of technology. Specifically, the relative or comparative opportunity cost analysis basically assumes that

1. a nation is 'constituted' by a limited factor endowment and a level of technology;
2. monadically individualistic maximizing actors 'own' different scarce factors and bring them to the production process;
3. minimal social relations exist between these actors and tend to be limited to free contracting in respect of factors and outputs;
4. the production process is constituted by a limited set of technically determined methods; and
5. factors are combined through that production process and commodity (owned and tradeable) outputs are generated.

This conception reflects scarcity's role as the leading lady of modern economics. Indeed, for the neoclassical economist, economic life in general is a response to her strictures, and the discipline in its modern guise has dedicated itself to generating solutions to the problems that she throws up.[34] We confront a world – according to mainstream economics – that imposes on us 'material' and 'physical' resource limitations. In its focus on scarcity, the neoclassical theory of comparative advantage is at one with its discipline's preoccupations. It is scarcity that creates the necessity of opportunity costs – in a situation of constraint it is not possible to produce more of one thing without giving up some of another. And as we have seen, in the Hecksche–Ohlin–Samuelson model it was price as an index of scarcity that formed the conceptual background for predictions concerning the election of productive technique and patterns of specialization.

However, is this background picture and conception accurate? My claim is that it is not – this is a sterile and fictitious understanding of the productive process that is deceptive and leads to a skewed and mistaken conception of the origins, nature and – most importantly – the malleability of production costs, opportunity costs and comparative advantages. Specifically, what have been sterilized from the conceptualization of the production process are its social aspects and in their place have been substituted some tall tales about the nature of economic scarcity.

The Cambridge Radicals, as we have seen, saw that something was amiss in how scarcity was conceptualized by the mainstream. We are now in a position to say more about what they were pointing to. As we will now see, scarcity is neither as 'given' nor as independently imperious as is often presupposed. Specifically, I claim that the experience by individual actors, or indeed at the economy-wide level, of 'scarcity' or 'costs' is not merely 'material' or 'physical' in nature. Specifically, scarcity has an additional aspect: a social, institutional aspect.[35]

The neoclassical economics' conceptualization of production detailed above is almost purely what might be termed a mechanical or 'clockwork' one. What I mean by this is that physical resources are imagined to interact with each other through a gross, physical process to produce material output. This approach tends to focus upon the relationship between physical productive inputs, within an overall context of an economy's level of technology – a relationship between 'Monsieur Le Capital and Madame La Terre' consummated through labour and mediated only by a given technological constraint.[36] As I have touched on in the previous chapter, economics becomes engineering:[37] an enterprise that aims to discover universal laws – akin to the laws of physical nature – of clockwork economic processes. The neoclassical approach treats production as precisely such a mechanical process. Circumscribed only by man's technical relation with the physical world, cost and opportunity costs that emerge from that process are understood to be a function of physical interactions and relations between mere objective, scarce things.

However, economic activity and production are concerned with *both* physical nature and human action, involving not only the relation between people and nature, but also relations *between* people.[38] What the mainstream approach seems to do is confuse the physical or material production of goods with the totality of the production process itself. The physical element assumes pride of place and the social nature of the process as a whole slips from view. Moreover, the mechanistic nature of the *analysis* seems to become reflected in a mechanistic understanding of the world *itself*. The exogeneity of variables (input supplies, level of technology, etc.) to the analysis comes to imply the exogeneity of these variables in the social world.

These confusions are easy to fall into. It can be tempting to think about physical, material, commodity resources being 'worked' in one way or another in the pursuit of physical, material, commodity outputs. However, this physical process is not all that is happening in production. Moreover, it is not even a good proxy for the process viewed as a whole. As Schmid has said – echoing Marx – the economy is not merely a universe of commodities, but also a universe of human relations.[39] Undue focus upon the universe of commodities and upon the implications of given resources (scarcity) and technology can cause analysis to miss important dynamics relevant to the understanding the production process, opportunity costs, comparative advantages and, thus, international trade more broadly. As we will see, little that is economic is in reality a matter of clockwork.

Piercing the Fiction: An Alternative Account of the Origins of Trade Advantage

To better grasp the nonfictional origins of comparative advantage we need to take account of that part of the economic story that tends to be deemphasized: that relations between people shape our relationship with the physical world. This fact has special relevance in the context of the production process, and hence comparative advantage analysis, as I will attempt to illustrate. Here we will bring social institutions into the story – those established and operative social rules that structure interhuman or social interactions. These are the 'working rules',[40] or 'rules of the game',[41] by which economic action takes place, and in which scarcity plays itself out and affects actual economic actors. The framework of these rules dictate the form and strategies for economic action in particular economies.

Social institutions can include anything from table manners to language to rules of private property.[42] I will particularly focus on one species of social intuitions – legal institutions. Other social institutions are very much important to the production process and its dynamics. Legal institutions, however, as a dominant form of socially effective normativity – backed as they are by society's 'legitimate' coercive powers – are a particularly interesting site for consideration, both analytically and (as I will discuss later) normatively. Critically for our present purposes – and as we shall see – legal institutions are a dominant policy medium through which the tussle for free trade is carried out.

Considering legal institutions and the rules of the economic game brings into view the fact that the distribution of sacrifice and aggregate social experience of scarcity are social and relational rather than purely the effect of physical 'facts', with significant implications for the origins of comparative advantage. To demonstrate this, let us start, as does the mainstream analysis, with 'factors of production'.

Factors of production

Take the basic question – how does production occur? The mainstream answer would be: through a process (the 'production process') in which various inputs or scarce or limited 'factors' of production are combined. But what precisely are these factors?[43] For mainstream analysis, these are usually understood to be labour, capital and sometimes land/ geographical elements. We have already seen that counting capital as a factor of production can be troublesome. So let us try to be a little more detailed than this.

Specifically, factors of production – those things that are used in the productive process to generate output – can usefully be understood (very roughly[44]) as belonging to three categories:[45]

1. *Raw materials* (broadly understood): including natural resources, geographical elements (such as climate, the fertility of soil and similar elements).
2. *Instruments of production* (or physical 'capital'): including plant and equipment, premises and spaces,[46] instrumental and intermediate materials.
3. *Labour power* (or human productive power): the productive ability of producing agents, including strength, skill, know-how and know-what, creativity, coordination.

As we have discussed, mainstream production analysis has a largely mechanical understanding of what happens through production. Factors are conceived of as physical quantities that are more or less physically scarce, and these factors are transformed into physical output at a rate defined by the subsisting level of technology. If economic production were solely about the transformation of inputs into output, this would all be well enough. However, this simple and mechanical exercise is not all that there is to economic production. Factors of production do not appear out of thin air and take themselves to be transformed into goods. Rather, they become involved in a social process; they become embroiled in relations between people.

The trouble starts with the very conception of 'factors' of production. As Coase has pointed out, a factor of production is 'usually thought of as a physical entity which the businessman acquires and uses (an acre of land, a ton of fertiliser)...'[47] However, Coase argues that this kind of thinking can lead us into misunderstanding: 'We may speak of a person owning land and using it as a factor of production but what the land-owner in fact possesses is the right to carry out a circumscribed list of actions'. Rather than conceiving of factors of production as mere physical things, Coase suggests that they are better understood as rights to perform certain actions.[48]

While on point, Coase's definition of a factor of production is itself wont to create some confusion. A factor of production – say timber – is in an important sense a physical object. The point is that conceding that a factor of production is a physical (or nonphysical but objective) thing does not tell us much about the implications of its employment in a production process. That is, it is not clear what it means to 'own' something, or what one is permitted to do with the thing that one owns.[49] What is deceiving is not so much the characterization of factors as physical objects, as much as the slippage in moving from the physical nature of a factor to the social nature of its employment and use in production.[50] It is to this social and relational nature of the production process that I now turn.

The production process as social, relational and political

Once the transition is made to considering how such a factor is actually employed or used in production, one is no longer dealing with purely material or physical considerations, but rather enters the world of social relations. And this world consists, in important part, of constellations of legal relations of entitlement and exposure.

Appreciation of the legal aspect of production is – as is the relational aspect generally – in the mainstream account, limited. The idea of commodified resources being brought to the production process and commodity outputs emerging from that process translates in legal terms to inputs and outputs being capable of being owned (private property) and freely exchanged (freedom of contact).[51] These are, for mainstream economists, the legal foundations of the market order, the 'baseline' for normal economic activity.[52] However, this description of the legal foundations of that order is a thin – and ultimately inadequate – way of describing the social relations that are at play in the modern production process, as we shall now see.

Ownership

Let us begin with ownership. Mainstream economic understandings of ownership and 'property rights' render these terms relatively determinate, in the sense that mainstream economists (especially international economists who seem to be relatively institutionally insensitive) tend to regard as obvious and simple the specification of the rights to which these terms refer. All things of value can be owned, and what it means to own something is uncontroversial – though often unspecified.[53]

But of course, property is itself a creature of the law. As Bentham put it 'Property and law are born together and must die together.'[54] That is, property is a social institution. Though this insight has floated around and animated various traditions of legal and philosophical thought that placed themselves in opposition to the Lockean tradition of natural rights, this insight received its most clear and elaborate articulation in the domain of legal thought by a group of legal scholars loosely gathered under the title of 'the American Legal Realists'.

Key among these was MR Cohen, who remarked,

> The legal term 'property' denotes not material things but certain rights [...] Further reflection shows that a property right is not to be identified with the fact of physical possession [...] we must recognize that a property right is a relation not between an owner and a thing but between an owner and other individuals [sometimes] in reference to things.[55]

That is, having 'property' or 'ownership' involves certain rights, under
certain circumstances, to call on the coercive power of the state to be
applied against another *person*, for example, to exclude them from an
object or land or something else, or to stop them from interfering with
the owner's possession in one way or another. So as well as being a
social phenomenon, owning something is invariably *relational*: it concerns
relations between people that influence the terms of interaction and
relative positioning of individual actors.

Moreover, the term 'property' itself provides little determinate content
or guidance concerning the precise particulars of these relations. It is
not the case that the rights that inhere in the party that has 'ownership'
can be easily or simply deduced from the concept of property. Nor does
the nature of the 'owned' object itself circumscribe or delineate the kind
of different jural entitlements that can be possessed between people with
respect to it. Kennedy has neatly encapsulated the point:

> It turns out that the concept is relative, so that you can have more
> or less protection depending on the kind of thing. The three main
> axes of variation are the number of people against whom you
> have protection, the 'mental element' required before we say that
> someone who has interfered with your thing has to compensate you
> for injury, and the kind of redress you can get for interference.[56]

The possible constellations of entitlements and relations that a party can
have in respect of others relevant to a particular object are exceedingly
broad and diverse. In the absence of a deductively reliable method
of choosing between those constellations, the settling of what rights a
particular person will have in relation to others will at base be a 'political'
matter involving setting the terms upon which the power of the state
(collective social power) can be invoked to enforce and empower the
interests of some rather than of others. To own factors of production is,
then, inescapably social, relational and political.

Use

Quite apart from questions concerning the ownership of certain factors
of production, social and institutional considerations also provide the
basis and ground rules for the permitted *use* of those factors. Particularly,
legal-institutional rules delineate and circumscribe the extent to which
factors can be used in ways that adversely affect the interests of others.

Again, the question of permitted use is a relational one. It involves the boundaries of allowed interpersonal interaction, and particularly interpersonal harm and cost imposition.

In terms of categories of legal rules, these sit at the interface of property and tort. The latter, specifically, spell out when harm caused by one to another will be legally compensable. Not all 'temporal damage' attracts legal remedy.[57] Sometimes the power of the state can be called upon to have harm redressed, and sometimes not. Think here about the ability to build upon or use one's land in a way that reduces the value of adjoining land (say, by blocking the latter's previously glorious evening views by erecting a communications tower, or by creating noise or chemical pollution). Alternatively, consider the manner in which one's means of production (e.g., tools, machines or a factory) can be withheld from use, causing harm to those who might otherwise use those means to produce or to earn. Or even consider the opening of a new, competing business next door to an already-existing one, which takes market share and causes economic or financial harm.[58]

Different legal-institutional arrangements and configurations differentially impose and remove limitations on behaviour – and importantly for our current purposes – condition how the 'owners' of factors of production can use their factors *in relation to* the interests of others. These configurations disperse costs relevant to economic action between actors. The scope of those configurations can, again, vary widely along a number of lines, including: the extent and scope of a privilege to harm, different mental elements required in respect of the infliction of harm before they become compensable, and the nexus of causation required between particular uses and any harm that might be caused. Of the universe of possibilities, which specific rules or sets of rules as to the extent of privileges to inflict harm will be instituted is a matter of policy – the output of sociopolitical decisions. Such decisions will delineate and answer the question of how an individual can use factors of production, and who is to bear the costs of one actor or another, or of certain types of economic action.[59]

Sale/transfer and allowing access

Again, factors of production do not merely present themselves to be incorporated into the production process. They are brought to that process by actors who then bargain, contract for, and exchange those factors. And while mainstream economic theorists understand that contracting is interactive and relational, they tend to see the institution of contract law as committed to and embodying the notion of enforcing voluntary agreements. Thus, the relations represented in exchange are, for the neoclassical economist, equal relations. Though the steps to this are a little more complicated than need be presented here, this allows the institution of contract law to be conceptualized as a neutral or efficient baseline for the operation of the market free from social or political intervention. Individuals relate, but they do so equally and on their own terms.

However, this means of reading out sociopolitical content from the institution of contract law is flawed. Contract law consists of the legal rules that condition terms and tactics of bargaining interaction, the kinds of bargains that will be recognized and on what bases. But once again, pure deduction fails us – the concepts of contract law, or of enforcing voluntary agreements, or even of efficiency, cannot conclusively and once and for all determine the content of those rules. There is no easy, deductive method that can be unproblematically called upon to settle what kind of activity is acceptable in the context of bargaining (e.g., what counts as 'coercive' or 'fraudulent'), the degree of tolerability of information asymmetries, prohibited/nonprohibited contacts, compulsory terms, or the formal and substantive elements of promises in relation to which a person is able to call on the power of the state to compel performance. Rather, all of these are subject to being concretized through a plurality of different arrangements of legal relations.[60] Any election or settlement of these relations is invariably a political and social act by whoever makes the decision, and one that differentially impacts upon economic actors in their dealings with one and other.

Other (regulatory) constraint on action

So far, the legal-institutional considerations that I have pointed to concerning the ownership, use and exchange of factors of production generally fall within the heading of rules of 'private law'. Quite apart from these rules, the legal system of any actually existing country will involve what may be termed 'regulatory' rules (as will become clear, I use the term broadly).[61]

While not always as obviously relational in the sense that the rules of property, tort and contract are, such regimes and webs of regulation do very much alter the positions of actors by impacting, populating and conditioning the courses of action available to the individual, and structuring the costs involved in particular actions. The law routinely prohibits certain kinds of action, burdens it in one way or another, or permits it freely. Consider licensing regimes, taxation arrangements or immigration regulation. Or environmental regulation, the regulation of trade practices and competition or rules about labour or working conditions. Indeed, consider even family law, social security or building regulations. Each of these kinds of regulation will affect certain production practices, and the relative positioning of those who engage in them. Moreover, law- and policymakers devise, implement and enforce the webs of regulation for a range of policy and political motivations that defy reduction to a single rationalization. Rather, particular settlements of regimes will be, again, a matter of political and social decision.

Beyond fiction: Production and the economy as an
interdependent network of mutually coercive relations

So, in contrast to neoclassical economics' clockwork, mechanical model of production in which costs appear as the result of the interaction between inputs – between things – and are defined by the scarcity of those inputs and levels of technology, the social and relational picture of production highlighted here tells a very different story about the nature of that process and the costs and burdens thrown up by it. I will return to the import of this point in the context of comparative advantage in a moment. First, however, it is worth noting that we are – in light of this perspective on production – in a position to elaborate upon the inadequacies of the neoclassical model of the economy that I mentioned in chapter 3.

As I discussed in that chapter, neoclassical economic theory tends to imagine that economic actors are basically identically characterized and motivated. These actors are the yeomen producers, the isolated Robinson Crusoes, of the comparative advantage models that I discussed earlier. In chapter 3, we saw the failure, albeit at a relatively high level of generality, of this model of the economy. Through our discussion in this chapter of the equally abstract and rarefied conceptualization of the production process that sits at the base of the comparative advantage analysis, we are now in a position to add some finer grain to the critique of the techniques of feverish individualism and high abstraction used by neoclassical economic models. In both cases, what is missing from the mainstream analysis is a consideration of the rules by which the economic game is played in any given economy. The legal-institutional factors that I have been highlighting here very much constitute those rules. Economic players act and interact within the framework created through those rules. In the absence of that framework, their actions fail to make sense. Far from individualism and abstraction, what results is a very different model of the economy – one of an 'interdependent network of mutually coercive relations'.[62]

In contrast to the abstract individualism of mainstream models, the analysis here points to the essential interconnectedness of actors in production and the modern economy. There are three key levels to this interconnectedness that bear mentioning. The first might be termed *legal-relational interconnectedness*. As will be clear, the legal-institutional elements that I have been discussing work relationally. They deal primarily with dynamics between different actors. Any allocation of an entitlement (of whatever nature or strength) must be correlated with a matching obligation on another. Rights for one are matched by duties on another. Privileges to harm are matched by corresponding a lack of rights to complain. Legal entitlement and exposure go hand in hand, creating a network of dependent relations.[63]

Moreover, this is barely surprising when one considers the nature of modern capitalist economies and their high degree of *productive interconnectedness*. A defining element of such economies is that markets are the primary vehicle (as opposed to, say, governmental command) for the coordination of social productive activity. Production of goods occurs for the purpose of, and with the intention of, exchange on the market. A producer does not produce to meet her own needs directly, but supplies her needs through market exchange. A high degree of specialization of labour abounds. Indeed, goods are often produced by or using machines – that is, through the use of commodities produced by others. All of this means that produced goods are jointly produced and seldom through the work of one isolated individual alone.

This legal-relational and productive interconnectedness is also exacerbated by what we might term *physical interconnectedness*. Again, in contrast to the Robinson Crusoe island model of living or the yeoman producer, forty-acres-and-a-mule conception, in our current mode of social life, individuals do not live physically isolated from each other (if they ever did). Our lands are 'thickly settled'.[64] We often live in close physical proximity to others, and what we do – and fail to do – affects those around us.

Given this multifaceted interconnectedness, it is unsurprising that questions of economic provisioning and of who gets what from the process of production and exchange is also determined relationally, through a network of connections in which various actors attempt to induce each other to lower the legal obstacles to access of particular goods, be they productive or consumptive. And lower these obstacles they must, for each individual is dependent on (at least some) others for the provisions of the basic necessities of life in capitalist economic organization.

But while each person in this web of relations 'coerces', in the sense of impinging on the freedom of action of others, the ability to coerce is distributed unequally through society.[65] That ability depends in part upon the unequal legal entitlements possessed by different actors within that network, which in turn results in inequality of distributive shares, or 'fruits' of bargaining.[66] In this sense, legal-institutional considerations and entitlements are 'weapons of coercion',[67] applied by some actors to shift economic costs, burdens and benefits from themselves to others. This is not to say that the party less able to coerce does *not* coerce the more powerful party. The point is, though, that coercion cannot be measured purely along qualitative axes: degree and extent of coercion are important. Certain actors in society are given, by reason of legal-institutional factors, disproportionate ability to dictate and make their interests count in terms of social life.[68] Thus, while economic actors are interconnected in a way that ensures that they must rely upon each other and on their interactions, they are differentially endowed and empowered as they face each other in those interactions.

Certainly, this is a simplified picture of how the economy works – that is, as a web-like set of coercive relations, in which parties have unequal entitlements and therefore, unequal bargaining power. However, as highlighted several times above, simplification in understanding economic matters is not itself a sin. The point is that the simplified model advanced here is far more appropriate for economic analysis of modern capitalist economic relations than are the Robinson Crusoe models relied upon by mainstream economics – models characterized by what Hunt has called 'extreme bourgeois individualism'.[69] It takes into account the necessarily relational and material intertwining of actors in a modern economy. The fictitious monadic individualism of imaginary deserted islands is simply an inadequate way to model modern economic and social relations – a distortion rather than a simplification.[70]

The social origins of scarcity and comparative advantage

How then does this nonfictional account of production – which highlights that legal-institutional considerations give form and shape to the inherently social and relational process of production – relate to issues of costs, opportunity costs and advantages in international trade? Keeping firmly in mind the fact that comparative advantages involve, and are functions of, differences in opportunity costs in the production of goods, the answer to this question starts to become clear.

Firstly, understanding the legal-institutional underpinnings of the economy provides important insights in relation to the experience of scarcity and costs in actually existing economies. Even in a situation of physical scarcity, there remains a question of how that scarcity – or more importantly, the sacrifice (i.e., the costs) entailed by that scarcity – will be 'distributed' through society. This is where legal entitlements and relations become important. The distribution of entitlements and content of particular legal relations between people (in relation to factors of production), when combined with other legal and institutional regulation, significantly influence costs that attach to particular activities, specifying and imposing costs, allocating them between actors and allowing certain actors increased power to impose their costs on others.

This perspective downplays the importance of 'sacrifice' as some ontologically given category when considering the effect of scarcity. A particular pattern of sacrifice (cost) is not inherent to 'scarcity' as much as it is forced upon parties who lack the ability to cause others – often through the use of legal entitlements – to behave in ways consistent with their interests. To a large extent, the actual experience of costs and scarcity in society, and what these in fact mean for economic actors, is a law-made dilemma,[71] a social experience, the result of sociopolitical decisions, actions and schemes.

Opportunity costs, too, are shaped importantly by these social and relational elements. Although mainstream theory tends to focus on private, individual decision making as the driver of economic activity, the context of individual action cannot be ignored. Individual decision making involves choosing between the sum of available options (which can be called an individual's opportunity set). Any choice within that opportunity set involves the incurring of opportunity costs – the relinquishing of the next best alternative made necessary by the choice.

But of course, an individual's opportunity set is limited by both external constraints on action, as well as by the opportunity sets of others. Legal-institutional considerations draw the boundary of an individual's opportunity set in an absolute sense by defining some actions as outside of that set. Such considerations also shape and influence opportunity costs within the opportunity sets of individuals. Legal institutions also empower certain actors over others in situations of conflicting opportunity sets. The inclusion, by legal-institutional means, of particular opportunities in an individual's opportunity set, will often involve taking it from the opportunity set of another. Refusing to impose a cost on one person, or one activity, will be to impose it on another. Differential options for action, entitlements, exposures and obligations constitute the basis of differential economic characterization, action and bargaining position. Indeed, the three levels of interconnectedness mentioned above combine to generate what might best be termed 'opportunity-set interconnectedness'.

The opportunity costs for a country in respect of the production of a given good depends on the aggregation of all individual opportunity sets and costs.[72] Thus, national or country opportunity costs are also, in part, the creatures of sociopolitical decision, as are relative opportunity costs and comparative advantages. Different distributions of legal entitlements, obligations and exposures will mean that individuals are confronted by different costs for action, can differentially cause others to bear costs and undertake certain actions rather than others. These aggregate to different production situations, possibilities, opportunity costs and comparative advantages for the nation as a whole.

At an even more profound level, if my reader glances back to the list of productive factors that I presented earlier in this chapter, it will be noticed that more than merely distributing the sacrifice entailed by scarce resources, legal-institutional considerations can condition and affect the very supply of factors themselves. For example, the development of certain aspects of labour power – say skill – is in part endogenous to legal and regulatory regimes such as public, subsidized or compulsory education. Particular healthcare regimes that deliver and regulate the provision of healthcare services will have an important influence on workforce capacity and productivity. The relative abundance or depletion of natural resources at a given time may be partially the result of the permissiveness (or not) of government regulation in the past concerning exploitation of such resources. The development of societal know-how or know-what may similarly be affected by education regulation and public infrastructure investment, so too the development of particular industry sectors and private collections of means and machines of production. That is, even if in any particular moment a country's supply of factors of production is limited or 'given' for the purposes of analysis, the supply itself is not completely asocial, prelegal or immutable.

The level of technology that exists in a particular economy also exhibits a similar partial dependency upon a legal-institutional environment, as does (in keeping with the Cambridge Capital Critique) the election of one productive technique over another. Cost is not related to technology in a straightforward sense,[73] but rather, a given level of technology can generate a number of different cost structures. Nor is it the case the one technology-driven cost structure can be understood as being the 'cheapest' or most 'efficient' in the abstract. Rather, as with resource endowments, differential legal-institutional background rules and entitlements can shift the costliness of particular technological configuration and cost structures. As Marglin has argued,

> Contrary to neoclassical logic – a new method of production does not need to be technologically superior to be adopted; innovation depends as much on economic and social institutions – on who is in control of production and under what constraints control is exercised.[74]

The point is that the 'givens' of mainstream analysis – whether resources, levels of technology or the trade-offs that are required in the face of scarcity of the former in light of the latter – are emphatically *not* exogenous from the social and institutional environment in which they present. In the final analysis, we see that it is the peculiar, fictional modelling of the economy and its processes as mechanistic, physicalistic and individualistic rather than institutional, social and relational that cause it to fail to grasp or understand the origins of comparative advantage.

Two Implications of the Social Origins of Comparative Advantage

At this point, the reader might be wondering what difference is made by this analysis of the social and relational aspects of scarcity, costs and comparative advantages. What does this imply for the case for free trade? Indeed, for many economists the retort might be: 'That's all fine, but it doesn't really matter. Irrespective of *where* patterns of costs and advantages come from, the point is that specialization and trade on that basis of comparative opportunity cost advantages leads to gains.'

This hypothetical retort is misguided. The analytical clarification involved in seeing costs as partially sociopolitically created has critical implications in respect of how to think about international trade and its economic analysis. Two key points bear further discussion, the import of which will become even more acute as we continue our investigation in the coming chapters.

Comparative advantages (and the gains from trade) are malleable and constructed: Troubling the optimality of market-generated outcomes

Comparative advantages are not – as we have seen – merely 'facts' that confront societies, the exogenous result of givens beyond human control. Quite the contrary: in important ways, comparative advantages are a function of human, sociopolitical choices. Further, given that potential gains from trade depend on relative opportunity cost differences between countries, the extent of potential gains from trade will also be a partial function of sociopolitical decision.

However, once it is recognized that opportunity costs and comparative advantages are the result of interaction between agents – rather than the mechanical result of the interaction of technology and inputs – the dynamic nature of comparative advantages presents itself more clearly.[75] Recognizing the social and political sources of comparative advantage forces us to recognize, too, the relative contingency of patterns of comparative advantage that predominate at any given time, and also for the possibility that different sociopolitical choices may to give rise to different patterns of comparative advantage. Changing the legal-institutional substructure of economic and productive activity may change costs and opportunity costs domestically, and comparative advantages between countries, shifting both the bases of specialization and the gains from trade.

But whereas the mainstream's fictional account of production encourages a 'hands-off' approach to productive specialization and trust in the market to seek out and optimize gains in light of existing circumstances, sensitivity to the social aspects of comparative advantage should cause us to worry about simply allowing the market to work with existing resources and technology. Just as we saw in chapter 3 in the context of international exchange, the market cannot alone be trusted to cause efficient or optimal outcomes. If a country can shape its comparative advantages, there is a strong argument that it should attempt to do so in ways that optimize benefit, rather than merely passively accept existing patterns of specialization and the gains that emerge from them.

It is not clear to what extent mainstream economists would acknowledge that that costs and comparative advantages are in some (perhaps even important) sense 'constructed'. Even sophisticated international economists such as Paul Krugman seem to fail to fully appreciate the extent to which advantages in international trade are 'created' phenomena. Krugman has written:

> Much international trade is driven by enduring national differences in resources, climate, and society. Brazil is a coffee exporter because of soil and climate, Saudi Arabia an oil exporter because of geology, Canada a wheat exporter because of the abundance of land relative to labor, and so on.[76]

Notice how Krugman's examples – resources, climate, geographical factors – track the Ricardian and Heckscher–Ohlin–Samuelson sources of comparative advantage that we encountered earlier in this chapter.[77] This is not to say that Krugman thinks that natural resources and factor endowments are all that matter:

> Trade in manufactured goods among advanced industrial countries is harder to explain. In many cases industries seem to create their own comparative advantages, through a process of positive feedback.[78]

For Krugman – and many of his followers and associates in the New International Economics and Strategic Trade Theory schools – what gives rise to the possibility of constructed comparative advantage is the existence of external economies (including technology spillover effects, and pecuniary external economies dependent upon the size of domestic markets). This perspective underscores the role of history, accident and government intervention in creating the bases of trade '*when external industries are powerful*'.[79]

Krugman does seem to appreciate and acknowledge the gravity for the case for free trade of the possibility that comparative advantages are constructed, and specifically, that it undercuts the 'generally benign', mutually beneficial and optimal picture of market-led specialization and trade.[80] What he fails to appreciate, however, is the ubiquity of the construction of particular patterns of costs, opportunity costs and comparative advantages. For Krugman, the presence of strong external industries is 'exceptional' – there are a limited range of circumstances in which comparative advantages are constructed by something other than resources and factor endowments. However, what the discussion above demonstrates is that social decision and institutions *always* influence the development of a country's comparative advantage.

But what then of the generally benign nature of free international trade and the patterns of specialization that it brings? As Krugman himself realizes, the phenomenon of constructed comparative advantage qualifies the picture. But as comparative advantage is always and everywhere constructed, the benign picture of, easy faith in, and passive acceptance of market-generated comparative advantages and trade outcomes must also be rejected. Knowingly or unknowingly, social decisions in part make patterns of production and comparative advantage, and as such dictate the magnitude of gains from trade.[81] And if gains are what are sought by the policy-maker or advocate of free trade, exercising social and political decisions differently to chase these gains must be a strategy on the table.

In terms more familiar to social theory, the failing of the mainstream in this regard is an instance of the consciousness-related effect that Marx termed the 'fetishism of commodities'. At a very basic level, to fetishize something is to invest it with powers or qualities that it does not inherently have.[82] Commodity fetishism involves attributing to commodities – to things – characteristics that are not inherent to those commodities but are rather the effect or result of human or social relations. This attribution leads to a mistake, a misunderstanding, a failure to see the role of social processes and historical contingency in the association of particular properties with commodities.[83] The results of social relations and processes (between people) are mistakenly thought to be the results of mere relations between things. The nature of social life is misunderstood, and the role of human agency in setting the terms of that life fails to be recognized. In this context, the fetishistic misapprehension is the failure to see that a country's actual production possibilities, the opportunity costs involved in certain activities, the construction of comparative advantages and the shape and gains from international trade are all the effect of social relations and institutions rather than mere responses to given and immutable scarcity and technological constraint. The economic world is largely our own. We are its authors and we author too many of its outcomes and implications globally, for nations and for individuals.

Comparative advantages are state sponsored: The fairy tale of 'free' trade itself

Understanding the role of legal rules and regulations in economic activity leads to the conclusion that the state – as definer, elaborator and enforcer of these rules and regulations – is omnipresent in the so-called 'private' domain of production and exchange.

So too in international trade. Comparative advantages are partially the effect of the state's power being called upon to protect the interests of some against others. However, acknowledging the place of the state in authoring and constructing comparative advantages starts to make unclear precisely what is meant by 'free' trade. When the state's role in shaping bases and patterns of international trade and specialization through legal-institutional means is acknowledged, it becomes tempting to announce the slogan 'there is no such thing as free trade', if by 'free' is meant the absence of the state. The state is *always* involved in trade.

Behind this slogan hides a more profound issue in the context of our current enquiry. Specifically, what is the *policy relevance* of the notion of free trade? What precisely is being advocated for when a policy of free trade is on the table? Generally, what is meant by this is that the state does not intervene to disturb the operation of supply and demand in the pricing and allocation of commodities and resources through interventions such as tariffs, subsidies, taxes, quotas and certain other 'nontariff barriers to trade'.

However, when thought about in light of the analysis we have explored, the waters become somewhat murkier. The problem is that of the absence of an economic yardstick with which to judge certain state actions 'deviant' or 'distortive.' Mainstream trade models tend to assume a baseline of 'normal', market-based economic activity, and a policy stance of free trade involves not acting in a way that disturbs that baseline. As we have seen on several occasions, this assumption fails to take into account the 'rules of the game' at play in a given economy: the manner in which actors – differentially empowered, constrained and characterized by a particular legal-institutional framework – interact with each other within that framework. Once the framework is brought into focus, it becomes clear that legal-institutional considerations are not 'imposed' on some otherwise normal mode of economic ordering. Rather, the framework in part *establishes* that ordering.

Thus, it cannot be said that the state is absent from the machinations of 'supply and demand' – the process of bargaining and the determination of prices and costs takes place in, and through, a legal-institutional framework that the state has a hand in crafting and enforcing. It becomes difficult, therefore, to know where the line between free and unfree trade should be drawn, and what criteria should be used to draw it. Tariffs and subsidies are impermissible. But what about public health or education regimes? What about property or asset entitlements? Or welfare payments? Or roads? Lines can, of course, be defined and imposed that characterize government action as either 'permissible' or 'impermissible'. However, simple reliance on the standard of 'free trade' does not help us to do so in a nonarbitrary fashion.[84]

The implication of this insight for the policy coherence of 'free trade' is immense. Free trade itself turns out to be a fiction – an imagined, unreal and ultimately empty concept. Indeed, to advocate a policy of free trade is a policy nonsense; in any number of ways the state can – and always does – tend the field from which trade sprouts forth. Trade is always and everywhere regulated, political and controversial.[85] That is, it is not at all clear to us any more what policy stance the advocate of free trade is actually calling for.

In addition to troubling the policy coherence of free trade, the social, relational and political understanding of production and trade has additional import in respect of the state's role in constructing the bases of trade. The analysis here suggests that we can reunderstand comparative advantages as the result of asymmetric social and economic power in production and more generally, not merely as a function of 'given' scarcity and technology. Affirming the desirability of a particular pattern of comparative advantage is more than merely affirming a commitment to the pursuit of efficiency and of the gains from trade. It is tantamount to affirming – through state power – the social-relational substructure that gives rise to those comparative advantages.[86] If the economy is understood, as it should be, as a network of mutual coercion, the role of the state is that of aider and abettor in that coercion. The state is the muscle that backs up the individual threats of economic actors.

Even more than merely a stand-over man, the state is partial *author* of patterns of production and opportunity cost and international trade. And if the state is in part responsible for the creation of costs and opportunity costs – and therefore the manner in which production occurs domestically and trade occurs internationally – it is also in part responsible for the various results and implications of particular patterns of production and exchange including, but not limited to, any gains from trade. I will return to this question in the following chapter. For now, it is sufficient to note that, given the role of legal-institutional considerations in constructing the bases of trade – and contrary to the usual framing – no recourse can be had to arguments that cast trade as a purely private economic response of individual actors to a particular resources and technological context to allow the state to shirk its partial responsibility for the results and outcomes of international trade.

Summary: The Unwitting Architects of Trade

Let me take a moment to summarize the argument I have advanced in this chapter.

The mainstream's origin-myths of comparative advantage have been shattered. I have argued that production cannot be conceptualized in the fictitious, clockwork and mechanistic fashion that mainstream approaches to understanding the sources of comparative advantage attempt. These approaches fail to predict – as they claim to – patterns of specialization and comparative advantage for the very reason that they are unable to grasp the actual sources of costs and opportunity costs in production. Blind to the economic rules of the game that privilege certain interests and set the terms of social interrelationship, these approaches mischaracterize costs and comparative advantages as exogenous and mechanically born.

However, by bringing these rules more clearly into focus and by interrogating the social, and especially legal-institutional preconditions of production, we are able to reunderstand costs, the origins of comparative advantages, and the gains from trade themselves as irreducibly social, relational and state sponsored – rather than clockwork or individualistic – phenomena. Though hidden by the fiction of mainstream models, each of these is in important ways, and to significant extents, 'made' by social institutions, decisions and relations. Made, that is, in part by us.

This insight builds upon and adds nuance to the argument against abstraction that I advanced in chapter 3 and pierces the fictional perception that trade advantages 'just are', in some sense optimal and relatively unsusceptible to alteration through human agency. Further, we now have reason to worry about even the policy stance of free trade – which starts to look decidedly fairy-tale in nature when the fiction of state absence from the origins of comparative advantage has been dispelled. Significant and fundamental fault lines are starting to show in the case for free trade as we now are forced to become less sure that we can define what the case is arguing *for*.

I will return to the import of these findings in chapter 6. Before doing so, however, we must first consider the normative component claim of the case for free trade, a consideration which will add further urgency to the result of our investigation here.

Chapter 5

'AND THEY LIVED HAPPILY EVER AFTER…': FICTIONS OF BEING BETTER OFF AND STORIES OF WHAT 'SHOULD' BE

It is characteristic of the low state of our philosophy that the merits of capitalism have been argued by both individualists and socialists exclusively from the point of view of the production and distribution of goods. To the profounder question as to what goods are ultimately worthwhile producing from the point of view of the social effects on the producers and consumers almost no attention is paid.

Morris Cohen[1]

The discussion in the previous chapters has focused on what are often termed the 'positive' aspects of international trade economics: the description and explanation of the economic phenomena of international trade and specialization.

Of course, and as I touched on earlier, the case for free trade that the principle of comparative advantage grounds goes beyond the realm of positive economics. The case is an inherently normative one: it argues about what 'should be' – that free trade *should be* adopted as a policy.

From its beginnings, the principle of comparative advantage's normative elements have been crucially important. Indeed, the principle's positive elements have always worked at the service of its normative argument, the latter representing the crescendo to which the former build. Recall that the principle was developed and deployed by Ricardo as an analytical weapon in a *policy* debate concerning whether or not England should repeal the Corn Laws. And the root of the normative argument incorporated in the comparative advantage model is to be found in the analysis of the predicted 'gains' from international trade.[2]

Thus, our focus now shifts to the final component claim of comparative advantage's case for free trade. Specifically:

1. In a situation of free trade, the direction and pattern of trade and specialization will be driven by comparative advantage.
2. Specialization on the basis of comparative advantage and trade will lead to gains.
3. *Gains from trade can potentially make each country better off as a whole.*
4. Therefore, a policy of free trade should be adopted.

When speaking about what 'should be' and about the garnering of gains from international trade, we are concerned with the ranking of different trade policies through assessment of the states of affairs to which they lead. Beyond positive economics, we are now in the realm of welfare economics – the analysis and maximization of social well-being. We ask: Will England and Portugal be 'better off' through adopting a policy of international trade or a policy of protection? To return to a point that I have insisted upon in previous chapters, advocates of free trade tend to make quite unambiguous claims concerning the welfare benefits of international trade – and therefore its normative compulsion – declaredly on the basis of comparative advantage. In this chapter we will unpack the supposed analytics here and explore the following question: Is a compelling account provided by the case for free trade for electing such policies as opposed to others?

As will become clear, the normative aspects of international trade and comparative advantage tend to be far less tidy and crisp than (at least superficially) some of the economic analysis considered to this point. Similarly, the views of economists in relation to these normative questions are also somewhat less uniform. I will argue that the normative analysis of international trade – though complicated and often ornate – fails to justify comparative advantage-driven free trade policies. I claim that the evaluative and conceptual apparatus used by economists in this area is limited and – in important ways – of only illusory force. These limitations encourage a distinctly unreal evaluation of policy choices in this area – failing to provide closure in respect of such choices and misestimating the welfare implications of particular trade policies.

Let us begin by discussing the manner in which the simple textbook account of the gains from trade becomes – when probed – immediately more complicated than usual presentations suggest.

Back to the Textbook Story

As we have discussed at length, free trade and specialization on the basis of comparative advantage has been argued since Ricardo to allow trading partners to realize 'gains' that leave them 'better off'. This is the economic equivalent of '…and England and Portugal lived happily ever after'. However, for all of the recitation of the mantra of gains and being 'better off', what it precisely means is often shrouded, assumed or passed over with relatively little interrogation.

To begin with, what is meant by the 'gains' from trade promised by comparative advantage theory? In fact, something quite limited. In simple terms, international trade – from a comparative advantage perspective – increases consumption possibilities, or put another way, causes real incomes in both countries to rise.

In autarky, a country can consume only what it produces – its consumption possibilities are circumscribed and limited by its production possibility set. According to the case for free trade, specialization and international trade allow for a country to specialize in its relatively less inefficiently produced good, and then to trade amounts of that good for other goods in relation to which it would be a relatively more inefficient producer. A country thus essentially 'piggybacks' off the productive efficiency of its trading partner, while also taking advantage of its own efficiencies. The result is that with no increase in productive input, total output and consumption possibilities for each country has increased to a point outside each country's production possibility frontier. Trade increases, in Ricardo's words, 'the mass of commodities' available and therefore the 'sum of enjoyments' domestically,[3] and each trading nation 'as a whole' reaches levels of consumption beyond that which it could enjoy without trade.

Note that these are very specific gains. There is a range of other gains that are often identified with trade and/or specialization. For example, trade may be said to increase the variety of goods on offer to consumers. International competition might be hoped to lower prices and increase innovation.[4] Specialization might also lead to dynamic gains if it allows countries to take advantage of greater efficiencies of scale and producers to develop task-specific skills (the benefits of the Smithian pin factory[5]).

However, these are *not* the gains with which comparative advantage is concerned.[6] This is an important point to bear in mind. Too often there is confusion in the advocacy for free trade between different types of gains (particularly, though not exclusively, in public discourse). When comparative advantage is argued to be the basis of the 'gains from trade', this confusion is wont to generate a misleading impression concerning what comparative advantage establishes. However the comparative advantage-based case for free trade is exclusively concerned with increased consumption possibilities and says absolutely nothing about these other categories of benefits.

Before delving more deeply into the normative case and theoretical treatment of the gains from international trade, it is worth noting a point here about the *actual* gains from trade. For all the promises concerning these gains made by economists, policy-makers and others, their measurement has proven notoriously difficult. Gains remain somewhat ghostly in the real world, in important senses dependent on the faith of economists to attest to their existence. In his rereleased (and remarkably chipper) defence of free trade, Douglas Irwin admits early on that while economists 'suspect' that the static gains from international trade and specialization are sizeable, for a number of reasons they are difficult to measure.[7] Further, Leamer and Levinsohn candidly acknowledge that while economists believe – for what they consider to be good theoretical reasons – that there are gains from trade, this is more of a fundamental premise of economics, 'not testable implication of a particular model.'[8]

As we have seen before, in the context of free trade and comparative advantage, there is a parasitic relationship between the 'real' and the 'theoretical': real-world actions or results are sought to be established through theory alone, and without recourse to examination of the real world or empirical evidence about it. Suffice it to say, much of the economic belief in the gains from trade and their particular distribution is based upon the robustness of the theoretical models that have been constructed and used. A failure in the coherence and strength of the models, therefore, has serious implications for faith in the existence of these gains and very high stakes for the case for free trade. Indeed, a failed theoretical model is nothing but a figment of the economist's imagination – a comfortable but misleading fiction. As we will see, the normative element of the case for free trade relies – as does much of the rest of the case – upon a chain of linked fictions. The first of these relate to issues of distribution, to which we will now turn.

Distribution and International Trade

So, comparative advantage suggests that opening trade allows each country to consume more than it could before. Thus far, the textbook story looks as though it has quite a happy ending. Or at least it might, if it ended here. Sadly, it does not.

Specifically, there are three key complications concerning these gains that must immediately be confronted:

1. The question of how gains are shared between trading partners.
2. The question of present, versus future, gains – the distribution of gains over time.
3. The question of sharing gains within a country and transcending the abstraction of the nation 'as a whole'.

These complications concern the distributive implications of international specialization and trade, both between and within countries. Of course, these implications are crucial to the persuasiveness of the case for free trade. Different distributive outcomes will affect how beneficial a policy of free trade can be considered to be for an individual trading country when compared to other policies that it might adopt.

It may quickly be retorted that 'no sophisticated economist' thinks that the normative story about free international trade ends where textbook presentations leave it, or that questions of distribution are irrelevant to that story. This retort notwithstanding, as I hope will become clearer as the discussion progresses, there is nonetheless a tendency among even the more sophisticated of economists to be somewhat coy in relation to the distributive implications of international trade.[9] We are encouraged to couch discussions of free trade and comparative advantage in terms of 'efficiency', of increased consumption possibilities and of mutually beneficial exchange in a way that implicitly conjures, invokes and reinforces the truncated and simplistic story of international trade.[10] As such, even where economists do attempt to present a more complicated picture of international trade-related distribution, they clamour to be heard against the loud confidence of a simplified and far more comforting first impression.[11]

As I have mentioned, the distribution of the gains from international trade can be understood on intercountry, temporal and intracountry bases. I will address each of these in turn.

Distribution between countries

The terms of trade and the mainstream perspective

The issue of distribution between countries leads us back to the question of the terms of trade between countries. It will be recalled from the discussion in chapter 2 that mainstream trade models start with the assumption that the terms of trade occur within what is called the 'feasible range' – that is, somewhere between the opportunity costs for the production of the relevant goods in each trading country.

Of course, the distribution of efficiency gains (the increased consumption possibilities) generated by specialization and trade between international trading partners will depend upon where the *actual* terms of trade fall within the feasible range. Imagine the feasible range as an interval bounded on one side by Country A's opportunity cost for the production of a given good, and on the other side by Country B's opportunity cost. The closer that the actual terms of trade are to Country A's opportunity cost, the greater will be Country B's share of the efficiency gains thrown up by trade, and vice versa.

Ricardo's early models set the terms of trade in a way that equally distributed the efficiency gain between trading partners. But this was just assumption – as we have touched on, it was John Stuart Mill who first clearly articulated the insight that where the actual terms of trade would fall within the feasible range depends upon the interaction between the relative strengths of the demand for commodities in trading nations.[12]

And here we arrive at a first wrinkle in the simplistic normative tale of international trade presented above. That is, if it is possible for a country to depart from a policy of free trade (for example by erecting a tariff), and by so doing shift the terms of trade for internationally traded goods in a direction that aggregates to it a greater share of the gains from trade, then a policy of free trade may cease to be compelling from the perspective of that country.

Though not often clearly articulated when the comparative advantage argument is first presented (that which is presented in chapter 2 of key international economics texts is not qualified until chapter 10, and even then only briefly in a couple of pages[13]), the notion that a departure from free trade could be justified on grounds of national interest has long haunted the literature concerning international trade. Indeed, during the 1840s Robert Torrens generated several works that pointed to the positive terms of trade effects that could be generated by imposing a tariff and thus raising the prices of imported goods, while exported goods continued to trade at unburdened prices.[14] For his then-heretical, nonunilateral free trade views, Torrens became something of a pariah in the annals of economic history for some 100 years.[15]

Notwithstanding Torrens' outsider status, following further development in the hands of John Stuart Mill and economists that followed, his insight blossomed into what has become known as 'optimum tariff theory' – which is now regarded as the 'most generally valid argument for tariffs'.[16] The argument goes something like this: a tariff may have the effect, other things being equal, of causing a fall in demand for the taxed good. The tariff-raising country thus conducts a smaller volume of trade but on more favourable terms. The optimal tariff is reached when the gain from the better terms of trade offsets the loss generated by the reduction in the volume of trade.

The question then becomes, *can* a country affect its terms of trade through levying a tariff? According to mainstream economic theory, the answer depends upon whether levying the tariff will have an effect on the world price of the relevant commodity. If a country is large enough in relation to competitive international markets, so the argument goes, a tariff raised by it may alter world relative prices – decreasing the world relative price of imports, or raising the world relative price of its exports. As a result, a large country might, through the imposition of a tariff, improve its terms of trade, and garner income at the expense of its trading partners.

The mechanism here can be helpfully understood by imagining the tariff-raising country as similar to the seller of a commodity who has monopoly power. By controlling supply, a monopolist is able to exert some influence over the prices of its commodities. A tariff has the effect of reducing a country's import demand (by raising prices domestically), and also therefore, the quantity of exports necessary to pay for those imports. That is, the supply of exports is being controlled in a sense by the tariff, with any resulting change in price altering the terms of trade.

The situation is somewhat different in the case of a tariff imposed by a small country. If a tariff-raising country is not large enough to influence the world price of the relevant commodity, the tariff will merely raise the domestic price of imports, decreasing both import demand and real income levels. There will be no counterbalancing terms of trade income augmentation, and thus, for the small country, the raising of a tariff is argued not to have meaningful welfare benefits over free international trade.

Although sophisticated economists are willing to grant that there is a technical argument that countries large enough to alter world prices might increase domestic income – that is, their distributional share of the efficiency gains from international specialization and trade – by levying an optimal tariff, they are also quick to urge caution in using tariffs as a means of effecting international redistribution. The reasons for this are essentially twofold.

Firstly, where a tariff does shift the terms of trade and augments the income of one country, it necessarily does so at the expense of that country's trading partner. The optimal tariff argument assumes that the relevant trading partner sits passively by while the tariff-imposing country adopts whatever trade policy it prefers.[17] There exists, however, the very real possibility that this trading partner will not be this compliant, and will rather raise its own tariff or undertake other retaliatory action. If that occurs, the advantageous position of the original tariff-raising country is no longer guaranteed, and any number of 'beggar-my-neighbour' trade wars and games of protectionist Russian roulette become very real possibilities.[18] Raising an optimal tariff might have the effect of harming *both* countries' positions as compared to the reciprocal pursuit of free trade policies. Thus, while a tariff might *seem* to be unilaterally beneficial to a country, there are good practical reasons – so counsel economists – that the unilateral benefit might in fact turn out to be evanescent.

Secondly, economists claim that even though a tariff may benefit one country at the expense of another, the gain to the tariff-raising country is likely to be *outweighed* by the losses endured by the country's trading partners. That is, from a global perspective, a tariff will hurt more than it will benefit. The reason for this is the standard 'deadweight loss' argument: a tariff is argued to create a distortion between domestic prices and international prices. Specifically, it raises the relative price of the protected good domestically, directing domestic production towards the production of that good and thus channelling resources to a less-efficient location. Production output therefore declines. From a consumption perspective, the distinction between domestic price and world prices for the relevant commodity that a tariff creates causes real incomes to decline in both countries. All told, the tariff causes world output and real income levels to settle at suboptimal levels the world over as compared to free trade on the basis of comparative advantage, and – to this extent– is argued to be normatively unjustifiable. Indeed, in discussing such tariffs, John Stuart Mill said, 'If international morality, therefore, were rightly understood and acted upon, such taxes, as being contrary to the universal weal, would not exist.'[19]

Now, it might be reasonably asked: Why should a country care about global efficiency in setting its trade policy? Though not entirely clear, the basic economic argument is because there are better ways to do international redistribution, if that is the goal, such as direct gifts, international aid, and so forth. It therefore makes sense that trade-distorting behaviours be foregone by all and alternative mechanisms be sought for accomplishing any desirable international redistribution.

I will return to the persuasiveness of arguments such as this in due course. For now, however, we can characterize the mainstream international economics' perspective on the distribution of gains from trade between trading partners in the following way: assuming competitive markets, the terms of international trade will be determined by the interaction of given tastes, technology and resources, and will settle upon the efficient level given those factors. If the resulting international distribution of the gains from trade is undesirable by reference to some external (noneconomic) value criterion, by all means address this, but do not try to do this by attempting to tinker with the terms of trade through tariff policy. Rather, find some less dangerous, less distortive means to achieve your distributive ends.

This is a benign picture of international exchange. Absent self-serving, politically fraught and economically distorting behaviour by states, free trade is imagined for the most part as doing a good job maximizing efficiency gains and distributing them on the basis of neutral, 'technical' market criteria.[20] Maximizing the size of the international pie prepares the ground for political discussion about how to cut it, an enquiry itself beyond the scope of that about which economics seeks to speak. While it is possible to argue that certain circumstances potentially license departure from free trade, these circumstances are narrow and indeed, dangerous in practice, undermining the basis of protectionist or non–free-trade policies, and confirming the case for free trade.

However, is this benign view of free trade accurate? Here I will introduce a perspective that undermines this comfortable picture of international exchange, and that will help to set the stage for our subsequent discussion.

Unequal exchange, exploitation and international trade

Although mainstream economic thought imagines the archetype of market exchange (and the setting of terms of trade and consequent distributional shares) to be 'equal' and devoid of power imbalances (in the absence, that is, of failures of perfect competition), in this section I will claim that there are good reasons to think that relying on the market to set terms of trade will tend to exacerbate international inequality. That is, even if it is the case that efficiency gains will be generated by international trade, the market mechanism for setting the terms of trade will tend to distribute the greater share of those gains to some countries rather than others. I will argue that this fact must be considered normatively significant. The intuition is this: if free trade, even though benefiting both trading partners, disproportionately benefits one of the partners, a party at the 'wrong end' of the dynamic might reasonably consider free trade to be less attractive than another policy that does not so disproportionately enrich its trading partner.

Heterodox and radical economists working in relation to international trade – often under the rubric of 'unequal exchange' or 'exploitation' – have long attempted to demonstrate that the dynamics of the global economy work behind the scenes of supposedly equal international exchange to effect a net transfer of wealth or value from certain parts of that economy to others.[21] Thinkers on the Left, and particularly those emerging from the Marxian tradition, have argued that international trade can be – and is – a means of exploitation by which the 'core', 'centre', 'Northern' or 'advanced capitalist' countries are enriched at the expense of 'peripheral', 'Southern', 'Third World' or 'developing' countries. Though quite heterogeneous, these approaches tend to share the view that even in the absence of violent or overtly coercive relations between international actors, behind seemingly or formally equal market interactions of exchange lies an exploitative and unequal dynamic. These approaches have often drawn (implicitly and expressly) upon an analogy to concepts of exploitation and inequality at the domestic level (usually within the wage contract).[22]

The concept of exploitation in social and political theory has a long and convoluted history.[23] Suffice it to say, in part for reasons of this complicated history, theories of exploitative or unequal international exchange have tended to encounter one or more of three stumbling blocks.

The first of these is the reliance on certain Marxian categories – most notably, specific understandings of the labour theory of value and related concepts – that have been the subject of deep controversy and uncertainty. Doubt in relation to the *building blocks* of international exploitation and unequal exchange theories has translated into academic and intellectual doubt concerning such theories more broadly.

A second stumbling block is what might be termed a 'subject–object'-based approach to exploitation. Again borrowing from Marxian rhetoric if not analysis, exploitation is conceived of as something that happens *by* one (sometimes though not always, individual) party and *to* another (sometimes though not always, individual) party, usually because the latter is denied something to which they are considered to be entitled,[24] and because the former in some sense compels or coerces the latter to forgo that entitlement.[25] Both as a reading of Marx,[26] and also as an analytical matter, this rendering of exploitation has fallen upon complicated – if not hard – times. Simply put, there are too many points at which it can be challenged or become unhinged. Can a clear line of extraction or denial be drawn between particular actors or groups of actors in relation to every instance of so-called exploitation? What gives rise to – or is the basis of – the entitlement that is denied? In a situation of joint production, where are the lines of entitlement to be drawn? What constitutes voluntariness and coercion in respect of the denial?[27] My point here is not to say that such questions cannot be answered, just that doing so is neither easy nor uncontroversial, and these difficulties have complicated and weakened unequal exchange and exploitation arguments in international trade.

A final difficulty that exploitation theories have often – at least in certain guises – confronted is a reliance upon particular empirical preconditions which may not always be present. For example, the Prebisch–Singer thesis (which predicts declining terms of trade for primary products as against manufactures) makes sense as a general theory of unequal international exchange only if 'subordinate' countries specialize in and export primary products. However, it is the case that, at least in recent decades, simple manufactures, rather than primary products, have tended to account for the bulk of developing country exports. Without modification, therefore, the Prebisch–Singer thesis, even if correct, fails to usefully describe the actual situation of many 'peripheral' economies.[28]

However, there is an interesting strand of social and economic thought that bears on the question of exploitation, and by extension, on theories of unequal international exchange, and deserves a little more discussion. I have in mind what might be termed the 'Roemerian' approach to exploitation.[29] This approach eschews reliance on *either* the labour theory of value/theory of prices *or* the subject–object approach to exploitation as the cornerstones of unequal exchange. Rather, the source of 'exploitation', or unequal returns to expended effort, is traced back to unequal 'class ownership', that is, to unequal access to the means of production. At the domestic level, exploitation is thus sourced in the entitlement background against which the wage bargain is struck, rather than in the wage bargain itself. Exploitation occurs at the class rather than the individual level, by reason of differential institutional empowerment, rather than revolving mainly or solely around different roles in the production process itself. Interesting analogies can be drawn in the context of international trade.

There is much baggage that comes with any definition or redefinition of Marxian concepts such as exploitation. I do not seek to engage in the debate concerning whether a Roemerian definition is what Marx 'really meant', or whether it can perform the function required of it by many Marxist scholars who seek analytical or schematic coherence from the Marxian toolkit. Rather, I merely seek to investigate whether a Roemerian model of international trade can add anything meaningful to the normative question concerning international exchange and distribution.

Given these purposes, it is helpful to isolate the core of what the Roemerian analysis is getting at. Specifically, the idea is that a certain group of actors, through its location within an institutional environment (in this case, for Roemer, in the domestic setting the relevant institutional environment is constituted by differentiated effective control of the means of production through property rights), is able to extract a share of exchange-related gains disproportionate to its sacrifice.[30]

In the context of attempting to understand the relationship between international trade and international inequality, Robin Hahnel[31] and Ron Baiman[32] have (separately[33]) employed something akin to a Roemerian exploitation model. Specifically, these theorists aim to show that even in the context of competitive markets, differential initial endowments of scarce factors of production can give rise to unequal or 'unfair' distributive outcomes in exchange alone. Such an approach sets itself against both a Marxian focus on production as the sole arena for exploitation, and also against the presumed equality of exchange posited by neoclassical accounts that focus on defects in competition (monopoly, monopoly-mimicking tariffs) as the source of iniquitous outcomes.

The contours of the approach are as follows: Imagine that the world is divided into Northern and Southern countries, and that two goods are produced – a consumption good ('corn') and a capital good ('machines'). Imagine further that there are three production technologies (combinations of labour and machines through which these goods can be produced) as presented in Table 5.1 below:

Table 5.1. Productive technologies, factor intensities and output

Productive technology	Resource intensity (in a single production cycle)		Output
	Labour	Machines	
1 Labour-intensive consumption + good technology	3 units	0	10 units of corn
2 Capital-intensive consumption + good technology	2 units	1	10 units of corn
3 More capital-intensive capital + good technology	1 unit	2	10 machines

Then, additionally assume the following:

1. Northern countries have an initial capital stock of 200 machines.
2. Southern countries have an initial capital stock of 50 machines.
3. There are more Southern countries than Northern countries.
4. Each country has an equal supply of homogenous labour.[34]
5. Producers in all countries seek to minimize their labour costs for production.

For present purposes, the result obtained through this model is more interesting than the mathematics.[35] That result is that free and competitive international markets and efficient international trade will aggravate international inequality and disproportionately benefit capital-rich Northern countries. The crux of this is that the global scarcity of machines creates a 'seller's market' for those machines. Assuming free international trade, Northern countries will specialize in the production of machines, the excess of which over capital replenishment will be sold on the international market. Southern countries, on the other hand, will specialize in the production of corn. They will use a capital-intensive technology to do so for as long as they have capital goods, but given their relative shortage of those goods, at some point will shift to a more a labour-intensive technology unless more capital goods can be secured. Having specialized in corn, Southern countries must go to the market to secure the machines that they need. However, given the international 'scarcity' of machines, Southern countries will compete among themselves for those scarce machines, bidding up prices (as far their reservation price/domestic opportunity cost), shifting the terms of trade closer (per Hahnel) or all the way (per Baiman) to the Southern countries' end of the feasible range, and thus 'turning the terms of trade against themselves.'[36]

While free international trade increases international efficiency (the amount of product that can be generated with the same labour input), such trade distributes, in this model, the efficiency gains (or saved labour) entirely or almost entirely to Northern countries, dramatically increasing (as compared to autarky) the inequality of work effort as between Northern and Southern countries.[37] Thus, even assuming the basics of comparative advantage, when one builds in relatively uncontroversial assumptions concerning differential initial capital endowments between countries, the market-driven and market-set terms of trade will tend to allocate the lion's share of efficiency gains to Northern countries. Free trade may not harm Southern countries in an absolute sense, but it certainly does in a relative sense. Moreover, Southern countries are working harder for Northern countries to be relatively enriched.

This is obviously a different claim from the terms of trade argument for a tariff that was discussed earlier, and behind it sits quite a different picture of international exchange. The thrust of the tariff argument was that a country might be able to cause its terms of trade to improve by intervening in the market. The market itself was conceived in that model as generating outcomes to which evaluative terms such as 'unequal' or 'exploitative' could not reasonably attach. Indeed, power entered the picture only in *deviating* from those market outcomes. Hahnel, Baiman and Roemer present quite a different picture. Differential initial allocations mean that the free market itself can generate outcomes that can – using the evaluative apparatus provided by such an approach – be described in a very real sense as unequal or exploitative. And this can be done without deviating from standard, core neoclassical assumptions.

Normative implications

The normative implications of this analysis are obvious. Market-driven free trade is claimed by its advocates to be beneficial to all countries (as wholes). However, it may be that some countries stand to disproportionately benefit from comparative advantage–based free international trade at the expense of others. It seems relatively uncontroversial that, viewed from the situation of the less-privileged party, engaging in a joint activity which leads to gains that are channelled almost in their entirety towards the other party is less than completely compelling. For what reason should a country adopt a policy that puts it into such a position?

Comparative advantage-based theories of international trade provide no such reason. While the Roemeresque analysis set out here brings the issue into stark relief, any market-based mechanism for setting the terms of trade and national trade-related incomes merely settles questions of international distribution by reference to the normativity of impersonal market logics.[38] Indeed, to claim that the market-determined distribution of gains from trade is compelling is to endorse a distributive entitlement of 'to each according to their bargaining power.' Such an endorsement requires providing, at the very least, an argument for the normative legitimacy of existing patterns of bargaining power (i.e., here particularly of endowments).[39]

Although to do so would be – in my view – something of a fool's errand, it might be claimed that countries with high capital or resource endowment 'deserved' their differential entitlements, and should be allowed the bargaining power and the fruits that those endowments bestow. To be clear, such an argument would not, even if it were correct, provide a normatively compelling reason for *nonbenefiting* states to pursue a policy of comparative advantage-based free trade if such a policy were to bring little if any absolute benefit but inflict significant relative harm. In any event, there are good reasons to be sceptical about any such claim of desert. Those reasons fall into two categories, the thrust of which might be summarized (in very truncated form) as follows:

1. The arbitrariness of the division of global resources and endowments: even assuming that the supply and quality of endowments and resources are partially influenced by legal-institutional factors,[40] these are distributed unevenly between countries, and this distribution is both contingent and normatively arbitrary. It is quite odd to say that nations or their people 'deserve', for example, the minerals that happen to be under 'their' ground. Indeed, the boundaries of these countries are themselves contingent and normatively arbitrary. Countries do not start from the same position in terms of resources or endowments, nor is there anything normatively compelling about those differential starting points that could ground any kind of desert-based entitlement to either the resources in question, or the increased bargaining power and distributive shares that result

from them. There is little normative relevance in the accident of endowment.[41]

2. The historical background that accompanies observed patterns in unequal country endowments and resources: there exist any number of works of colonial and economic history that highlight the fact that colonial and imperial relations of domination, extraction and repression of autonomy and industry often explain and are the sources of differential resource endowments between countries (again, even as shaped and conditioned by legal-institutional factors).[42] This, of course, adds colour to point (1) above – resource endowments are at best arbitrarily distributed and at worst, blood-soaked. The 'ill-gotten' gains of the past can barely be seen as a normatively compelling reason for present-day unequal distribution.

There exists an extensive and growing literature concerning 'global justice' – and of the obligations that might be properly owed between and across countries – in which arguments such as the above naturally find their home. Leaving aside whether the multilevel international integration brought about by modern globalization constitutes the international domain as a scheme of social cooperation that necessitates obligations of distributional justice writ large between countries,[43] the question that we must confront here – in the context of the normative compulsion of free trade – is much simpler. When we consider trade we are talking very clearly about a joint activity which produces gains that neither party would be able to realize alone. International trade alone constitutes a specific form of cooperative activity. The question remains: Why should a country participate in that scheme – what is the normative compulsion – particularly where it risks relative harm to itself and disproportionate advantage to its trading partner? World welfare arguments are often thrown around in relation to this question – the international pie is made bigger through cooperation. Of course, this cannot be considered even slightly normatively compelling from the perspective of a country in considering its policy stance unless any 'maldistribution' of gains is to be corrected through some other mechanism. In the absence of any such mechanism, the normative case for being 'exploited' seems nonexistent.

So, our first foray into the normative element of the case for free trade – examining the question of distribution of gains between trading partners – immediately turns up complications that undermine confident assertions of the normative desirability of free trade policies.

Properly understood, and accepting its assumptions about free and competitive markets, the comparative advantage-based case for free trade may well, in effect, instruct certain countries to engage in a scheme of cooperation from which they may fail to derive much (if any) absolute benefit and which may cause them significant relative harm. The determinants of this unequal distribution are themselves arbitrary, contingent or coloured by a history of extractive, imperialist relations so as to rob them of any normative import. In the absence of a guarantee of redistribution from those who aggregate the lion's share of the efficiency gains realized through cooperation, there is no normatively compelling reason provided by comparative advantage-based justifications for countries to participate in such cooperation rather than adopting some other policy (be it managed trade, protection or something else).

Distribution over time: Present versus future gains

In addition to problems concerning the sharing of gains *between* trading partners, there exists the further question of pursuit of trade-related gains over *time*. As I have mentioned, comparative advantage analysis concerns static consumptive efficiency gains. That is, the analysis takes a snapshot of the economy at a particular 'moment' and asks how to best organise then-available resources, production and output to generate the highest levels of efficiency. The discussion above deals with the sharing and distribution of those efficiency gains internationally. However, as developmentalists are quick to point out, there are economic objectives that might be pursued other than static and short-run consumptive efficiency gains using existing resources. Specifically, in its modern guise, the principle of comparative advantage and the case for free trade has little if anything to say about dynamic gains or the increase or accumulation or resources – that is, economic growth.[44]

The problem is one of considering or assessing an economic system over time. As Robinson neatly pointed out in the context of the Ricardian example, building in issues of real time and especially dynamic questions of accumulation and growth, is problematic for the case for free trade:

> When accumulation is brought into the story, it is evident that Portugal is not going to benefit from free trade [...] [English i]nvestment in expanding manufacture leads to technical advance, learning by doing, specialisation of industries and accelerating accumulation, while investment in wine runs up a blind alley into stagnation.[45]

Of course, considered in dynamic relief, specialization on the basis of comparative advantage will have effects that are left unaccounted for by the mainstream's static approach. Gains to be had (and ills to be avoided) over time are simply not questions which are measured by comparative advantage or that feature in its related normative calculus. That is, even granting that free trade might be a good policy to increase a country's short-run consumption possibilities, there is no reason at all to think that it is the best way to pursue development or longer-term welfare goals.[46] This point is made all the more acute by the analysis in the previous chapter. If comparative advantages are partially endogenous to particular legal-institutional frameworks and to some extent malleable and changeable, it is plausible to think that a country might see benefit in forgoing the gains realizable on the basis of existing comparative advantage so as to construct some future comparative advantage.

It is this notion that stands behind Mill's 'infant industries argument,'[47] of which Krugman's and the New International Economics school's economies of scale argument is a descendant. These arguments point to future gains that might be garnered by the protectionist sacrifice of short-term static efficiencies and consumption gains. Take the archetypal example – a country has a developing, fledgling, high-technology industry. If that industry is immediately subjected to international competition it may suffer from insufficiently developed capacities, scale, and so forth to allow it to successfully withstand the challenge from foreign imports. It is possible, therefore, for an industry that may – in the long run – bring significant gain, to be battered into oblivion by foreign commodities before having the chance to develop the ability to compete. The normative import is the following: Why should a country choose short-term consumptive benefits over long-term benefits? In what instances will dynamic gains from protection swamp any static losses, or vice versa?

Now, to be clear, the comparative advantage-based case for free trade does not purport to answer this question. It might be thought that I am therefore being uncharitable by raising the question of dynamic gains in a way that seems to trouble the comparative advantage analysis, particularly given my stated intention to take comparative advantage 'on its own terms'. This, however, would be incorrect. When we keep in mind comparative advantage's role in the case for free trade, the problem becomes apparent. While it is itself unobjectionable to focus on and analyse only static gains, the *normative* element of the case for free trade that comparative advantage seeks to establish cannot be borne out in the absence of a consideration of dynamic issues. That is, in moving from the prediction of static efficiency gains from free trade, to the normative prescription of free trade, mainstream analysis skips a beat.

Although it is possible to build dynamic issues into the relevant normative analysis,[48] this is not usually done by mainstream analysts. Indeed, economists have tended to ignore the normative complications that come as a result of the possibilities of dynamic gains at least (though not only) in basic presentations. The tendency is to do so by casting suspicion and doubt on either the efficacy of the economics behind such dynamic arguments (by claiming, for example, the market for firm ownership will properly price the long-term benefits of the firm such that owners are willing to accept short-term losses for long-term gain[49]), by pointing to practical difficulties in properly targeting protection to infant or struggling industries so as to produce dynamic gains,[50] by downplaying the importance of scale economies,[51] or, finally, by invoking history as a teacher that infant industries can survive the ravages of international competition.[52]

These suspicions from mainstream economists can and have been powerfully contradicted.[53] Of course, the problem for these suspicions is that they are precisely that – *suspicions*. When articulated, they are seldom done so with theoretical or justificatory rigour,[54] reducing to little more than asserted fictions, alone insufficient to close the justificatory circle on the normative question here.

The point is that it seems difficult, if not impossible, to justify disregarding the normative implications of dynamic gains in a once-and-for-all manner in the welfare analysis of the gains from trade. Failing to address these issues does not itself make static comparative advantage analysis useless or unimportant, but it does make it normatively incomplete and unable to bear the weight of justifying a conclusive normative proposition in favour of free trade. We must add this failure to consider dynamic issues to the list of areas – along with the question of relative harm – in which the comparative advantage story provides an incomplete normative basis for policies of free trade.

Distribution within countries: Beyond the fiction of the country 'as a whole'

To demonstrate a third, and far more profound incompleteness in the case for free trade's normative treatment of the gains from trade, let us return to our basic comparative advantage model which depicts England as trading with Portugal. From here, demonstration of an increase in production and consumption possibilities appears at least superficially (and particularly given Ricardian equal splitting of the gains from trade) to make the question of gain a relatively simple and uncontroversial one. Both parties experience gains and therefore both parties benefit. However, in addition to the terms of trade and dynamic issues discussed in the previous pages, the confident simplicity of the assertion that international trade benefits each trading country 'as a whole' is again shaken when the aggregation to the whole-of-country level is considered for more than a moment.

Of course, England does not trade with Portugal. International trade is, for the most part, not undertaken by countries, but by individual profit-maximizing actors. 'Trading countries' are composed of numerous actors, and international trade asymmetrically affects those actors. Depending on context, free trade may hurt some economic players and benefit others – farmers, auto manufacturers, importers or exporters. This point is obvious and well acknowledged by mainstream. Indeed, this is the whole point of the Stopler–Samuelson theorem (which, my reader will recall, is one of the key theorems that comprise the Heckscher–Ohlin–Samuelson approach to international trade discussed in the previous chapter), which states that (given the usual assumptions) a rise in the relative price of a good will lead to a rise in the return to that factor which is used most intensively in the production of the good, and conversely, to a fall in the return to the other factor.[55]

These domestic distributive effects should not be a source of surprise. From its very inception, comparative advantage's case for free trade has been deeply implicated in questions of distribution. Recall, once again, that this case was forged by Ricardo in the heat of a debate concerning the repeal of the English Corn Laws. Ricardo opposed those laws on the basis that they diverted income to landowners in the form of rents, and away from 'productive' capitalists.[56] The comparative advantage argument was important to Ricardo for the very *reason* of its in-country distributive effects.

When the asymmetric domestic effects of international trade policies, and the creation of both in-country winners and losers is considered, even if total national income or wealth can be said to have increased through trade, in what sense can it be said that the nation is made 'better off'? Specifically, what is required is some standard by which states of affairs (pre-trade, post-trade) can be measured against each other so as to answer the question as to which leaves a country – or more properly the people within it – 'better off'. This is where we squarely and unambiguously enter the terrain of welfare (or normative) economics.

As we have seen, the question of the welfare effects of international trade tends to be described in basic presentations in terms of enlarged consumption possibilities or *wealth*. However, enlarged consumption possibilities generated by productive efficiency require some intermediate analytical steps before they can be successfully linked to an increase in economic 'better offness' for a country *as a whole*. That is, there is a leap to be made across a conceptual canyon marked by the distinction between 'wealth' and 'welfare'. Wealth concerns quantities and values of goods or commodities. Welfare, on the other hand involves – in the mainstream analysis – individual (or aggregate in the case of social welfare) well-being generated by preference satisfaction through consumption of those goods or commodities. The classical economists – such as Smith, Ricardo and to some extent John Stuart Mill – struggled to adequately grapple with this distinction and tended simply to assume without demonstrating that an increase in economic wealth implied an increase in welfare.[57]

Welfare comparison and assessment is difficult and complicated. To start with, how shall we measure aggregate welfare? The problem that neoclassical welfare analysis of international trade faces here is the replication of one generally applicable to the approach of welfare economics: the problem of interpersonal comparisons of utility. Unlike the utilitarians before them, neoclassical welfare theorists are on the whole sceptical of the social analyst's ability to measure mental states such as utility (happiness/preference satisfaction) and to find a satisfactory yardstick for comparisons of utility across persons.[58] Trying to aggregate welfare of multiple persons (or a nation of persons) becomes a task of adding apples and oranges.

The so-called 'New Welfare Economics' of Pareto, Hicks and Kaldor (that succeeded the earlier neoclassical approaches of Edgeworth, Sidgwick, Marshall and Pigou) set itself the task of providing evaluative standards that avoided both interpersonal comparisons of utility *and* the mistake of eliding wealth and welfare. In doing so it promised to put normative economic analysis on value-free,[59] efficiency-maximizing and comprehensive (in the sense of applicable to all circumstances and problems) foundations.

The first such standard for the comparison of states of affairs thrown up by welfare economics is the Pareto criterion. The Pareto criterion seeks to avoid making interpersonal comparisons of utility by holding that an efficient or optimal situation is one in which no change can be made to make (at least) one individual better off without making another individual worse off. In the context of international trade, however, this criterion is relatively unhelpful – as we have noted, and as the Stopler–Samuelson theorem holds – a move from protection to free trade will invariably make some actors worse off. Therefore, free trade cannot be recommended in any general way as a Pareto improvement over a situation of autarky (or, indeed, vice versa), nor in that sense be seen as an optimal policy from a welfare perspective.

An alternative standard for comparison provided by welfare economic analysis is the 'potential Pareto' criterion. According to that criterion, a move is considered more efficient if a Pareto optimal outcome could *potentially* be reached if sufficient compensation were paid by those made better off by the move to those made worse off. That is, winners win to such an extent that they are able to compensate losers for their loss and still be better off. Specifically, according to a test developed by Nicholas Kaldor, an activity can be justified if the maximum amount the gainers are prepared to pay is greater than the minimum amount that the losers are prepared to accept.[60] Shortly after Kaldor's articulation, John Hicks suggested a related formulation – a move constitutes a potential Pareto improvement if those harmed by that move are not willing to bribe those who gained to forgo the change.[61] At base, the Hicks compensation test views the situation from the point of view of the losers, while Kaldor's adopts the perspective of those who gain. Again, the point of both of these criteria is – in a fashion more practicable than the Pareto criterion – to transcend the distinction between wealth and welfare while at the same time avoiding the problem of making interpersonal comparisons of utility.

Although popularized by Kaldor and Hicks in the late 1930s and 1940s, it is interesting to note that this concept of winners compensating losers was one that had been alive in the literature concerning international trade for some time. Indeed, in 1825 John Stuart Mill introduced the notion in the context of the repeal of the Corn Laws.[62] Specifically, he argued that it would be better that the economic waste entailed by the Corn Laws (that is, the failure to generate productive efficiency) be avoided, even if landlords who benefited from the Corn Laws were compensated for their lost revenues by the consumer and capitalist. At least then no one would lose, and some would gain (as opposed to the inverse situation that prevailed under the Corn Laws in which gains to landlords were outweighed by losses to capitalists and consumers).[63]

In keeping with the tendency of economists as a whole to downplay the importance of the distributive implications attending comparative advantage,[64] the analysis suggested by the Kaldor and Hicks tends to be *assumed* to work out favourably for free trade. That is, it is assumed that winnings from free trade *will* outweigh losses. As Samuelson – once the darling, and more recently the villain of international trade economics[65] – has paraphrased the arguments of prominent and sophisticated mainstream protrade/proglobalization economists such as Bhagwati, Mankiw, Irwin, Greenspan or economist 'John or Jane Doe':[66]

> Yes, good jobs may be lost here in the short run. But still total U.S. net national product must, by the economic laws of comparative advantage, be raised in the long run ... The gains of the winners from free trade, properly measured, work out to exceed the losses of the losers. This is not by mysterious fuzzy magic, but rather comes from a sharing of the trade-induced rise in total global vectors of the goods and services that people in a democracy want. Never forget to tally the real gains of consumers alongside admitted possible losses of some producers in this working out of what Schumpeter called 'creative capitalist destruction'.
>
> Correct economic law recognizes that some American groups can be hurt by dynamic free trade. But correct economic law vindicates the word 'creative' destruction by its proof [sic] that the gains of the American winners are big enough to more than compensate the losers.[67]

The point is that the economic mainstream tends to resolve the problem of distribution by assuming that it is not a problem after all: gains to winners will outweigh losses of losers and so the latter can potentially be compensated and everyone is still 'better off'. But here lurks fiction. As Samuelson rightly goes on to say, 'The last paragraph can be only an innuendo. For it is dead wrong about necessary surplus of winnings over losings.'[68]

Even leaving aside the flawed and complacent assumption that winnings will necessarily outweigh losses, the Kaldor–Hicks rendition of the compensation principle runs into two distinct problems. The first is a technical or analytical one, and has been termed the Scitovsky reversal paradox.[69] The Scitovsky paradox is the problem created where a method of aggregating social welfare makes it possible that a switch from allocation A to allocation B seems like an improvement in social welfare, but so too does a move back. For example, if a situation of protection is changed to free trade, those who suffer in the move (say, landowners) may be compensated by winners (say, capitalists). However, landowners might in fact still gain enough by returning to protection even after paying to capitalists some of the difference between the two allocations as to make a switchback efficient according to the Kaldor test. In order to avoid this difficulty, it is necessary for a shift between states of affairs to satisfy *both* Kaldor and Hicks principles. Problematically, Kaldor, Hicks or even the post-Scitovsky 'double-edged' Kaldor–Hicks tests fail to give clear guidance in relation to questions of distribution – to different divisions of the same economic pie. As was highlighted by Little, either would approve of making the richest man in England richer by £1 billion, even at the expense of making the poorest million men in the country poorer by £900.[70] Of course, as even advocates of free trade acknowledge, this undermines the usefulness of the individual Kaldor and Hicks criteria as easy unique standards for making comparisons between states of affairs and making a normative recommendation in favour of one or another.[71]

The second problem is an analytical-cum-normative one that is even more salient for our present purposes. More importantly, where the Kaldor and Hicks tests differ from Mill's compensation test, mentioned above, is on the question of whether compensation need *actually* be paid by winners to losers. The former two tests define the economic question to have ended at the point where potential compensation has been shown to be *feasible*. The question of whether compensation was in fact paid is seen from this perspective to be a 'political' question on which the 'economist, qua economist, could hardly pronounce an opinion'.[72] The normative compulsion of the Kaldor–Hicks criterion is that it promises to discriminate between states of affairs so as to guide policy action without recourse to either interpersonal comparisons of utility, and without simplistically conflating wealth and welfare maximization. But, in contrast to the Pareto criterion, using the potential Pareto criterion, a judgement concerning the desirability of a later situation does not hinge on it being *actually* better than the former. Rather, it hinges on the *potential* to be better. However, without the actual payment of compensation, it is difficult to justify the move as a positive one other than in a hypothetical state of affairs irrelevant to the world in which some have *in fact* been harmed by the move. Rather, the machinery of the Kaldor–Hicks test has merely redescribed the initial problem in more pleasing terms. It is yet another exercise in fiction – a fairy tale of compensation is deployed to soften the reality of loss. The problem, however, remains: some have won, and some have lost – how does one make an unambiguous welfare claim that the new situation is better than the last if no compensation is actually paid?[73]

In light of these deficiencies, we find that the New Welfare Economics – even post-Kaldor and Hicks – still fails to provide closure as a theory of social choice. That is, it is not able to provide a normative recommendation as to how to decide between states of affairs and policies. One final solution that has been explored by welfare economists is the positing of a social welfare function – that is, a measure of social welfare usually postulated as function of the ordinal personal utility levels attained by the component individual members of the society in question. Based purely on information concerning individual welfare in respect of particular situations, the idea is that the specification of a social welfare function will aid the welfare analyst in the task of assessing and making judgments about how to evaluate losses by some actors against the gains made by others.

Economists acknowledge that the selection of one rather than another social welfare function (that is the particular way in which to aggregate and weigh individual utilities) is an inherently value-laden exercise. That is the determination of the precise welfare function itself (be it utilitarian, egalitarian, prioritarian or otherwise) – and its relative weightings – is a matter in relation to which economic science must remain silent. The role of economics is, once such as function has been settled upon, to evaluate two states of affairs pursuant to that function with regard to individual welfare and nothing else.[74] The use of a social welfare function thus attempts to solve the distributive dilemma thrown up by the New Welfare Economics in at least two ways: firstly, by defining a weighting of different utilities within the social welfare function, and secondly, by evaluating states of affairs by reference to individual welfare, which may for some be premised on certain outcomes in respect of distribution.

What this means in the context of international trade is something like the following: Assume that a move is made from a situation of protection to one of free trade according to comparative advantage. There will be domestic winners and losers. A social welfare function will unambiguously rank both situations on the basis of aggregate social welfare, evaluating the winnings of the winners as against the losses of the losers, and therefore clearly recommending one or other policy choice.

It is worth noting that this technique will not necessarily save the case for free trade – it acknowledges from the outset that the normative persuasiveness of comparative advantage-based trade cannot be determined in a once-and-for-all manner. The normative compulsion of a policy of free trade is not automatic, but rather depends on how a *particular* social welfare function assesses winnings and losses. Different attitudes to these winnings and losses (encapsulated in different social welfare functions) will produce different normative attitudes towards free international trade.

Moreover, and unfortunately for the welfare economist, even this method of normative prescription has run aground upon difficult logical and practical difficulties. The former can be described as 'impossibility' results, the most famous of these being the Arrow's Impossibility Theorem.[75] The crux of these is that it is impossible to specify a social welfare function that satisfies without contradiction even minimal criteria.[76] There has been a raging debate within the economic literature concerning what kind of minimal criteria are indeed necessary, whether some softening or relaxing of them might be possible and therefore, whether there might be ways out of the impossibility paradox.

And even if such a social welfare function were to be in theory capable of being specified, there remains the practical point as to how a society goes about deciding on such a function. As was pointed out by J. de V. Graaff,[77] there are reasons to be highly sceptical of the possibility of finding sufficient consensus for the building of a social welfare function, given the multitude of issues that would need to be considered.[78] The analyst's assumption of some unspecified but simultaneously abstractly determinative function merely hides the irrelevance of welfare economic analysis and the potential impossibility of its project. Even committed and sophisticated welfare economists admit, in the context of normative economic analysis, that the

> depressing conclusion has remained more or less inescapable: there is no logically infallible way to aggregate the preferences of diverse individuals [...] there is no logically infallible way to solve the problem of distribution.[79]

All of this goes to show the incompleteness of modern welfare economic analysis as a theory of social choice, *even on its own terms*. And while this is frustrating for the project of welfare economics, it is devastating for the case for free trade. In a situation in which trade on the basis of comparative advantage creates winners and losers, in the absence of compensation actually being paid to those who lose, economic theorists fail to provide a clear answer to the question of why and according to what criteria, pre- and post-trade situations can be compared, and a welfare proposition can be expressed recommending a policy of trade. Not only can the normative persuasiveness of the case for trade not be established in a once-and-for-all sense, the analysis required to so establish it at all is fraught with logical and pragmatic fiction.

Somewhat bizarrely, neoclassical economists acknowledge the incompleteness and limits of their welfare analysis and the concessions that might need to be made in order to make policy recommendations in the face of the problems inherent in welfare economics as it currently stands,[80] even – perhaps especially – in the context of international trade.[81] What then explains the certainty that often accompanies the claims that free trade is welfare enhancing, or the constant use of economic analysis in support of propositions such as this? An interesting hint is provided by Bhagwati:

> Since these questions are of interest to policy-makers, the trade theorist has eschewed [...] scruples and [...] decided to handle income distribution in a non-purist fashion so as to enable him to get along with the business of ranking the contrasting policies.[82]

The implication here is that the normative concerns of policy formulation – the need to provide advice concerning what to *do* – sometimes lead economists to put aside their worries concerning theoretical inadequacies and provide recommendations nonetheless. However, while jerry-rigging available concepts in the absence of better ones in order to perform analysis is one thing, trumpeting the results of that analysis as ironclad truths is another. This is particularly so – as we shall soon discover – when there are high stakes involved in such trumpeting.

Where Welfare Economics – and the Normative Case – Run Out: The Fiction of Being 'Better Off'

Beyond its internal, analytical difficulties, there is another – more profound – problem that mainstream welfare analysis must face and that goes to the heart of its role as the primary normative discourse in relation to economic arrangements and policies. The high water mark of mainstream analysis' deceptive partiality concerns the very meaning of being 'better off'. Specifically, the fiction that we excavate and confront here is that 'better offness' is exhausted by a discussion of gains in consumption.

As will be clear from the discussion above, unlike the analysis of Smith, Ricardo and the other classicals, neoclassical economics does not focus on wealth generation (and its distribution as between classes) as much as it does on the efficient allocation of scarce resources (and the distribution of income) so as to maximize the sum of human satisfactions generated by those resources.[83] Again, welfare economics is very much the child of the ongoing economic project of attempting to show the essentially beneficent channelling role of markets – their alchemic ability to transmute individual maximizing behaviour to towards society-wide benefits – thereby justifying their starring role in the solution to *the* economic problem. That is, welfare economics is the 'final and most elaborate apotheosis of Adam Smith's invisible-hand argument',[84] and the culmination – the end – to which the entire edifice of neoclassical microeconomics points.[85] This includes the neoclassical analysis of international trade and its supposed gains.[86] Just as we have witnessed in chapter 3 the fictitiousness of the invisible hand in international exchange, we are now in a position to address the downstream normative fictions to which it is related.

However, as is the case with neoclassical economics more broadly (as we have seen elsewhere), welfare economics relies upon a limited, stylized and ultimately fictional conception of the economy as a whole, and the production process in particular. I claim that these misconceptions blind welfare analysis to elements of socioeconomic arrangements that are properly considered of normative import in assessing and deciding between such arrangements. Thus, in order to demonstrate the inadequacies of mainstream welfare/normative economic analysis and what it fails to consider, we must return to the neoclassical understanding of the economy and of the production process.[87]

The partiality of welfare economic analysis

It will be recalled that in chapters 3 and 4, I presented neoclassical economics' peculiar modelling of the economy as being monadically individualistic, with production activities being similarly individualistic and nonrelational. Moreover, the production process is conceptualized as mechanistic and simplistic – little other than another form of consumptive activity – inputs enter and are consumed by the process and outputs are expelled at the other end. Neoclassical economics remains blind to the workings of the 'black box' of the production process while nonetheless committed to the notion that markets cause efficient production that optimizes output in light of resource and technical starting points.[88] Such economics – and importantly for my present purposes, welfare economics – becomes therefore focused upon exchange. As Hunt has noted, Bastiat's slogan 'political economy is exchange' has come, through the marginal revolution and neoclassical economics, to describe almost the entirety of economic analysis.[89]

The fundamental thrust of welfare economics is to demonstrate that, under competitive conditions, the market-based exchange actions and interactions of utility-maximizing consumers and profit-maximizing firms will optimize social welfare. The steps to that demonstration may be roughly summarized as follows[90]:

1. Taking as given available capital and labour inputs, and assuming a two-commodity economy, profit-maximizing firms will drive a nation's output to that its production possibility frontier.

2. Any point on the production possibility frontier represents (as discussed in chapter 4) a total output in terms the two produced commodities, and it is possible to derive from that point the marginal rate of transformation in production (opportunity cost of one in terms of another) for those two commodities.

3. Under competitive conditions, the marginal rate of transformation of one good into another will always reflect their prices, and if markets are competitive, prices will clear markets and supply will equal demand in each market.

4. When consumers exchange so as to maximize their utility, the price ratio between produced commodities will reflect the ratio of marginal utilities of those commodities to consumers.

5. Thus, the equilibrium level and composition of production, and the resultant exchange of that production, will lead to a point on a society's utility–possibility frontier, each such point representing a situation in which no change in production and no additional amount of commodity exchange could make a single individual better off without making some other individual worse off (given an initial distribution of wealth).

The virtual absence of the production process in this demonstration – and its individualistic focus – should be clear. Specifically, it relies on the following (related) propositions as to the nature of the economy under question:

1. All sources of utility are commodities.
2. All outputs of the production process are commodities.
3. The activities of production and consumption of commodities have no effects beyond those individuals directly involved in that production and consumption.

It is by virtue of these propositions and in this fashion, that welfare economics can justify its sole focus on commodities and their exchange. The problem is, however, that each of these propositions is fictional rather than factual, and that this simplistic model of production and of the commodified economy leads welfare economic analysis up the garden path in considering actual socioeconomic arrangements. The actual social phenomenon of production generates (noncommodified) effects beyond the commodities that emerge from that that process. Moreover, consumption activities have effects not only for direct consumers, but also for third parties. Those (again, noncommodified) effects result in utilities and disutilities to not only direct producers and consumers, but also to third parties, and to society as a whole.

The best way to explain this is through the concept of externalities. In mainstream analysis, an externality (or external effect) is seen to occur when the utility function of one consumer is affected by another consumer's consumption, the production function of one firm is affected by the production of another or the utility of an individual is affected by a production process with which she has no connection.[91] In line with the propositions stated above, mainstream welfare economic analysis seems to assume that externalities are an exceptional phenomenon.[92] When an external effect is found, the economist will try to use either Piguvian taxes or Coasean allocation of rights guided by cost–benefit analysis to repair the market failure and 'internalize' the cost in one way or another.[93] A contemporary example of this is creating tradeable and priced pollution rights in order to internalize otherwise externalized environmental costs in production.

The problem is, when understood as broadly as they are according to mainstream definition, externalities are ubiquitous rather than exceptional. Following Coase's innovations in welfare economics, it is possible to see a multitude of externalities (in the sense of unpriced utility/disutility effects on others) in almost all acts of production and consumption.[94] Sources of utility and disutility can be material objects, or they can be the actions of others, or indeed psychological effects.[95] Consider such effects in the realm of production and different utility effects generated by different kinds and arrangements of work. Drudgerous work often has different utility effects for workers and, interestingly, their families and communities than work that is considered by the individual in question meaningful or rewarding. The same might be said of organizational or labour environments that are highly regimented or hierarchical, as opposed to those which allow a high degree of autonomy or participation.

Further, aesthetic offence taken at the destruction of natural environments, or the mental or emotional anguish of seeing or hearing about workplace accidents, are each 'externalities' in the mainstream sense. As are the several economic and social effects of a business choosing to relocate from a given area, or moral outrage at existence of certain industries or practices.

The same pervasiveness of noncommodity external effects presents itself in the domain of consumption. Thus, perhaps less obviously, but nonetheless completely accurately,

> Our table manners in a restaurant, the general appearance of our house, our yard or our person, our personal hygiene, the route we pick for a joy ride, the time of day we mow our lawn, or nearly any one of the thousands of ordinary daily acts, all affect, to some degree, the pleasures or happiness of others.[96]

Recognizing the ubiquity of externalities poses a significant evaluative problem for normative economic analysis. This recognition reveals a plethora of 'uncounted' utility effects that emerge from particular patterns of production and consumption. They are uncounted in the sense that they do not enter the normative or evaluative calculus pointed to by welfare economics. However, the absence of these effects from that calculus strips welfare economic analysis of its prescriptive ability. These effects cannot be ignored if efficiency predictions concerning utility maximization are to be generated.[97]

Critically, in addition to pure counting issues thrown up by the prevalence of noncommodified outputs from production and consumption, there is an additional problem of evaluation and assessment, particularly in light of the discussion above concerning dynamic issues. That is, developmentally or dynamically, socioeconomic arrangements and production practices have a range of human and (when aggregated) social-shaping effects that hide from mainstream analysis in the world of externalities. Socioeconomic practices and institutions have important effects on the personalities of those involved in those practices and with those institutions.[98] Indeed, there is a line of thought that extends as far back as Aristotle affirming the existence of various feedback effects between an individual's actions and environment, and the formation of his or her character or personality (a diverse set of individual valuations, skills, tendencies, beliefs, assumptions and habits). Nor is that line constituted by the weak-minded – no less than Smith, Mill, Hegel, Marx and Veblen have pointed to the effect on the development of personality that can be exerted by the kind of work that a person does, and the kind of socioeconomic institutions and context in which they are situated. Much of this literature has been advanced under the heading of 'endogenous preference theory', as well as Marxian and post-Marxian theorizing of the effect on producers of particular kinds of production processes.[99] These approaches seek to investigate the human effects (not merely the commodity allocation effects) of socioeconomic arrangements.

Indeed, the ills of patterns and methods of production were well recognized by Smith:

In the progress of the division of labour, the employment of the far greater part of those who live by labour, that is, of the great body of the people, comes to be confined to a few very simple operations, frequently to one or two. But the understandings of the greater part of men are necessarily formed by their ordinary employments. The man whose whole life is spent in performing a few simple operations, of which the effects are perhaps always the same, or very nearly the same, has no occasion to exert his understanding or to exercise his invention in finding out expedients for removing difficulties which never occur. He naturally loses, therefore, the habit of such exertion, and generally becomes as stupid and ignorant as it is possible for a human creature to become. The torpor of his mind renders him not only incapable of relishing or bearing a part in any rational conversation, but of conceiving any generous, noble, or tender sentiment, and consequently of forming any just judgment concerning many even of the ordinary duties of private life. Of the great and extensive interests of his country he is altogether incapable of judging, and unless very particular pains have been taken to render him otherwise, he is equally incapable of defending his country in war...It corrupts even the activity of his body, and renders him incapable of exerting his strength with vigour and perseverance in any other employment than that to which he has been bred. His dexterity at his own particular trade seems, in this manner, to be acquired at the expense of his intellectual, social, and martial virtues.[100]

For the purposes of my argument here, a complex philosophical apparatus – such as the concept of 'substantive goods',[101] or the Aristotelian distinction between 'man-as-he-happens-to-be' and 'man-as-he-should-be' – need not be invoked. One does not need to affirm a determinate conception of human good or *telos* in order to take seriously the argument that I am advancing. It is enough to accept that there is a meaningful distinction between 'man-as-he-happens-to-be' under current socioeconomic arrangements and 'man-as-he-might-be' under other arrangements, and that different possibilities as to the latter should be part of the calculus in evaluating which economic policies or institutions to pursue.

This kind of thinking has tended to be frowned upon by mainstream neoclassical economics for fear that it might lead economists to inappropriately trespass into questions of where individual preferences come from,[102] to fail to 'take individuals as they are' and to misunderstand the production process as something other than just another consumption activity. However, my claim is that – in the domain of normative analysis – economists cannot avoid concerning themselves with issues of outputs of the production process and of particular constellations of socioeconomic arrangements in general. Why? Because failure to do so will cause normative analysis to drastically misestimate the welfare effects of those institutions and policies.[103] Particular economic policies or institutions may affect the personalities of individuals. Socioeconomic institutions and policies are not neutral with respect to personality and preference formation and development. This is a problem for mainstream welfare economic analysis. Indeed, as Herb Gintis has written,

The apparent mutual determination of a social structure (and economic structure in particular) and individual personality systems [...] presents severe problems for a purely atomistic welfare theory.[104]

Specifically, certain personality and preference-formation effects – human externalities – will impact the normative compellingness of one rather than another institution or policy. The unacknowledged prevalence of these kinds of externalities only underscores the poverty, absurdity and fictitiousness of the treatment of both and of normative prescription under the traditional welfare paradigm.[105]

Of course, when aggregated, these kinds of human and other externalities can operate to create economy- and society-wide effects. As we have seen, the possibility of domestic external or spillover effects is recognized by international trade theorists, particularly those aligned with the New International Economics school; however, their pervasiveness and omnipresence is not.[106] Certain negative effects of aggregated human externalities were pointed to by Smith in the passage quoted above – a degradation in the ability to participate in public discourse at the individual level that manifests at the social level, and also the decline in individual 'martial spirit' and hence, the security of the state as a whole. That is, certain production patterns and socioeconomic arrangements can create patterns of international dependence and can influence a country's relative geopolitical or strategic positioning vis-à-vis other countries.[107]

All of this together leads to the conclusion that production and consumption arrangements have a multitude of effects that are ignored by mainstream welfare economic analysis, but nonetheless have immense importance for the way in which we might normatively assess particular policies and socioeconomic structures. These effects are felt, both evaluatively and dynamically, by producing and consuming individuals themselves, by third party individuals, and at an aggregate level by the society 'as a whole'.

To hearken back to a theme we have encountered before, the ubiquity of externalities and neoclassical welfare economics' inability to properly recognize this ubiquity is sourced in the fact that *actual* economic activities such as production and consumption are primarily social and relational rather than monadically individualistic. These activities both involve more than a single individual producing and consuming alone. Rather, the interconnectedness of social productive and consumptive life mean these activities and the individuals involved in them constantly create utility or disutility for others.[108] Utility function interconnectedness is nothing other than the utility or welfare reflection of the sociolegal, material, productive and opportunity-set interconnectedness that I presented in the previous chapter. The actuality of social and economic interconnectedness thus cuts across and troubles both positive and normative dimensions of economic analysis.

In order to illustrate the importance of this in the context of our primary concern, I will return to the question of international trade, or perhaps more importantly, to international *specialization*.

Normative and evaluative insufficiency illustrated: International specialization

I have attempted to show that normative economics, in its neoclassical form, is an exchange-based theory – it is interested in assessing policies from the perspective of the most efficient satisfaction of individual preferences gained from commodities that are traded and consumed by economic actors. The normativity of welfare economics is the normativity of the market, of exchange and consumption. However, the totality of the economic process is not exhausted by exchange and consumption – production is vital to any actual economy. Its absence from the normative assessment of particular modes of socioeconomic organization is both myopic and has the propensity to mislead policy analysis and assessment.

In the context of international trade, the dangers of deemphasising production are immense. Comparative advantage is over and again touted as a justification for international *specialization* and *trade*, and yet it is primarily the trade-related aspect of that dynamic that receives consideration in the context of normative economic assessment. However, quite apart from the question of efficiency gains from trade and their distribution between and within trading countries, there are other criteria by which economic and social arrangements can, and indeed should, be evaluated. Trade and specialization have outcomes other than those relating to efficiency.

It is important to remember that the flip side of comparative advantage's case for free trade is its case for an international division of labour – of specialization *of production*. The question is, are all such divisions equally normatively acceptable? In light of the discussion above, I claim that this question must be answered in the negative. As we have seen, production does not merely produce goods or commodities for consumption. Different patterns of production and consumption generate different utility and developmental effects for producers, consumers, third parties and societies more broadly. Yet, at the same time, these effects are often external to the process of valuing commodity outputs from those arrangements. The evaluative and normative predicament created by the fictional model that allows this is acute.

For example, imagine two alternative specializations: the mining of coal, and the production of fictional literature. Imagine that the mining of coal is a dangerous activity in which the individuals involved spend hours involved in risky, hard labour. When these miners return home at the end of the day, they are exhausted. Given that exhaustion, it is all that they can manage to eat some food, drink a couple of beers, watch an hour of television and then collapse into bed. At the same time, imagine that the process of mining is leaving an aesthetic and environmental scar on the countryside. This has caused many to leave the area, and is causing many who remain to become depressed and despondent.

On the other hand, let us say that those involved in the production of fictional literature work a comfortable day exercising their imaginations and creativity in a library or office. At the end of the day, these workers – excited and invigorated by a day of creative-productive endeavour – engage in some social or recreational activity such as a sport, a book club, or a public-speaking group. They find that the kind of work that they do develops in them skills of articulateness and insightfulness, and they see themselves as intelligent and thoughtful. Imagine that this encourages these workers to be inclined to participate in political life in an engaged fashion. At the end of the day, they go home, have a stimulating conversation over dinner with whomever they live and then go to bed.

Or imagine another pair of specializations – say specialization in the production of processed chicken and the production of innovative, life-saving medicines to combat cancer. Imagine workers at the chicken-processing factory spend their days killing, plucking, gutting and cleaning chickens. This work is done through an assembly/disassembly line process that is geared towards mass production and in which each worker performs a single task that is repeated many times in one day. Imagine further that the workplace is organized pursuant to a highly regimented system of hierarchy: responsibility and autonomy is kept to a minimum for line workers who are heavily supervised and monitored. Success at work means that your name is put on a whiteboard for the week and that you don't get fired. After a day of repetitive, mind- and emotion-numbing labour of blood and entrails, workers go home, read the local tabloid and worry about the 'threat' to their jobs posed both by the worker who works at the next station down on the assembly line and also by immigrants. This translates to a high degree of fractiousness in the workplace, interracial ill feeling and violence in the community more broadly. Imagine that many of the workers in this factory left the countryside in order to seek work following the decimation of the farming industry by reason of cheaper foreign produce imports. They miss the country and feel caged and uncomfortable in the semiurban surrounds of the factory in which most of them live.

On the other hand, those who work in the medical research industry do so in small collaborative teams to solve puzzles thrown up in the course of their research. They tend to see their work as either a social or intellectual 'calling', and have a feeling that the work that they do is meaningful and important to society. Success at your job means that you might just cure cancer, make a lot of money and be awarded a Nobel Prize. After a day of tackling the greatest health scourge of the modern age, workers tend to meet old friends from their PhD years and swap research stories and insights. It turns out that many of these old friends now work in health and innovation policy roles within government and also in other public and private research roles. As a result of the constant interconnections and interchange, there has grown up a set of related research industries in the country, constantly reinforced by feedback effects between the other industries and government policy.

Now, I am not, of course, offering these examples up as necessary conditions or lifestyles that will be thrown up by these different specializations, or that the choice to be made between possible specializations is as stark as the hypothetical alternatives here. Nor does my argument here rely on having a preference for one rather than the other specialization in each of the two pairs (although I clearly do). The examples are somewhat absurd. What I claim is even more absurd, however, is the fact that – assuming that each specialization is equally 'efficient' – mainstream normative economic analysis will have nothing to say about the kinds of social and individual effects that I am pointing to through these examples. They do not, for the most part, even get close to entering into the normative calculus from a welfare economic point of view. The character of these examples does not relate to efficiency or income distribution (conventionally understood), and they occur in the hidden world of production and of unacknowledged externalities. However, I argue that these 'side effects' of socioeconomic arrangements seem every bit as normatively important and relevant to the question of whether aggregate social goods have been maximized and appropriately distributed.

At this point, the quick response from the defender of neoclassical economics might be something like the following:

'Look, no one ever said that there weren't considerations other than efficiency that might be pursued through socioeconomic arrangements. Just look at this quote from Coase:

> It is, of course, desirable that the choice between social arrangements for the solution of economic problems should be carried out in broader terms [...] and that the total effect of these arrangements in all spheres of life should be taken into account. As Frank H. Knight has so often emphasized, the problems of welfare economics must ultimately dissolve into a study of aesthetics and morals.[109]

Economists have always acknowledged that nonefficiency criteria are important, we just don't think that the economist has any business talking about them: that's politics – go speak to a statesman or a philosopher.'

This response is flawed in at least three senses. Firstly, the point here is that even if efficiency in the welfare economics sense were *a* goal (and not the only goal), the current incarnation of welfare economics is a bad way to go about pursuing it. Welfare economic analysis – and economic analysis generally – tends to evaluate economic arrangements solely or mainly on the basis of their efficiency in providing *material* and commoditized goods.[110] But it is ultimately arbitrary to focus only on material or commodity goods (and 'bads'). Economic processes not only transform material inputs into material outputs, they simultaneously alter human states at both individual and group levels as well. Noncommodity goods exist, and economic arrangements are not neutral in respect of such goods. It is a narrow, artificial and ultimately unhelpful welfare theory that seeks to make normative prescriptions without paying attention to these issues.

Second, and related to this, is not the case that the nuanced position suggested by the retort above – a position appropriately modest about what is and what is not shown by economics – is the usual position adopted by advocates of free trade and its benefits. It is often the case that in the realm of economic arrangements and free trade, efficiency is claimed (at least implicitly) to be the relevant evaluative consideration, to the exclusion of others. As even Krugman has said, 'trade policy should be debated in terms of its impact on efficiency.'[111]

Thirdly, and more fundamentally, the retort above relies on a misconceived distinction (though it is not clear that Coase and Knight relied upon this distinction, at least in the quoted passage). What sits behind this retort is the notion that the efficiency of social arrangements can meaningfully be separated from other aspects of those arrangements; that efficiency is maximized through the socioeconomic institutions recommended by economic science, and that trade-offs should be seen in that light. And of course, the premise itself – that efficiency is maximized through free trade – is misguided: for the reasons mentioned in this and previous chapters, the socioeconomic arrangements that result from free trade are not clearly justified as the efficient ones. I will return to the fallacious separation of economic and other social arrangements in our final chapter together.

Insufficiency exacerbated – welfare and the role of the state

The normative punch of this analysis is made more acute when we recall, as was discussed in the previous chapter, the state's role – through a multitude of different legal-institutional means – in constructing and influencing domestic opportunity costs, and thus patterns of comparative advantage and specialization. Different specializations will have markedly different outputs, outputs obscured by the dominant form of normative economic analysis, but for which the state must take some partial responsibility. Just as the bases of trade and patterns of specialization are in very significant sense 'man-made', so too are the negative (and indeed, the positive) outputs of particular kinds of specialization. The problem with welfare economic analysis is that it simultaneous obscures from policy-makers the combined effect of state policy in some areas, while purporting to guide it in another area. Given the stakes, policy might more helpfully and compellingly be directed towards garnering the benefits – and avoiding the detriments – of particular specializations, rather than allowing legal-institutional factors through the anarchy of the market to pick – willy-nilly – patterns of specialization and the direction of society, and allowing welfare economics to mask the problem.

Now, at this point it might be argued that even if the state is involved in constructing comparative advantages in all of the ways that I have suggested in chapter 4, the state does not do so willy-nilly, as I seem to be implying. Or at least, even if it does so, there is a happy order that emerges from that willy-nilliness. The argument might advance something like this: state regulation will itself in fact be efficient in a welfare economic sense, by reason of inter-jurisdictional (that is, international) regulatory competition.

Such arguments grow from the literature based on and around what has been called the 'Tiebout model' of the provision of public goods, and specifically, its extension into the realm of law and regulation. That model basically argues that citizens, owners of factors of production and so on, express their preferences regarding different packages of public goods by 'shopping' from jurisdiction to jurisdiction, each such jurisdiction competing to attract the shopper with its specific package of public goods.[112] The logic of market competition is thus imported into the domain of public goods. The state is a producer of such goods in the same way that Toyota is a producer of cars. In its application to regulation, the Tiebout model is argued to establish, by analogous logic, that regulatory competition between jurisdictions will ensure that only 'efficient' regulations will survive as mobile economic actors force regulation setters to respond to their preferences. Regulation will be efficient in the sense of meeting the preferences of 'consumers' of that regulation.[113]

However, the Tiebout model has been brutalized in both the economic literature and also by legal scholars in its application to regulatory issues.[114] As Bratton and McCahery have forcefully argued, for reasons theoretical, empirical and practical,

> To put it bluntly: the Tiebout model, viewed in isolation, provides no basis for predicting that competitive behaviour by government leads to optimal preference matching. Instead, the model predicts instability – competition may make residents better or worse off depending on a dynamic and complex mix of factors [...][115]

As has been well demonstrated by the technical economic and legal literature, the Tiebout model relies on (domain) assumptions that are seldom if ever established in the real world,[116] and moreover, fails to maintain its theoretical coherence as a general equilibrium model even when more restrictive assumptions are introduced.[117]

However, as is often the case, and as I have attempted to demonstrate above, policy-orientated analysis seems to sometimes to relax the rigours – and overlook the flaws – of economic models, holding fast to what little remains of them when the need for normative prescription predominates.[118] As a result, the Tiebout model, and arguments founded in it concerning the market-like welfare maximizing effect of state-made regulation continue to drift around in the policy literature. They lack, however, robust foundation in economic theory. The state remains the architect of trade and its effects, but in a normatively blinkered and scattergun fashion.

Summary: Confidence in Blindfolds

The normative element of the case for free trade now stands before us in a somewhat embarrassed state, frustratingly unable to cash out the confident assertions of mainstream economic and policy analysts concerning the desirability of free trade policies. Model after model is suggested by mainstream analysis to bear out the claim of normative compulsion – story after story is told. But as we have seen, these stories are superficial and do not withstand close examination. They rely upon concepts that are unhelpfully abstract or misleadingly incomplete – all the while claiming to establish a proposition that is put with force and confidence.

Whether as between trading partners, within countries or over time, the apparatus of welfare economics fails to provide an unambiguous and complete normative basis for free trade, even granting standard assumptions concerning the completeness and competitiveness of markets. Even more dangerously, mainstream theory lacks the tools to see (let alone address) important and relevant normative aspects of the states of affairs created by specific policy settings. Blinded to the prevalence of externalities and of noncommodity sources of utility and disutility, neoclassical welfare analysis systematically misjudges the welfare effects of particular production and socioeconomic arrangements, providing an arbitrarily narrow form of normative evaluation and prescription.

Thus, in its normative, supposedly policy-relevant guise, neoclassical economic analysis is unable to justify the unconditional or confident welfare-based recommendations that we often see in respect of free trade policies. The mainstream's models are archetypically fictitious – unmoored from reality. Problematically, however, they are used in ways that offer false comfort to those who rely upon them. The state and its policy-makers who look to welfare economic analysis for guidance are simultaneously responsible for – and blinded to – the effects of particular patterns of specialization and trade. Confidence and faith in those models is nothing less than singing odes to blindfolds in praise of clear vision.

Chapter 6

CONCLUSION BY WAY OF *IDEOLOGIEKRITIK*: FICTION AND RATIONALIZATION

> I don't care who writes a nation's laws, or crafts its advanced treatises, if I can write its economics textbooks.
>
> Paul Samuelson[1]

In the foregoing chapters we have seen the twofold use or effect of the case for free trade. Specifically, the case is deployed both to *explain* patterns of international trade and specialization, and to *advocate* for a particular set of policy settings – what we call (though now can be less sure we can define) free trade policies. And it does so using the touchstones of efficiency gains and welfare improvements. I hope that by now my reader will be deeply sceptical of the mainstream's argumentative strategy here.

By way of recapping and summarizing the reasons for this scepticism, I want to point out a third – less often highlighted – effect of the case for free trade. This effect becomes more clear when we place the case for free trade and its component claims in their social-theoretical – rather than a purely technical-economic – context.

Notwithstanding the fragility that I have pointed to, the comparative advantage–based case for free trade has a high degree of intellectual, policy and, indeed, social currency. It is thought to be *true* and people behave differently *because* they so believe. In our final chapter together, I aim to bring together the various themes and strands of argument advanced in earlier chapters of this book in order to make an encompassing claim about the operation of – and the stakes involved in – this aspect of the case for free trade, and the social actions and arrangements to which it purports to speak, explain and justify.

Comparative Advantage as Ideology

The principle of comparative advantage and the mainstream case for free trade is part of an ideology. I use the term ideology in a particular sense here and a few words of clarification may be helpful. What I mean is that comparative advantage both comprises, and is related to, a set of interconnected categories, concepts and tools that are used to – and have the effect of – making sense of particular socioeconomic arrangements and practices.[2] While existing arrangements can be made sense of through multiple strategies and on various grounds, I am here interested specifically in the manner in which comparative advantage *rationalizes* – gives a justification and reason for – certain arrangements and practices.[3]

It is worth pointing to the difference between my use of the term ideology here, and the concept of 'propaganda'. The latter connotes the cynical or rhetorical deployment of argumentative tools and resources to manipulate a person, or a group of persons. Ideology in the sense in which I use it may also be propaganda.[4] However, I am more interested here in the manner in which the case for free trade is *believed* (albeit – perhaps – unselfconsciously) by economists, policy-makers or consumers of public discourse writ large, and the consequences of it being so believed.

Two levels of rationalization

There are two levels of the rationalization performed by the case for free trade that I would like highlight. The first might be termed 'technical' rationalization. That is, the principle of comparative advantage provides a reason, based in technical economic analysis and using that discipline's technical expertise and tools, for particular social arrangements, policies and practices. By now, I hope that my reader will be well placed to appreciate the rationalizing role of comparative advantage in respect of free international trade and the socioeconomic arrangements that result from it. As we have discussed, comparative advantage analysis claims to support the conclusions that a policy of free trade generates efficiency and welfare gains for trading countries. The technical economic analysis of efficiency and welfare gains provides the *reason* for pursuing such a policy, and for the socioeconomic arrangements that emerge as a consequence of doing so.

Beyond this 'technical' dimension, the case for free trade rationalizes at a second level. Specifically, it also gives reason to a particular kind of conduct – that is, self-regarding, individualistically motivated production and trade – in a particular way. The pursuit of individual advantage, at both personal and country levels, is interpreted through the lens of the comparative advantage analytic as working (albeit through happy coincidence rather than by design) towards the good of all. Again, as Ricardo wrote, echoing and adding an international flavour to Smith:

> Under a system of perfectly free commerce, each country naturally devotes its capital and labour to such employments as are most beneficial to each. This pursuit of individual advantage is admirably connected with the universal good of the whole.

As we have seen, the benefits of individual maximizing behaviour at the domestic level are seen to have global benefits. The invisible hand 'works its magic,'[5] and the interests of all are, at least potentially, advanced.

This second level of rationalization – the reunderstanding of self-interested productive and trading behaviour as being in line with the social good – bears a little more discussion. Firstly, it should be noted that this rationalization operates at a *moral* level. In a sense, what Ricardo did was make respectable a form of self-interested behaviour in both domestic production and international trade. Whereas the mercantilists against whom he (along with Smith) pitted himself developed and advocated a pro-trade (though not *free* trade) policy stance, trade was in that conception understood to be a zero-sum game. Augmenting the coffers of England was to come at the cost of depleting those of Portugal. The *realpolitik* embodied in this theory and in the picture of international relations implied by it stood in contrast to earlier scholastic attempts to discern an economic system and mode of organization that embodied and reflected Christian notions of justice and piety.[6]

Smith, Ricardo and those that followed essentially regenerated a quasi-ethical basis for economic behaviour, but on secular and individualistic terms. After them, the self-regarding and self-interested pursuit of individual advantage through free international trade becomes linked – via stories about invisible hands and comparative advantages – to social well-being. This linkage works to excuse or salve any sense of moral unease that might be felt in respect of these behaviours and their immediate outputs that was so keenly felt by the scholastics. These behaviours and immediate outputs – even if superficially troubling – now are shown to have an unplanned purpose, an end that benefits (or potentially benefits) the whole. As Foley has nicely put the matter, the Smithian–Ricardian position 'urges us to accept direct and concrete evil in order that indirect and abstract good may come of it'.[7]

It will be recalled that an often-played retort to the critic of free trade will be that of 'perversity of outcome', the notion that impeding free trade ends up harming those whom the critic seeks to help. This retort, by reason of this second level of rationalization, gains moral steam. The case for free trade now operates as a form of a moral shield – whatever action or outcome is complained of, the comparative advantage analysis offers an excuse by appeal to a higher-order moral purpose as justification. Interference with free trade becomes not only technically but implicitly *morally* problematic – a 'partisan' preference to some interest group that involves sacrificing the good of the whole at the altar of the benefit of the few.[8]

A related characteristic of this 'moral' rationalization – and another sense in which the comparative advantage–based case for free trade differs from the economic thought that preceded it – is the relationship that it posits between the economic sphere and other aspects of society, and the criteria that it sets for the evaluation of action in the former as opposed to the latter. It should be noted that the father[9] of the modern invisible hand explanations Adam Smith was, by training, a moral philosopher. And he was no simple-minded apologist for free market capitalism or commercial society, awake as he was to the detriments that such society had both on the capacity for and nature of moral evaluation by those who lived through it.[10] However, Smith's point was that the moral costs of commercial society, in the end, were overpowered by the material benefits that could be garnered through this mode of socioeconomic organization.[11]

The subtlety of the Smithian position, however, became somewhat lost in translation via Ricardo and the marginalists. Specifically, by the time we reach neoclassicism and modern economics, the moral dilemma has dropped from view and has transformed in nature. Whereas for Smith the moral costs of individualistic economic action are *excused* by material benefit, for those that followed and established economic science through mimicry of the natural sciences, economic action was in important senses *amoral*. That is, such action is not the type of conduct to which moral evaluation is properly applied. Asking whether economic action, the economic laws that govern it, or its outputs, are 'moral' is a nonsense – akin to asking whether such conduct is 'yellow'. Or perhaps more precisely, asking whether comparative advantage and its outputs are 'moral' is similar to asking whether Boyle's Law – which explains the behaviour of gases under pressure – is moral.

The economic domain, the rules that govern it and action taken within it are understood from this perspective as matters of cause and effect. They are amendable to description, as we have seen, through law-like predictive claims. They give themselves over to mechanistic understanding. As a result, 'effectiveness' or 'efficiency' rather than morality is the appropriate standard by which to judge economic action. And the role of the economist is to provide expert knowledge in relation to the effective achievement of an end – welfare – that itself remains beyond her (mechanistic) science.[12] Any trade-off to be made between that end and any other goal (moral or otherwise), is outside her mandate and must be remitted back to the realm of politics for settlement.

Permeating both Smithian and post-Smithian incarnations of this argument is the assumed possibility (touched on in the previous chapter) of separating the economic sphere from the rest of society. Self-regarding or individualistic economic action attracts either (for Smith and Ricardo) moral excuse or (for modern economics) nonevaluation, irrespective of any immediate negative consequences, and is measured by reference primarily to effectiveness in providing commodified goods and satisfied consumption preferences. This distinction pervades John Stuart Mill's acknowledgement (discussed in the previous chapter) of the relevance of cultural and political institutions to preference development, but failure to see the role of socioeconomic institutions in that formation.[13] It can also be seen in Krugman's arguments, mentioned above, that free trade policies should be debated primarily in terms of their efficiency results.[14] And it rears its head once more in the limited conception of normative analysis encapsulated in the welfare economics and its treatment of gains from trade, which aims to make normative evaluation depend upon the *efficient* allocation and distribution of commodity outputs.

The difference between previous modes of economic thought and the Smithian–Ricardian tradition is stark. Whereas for the scholastics economic activity was to be made to conform to the universal ethical imprimaturs of religious dogma, mercantilism involved an economics of subjectivism or relativism – everyone his own economist[15] – with economic thought a collection of pamphlets generated in response to particular economic problems with particular economic interests in mind. Those that followed Smith and Ricardo, in addition to eviscerating moral content from economic action, also reformulated the universality of economic thought lost during mercantilism. They did so by replacing ethical or religious universality upon which the scholastics relied with a secular, mechanistic/scientific universality.

Thus, the rationalization provided by the comparative advantage analysis is both technical and moral. It is a way in which socioeconomic arrangements and practices are understood, explained, given reason and the manner in which their various outputs and effects are evaluated in broader contexts. The rationalizing effect of the principle of comparative advantage gives rise to another related effect – specifically, the 'universalization' of certain interests. That is, the rationalization provided by that principle importantly provides the mechanics for reading the interests of a particular group in society as indirectly linked to the interests of the whole. As we have seen, countries do not trade, individual agents do. And, moreover, not all individuals in a country do. Indeed, in the modern international economy, most trade is undertaken by capitalistic corporations. By operation of the twofold rationalization that comparative advantage provides for free trade and specialization, the interests of trading actors are read as being in line with the interests of all. The particular becomes representative of the universal – that which is good for international traders is potentially good for everyone. In effect, the case for free trade provides an argument to justify allowing the free rein of particular interests on the basis that they are in line with common interests.[16]

Giving the rationalization teeth: Scarcity, sacrifice and efficiency

So, the case for free trade uses efficiency as the justificatory mantra. But why, it might be asked, do we care about efficiency? Why should efficient allocation and distribution of production and resources be compelling as a reason, either explanatory or normative, for socioeconomic arrangements and practices? In other words, whence does comparative advantage's efficiency rationale gain traction? The answer to this too is provided by the concepts and categories associated with comparative advantage.

The case for free trade importantly relies upon, and indeed is provided its element of urgency by, the perception of scarcity. As was discussed in chapter 4, the material benefits that are promised by the principle of comparative advantage are argued to be compelling in very large part because of the need to efficiently use *scarce* resources. The global economy is not one of abundance. Trade-offs and sacrifices need to be made. There are opportunity costs in production. Again, as we have seen, scarcity, trade-offs and comparative advantages are generally posited, by even sophisticated mainstream economists, as exogenous or, in a sense, 'given'. Although this need not be the case, the *impression* created by mainstream analysis is that comparative advantages 'just are', the effect of nonhuman, nonsocial variables, of the interaction of different material commodities given a level of technology. It is this 'fact' of scarcity that sits behind the need to use social forms that most efficiently generate well-being, and upon which the technical and moral rationalizations of free international trade and individualistic, self-regarding behaviour rest. The practical exercise of managing and provisioning with limited resources and a particular level of technology takes centre stage, with resources, technology and sacrifice themselves appearing to be beyond human or social influence or control.

Surely, the argument goes, a mode of social organization that takes advantage of differences in opportunity costs between countries and that maximizes the benefits that can be gained from scarce resources is a compelling one? Fortuitously – we are told by modern economics – we have discovered the social institution best placed to solve the dilemmas thrown up by scarcity: the market. The relationship between scarcity and free trade is thus the relationship between problem and solution. The conceptual apparatus that highlights scarcity and sacrifice is that from which comparative advantage derives its force and 'necessaryness'.

The Rationalization Is Mistaken

Economists are involved in the production of knowledge, knowledge that aims and purports to explain the social world and action within it. The question is, though, are the tools and resources provided by this knowledge up to the task? My claim, on the basis of the analysis contained in the preceding chapters, is that they are not. The rationalization that is provided for patterns of international trade and specialization is defective. It is wrong. In the previous chapters we have witnessed the disintegration of the case for free trade under the weight of careful consideration. We have seen that – time and again – the component claims that must be established in order to bear out an argument to adopt policies of free trade are based upon a suite of related and intertwined fictional claims about trade and its related economic phenomena or activity. These fictions are incomplete and tell only part of the story. They focus on some, rather than all, dynamics of economic phenomena, simplifying matters to a misleading degree. They skew the analysis, focus attention in the wrong places, and empty the case for free trade of its compelling force.

In chapter 3, I explored the linked fictions of international trade's invisible hand and the abstract barter model of international trade that underlies it. We saw that these fictions incorrectly and artificially screen out the monetary side of that trade, and the differential empowerment and motivations of economic actors involved in it. This causes economic analysis to lose sight of driving dynamics in international trade and the global economy, to assume without basis that free trade leads to specialization and comparative advantage, and to misestimate the efficiency of patterns of free trade–led specialization.

In chapter 4, I delved in more detail into the origins of advantages in trade and the failure of mainstream analysis to cognize and come to terms with the rules that condition the economic game in actually existing economies. Here we discovered a fictional, clockwork picture of production that leads the economic analyst to simplistic and hollow policy recommendations. Indeed, piercing this fiction – and recognizing the inherently relational, social and institutionally based nature of production and comparative advantages – revealed very real difficulties in even specifying the meaning of a policy stance of free trade. In a sense, it becomes difficult to grasp what the rationalization aims at rationalizing.

Finally, in chapter 5 I discussed the manner in which mainstream normative economic analysis fails – even on its own terms – to properly generate unambiguous welfare propositions in favour of a policy of free international trade (assuming we are able to delineate what that would mean). This is only exacerbated by that fact that mainstream analysis takes account of only certain aspects of the international trade process, dropping from sight dynamic issues, noncommodity sources of utility and disutility, and human and social outputs of production processes and economic organization. Welfare economics provides model after model to produce its normative recommendations, but time and again we find the economic analysts' imagination has run away with them – these models turn out to be little more than incomplete and unreal stories that disclose their fictional nature under careful examination.

The discussion and analyses in these chapters puncture the efficiency and welfare rationalization – at technical and moral levels – that comparative advantage provides for free trade, specialization and their outputs. Even more than this, however, we can see that the basis of the rationale – the notion of asocial and exogenously determined scarcity, technology and sacrifice – is also mistakenly portrayed by mainstream economic analysis. Specifically, the mainstream perspective of specialization and international trade obscures the social in favour of the asocial, and the endogenous in favour of the exogenous nature of comparative advantages, technology and supplies of resources. As we saw clearly in chapter 4, how production occurs, the costs that are associated with different actions, the availability of resources and the election of technology are all in part the product of social relations between people, rather than of purely physical or material properties or relations between things. S*ocial* relations (often concretized through legal-institutional frameworks) valorize certain interests, create cost structures, condition the availability of inputs and define allowable actions. They influence the technical processes that are selected for the production of outputs and shape the kind and distribution of those outputs. Far from the original and simple picture of constrained production possibility in a situation of scarcity, we now see the contingent, social and political aspects of the production process, and of the generation of opportunity costs and comparative advantages. Comparative advantages do not merely emerge from scarcity – they emerge in part from society. Society does not merely respond to scarcity – it has a hand in making it.

Patterns of specialization and trade are – as we have seen – robbed, therefore, of their supposed garb of efficiency. So too is the conceptual substructure that lends their efficiency its urgency, and the easy connection that links the aggrandizement of the few to the good of the many. The case for free trade's rationalization and advocacy that once looked so compellingly airtight and dominant now appears to us worryingly insecure.

This Mistaken Rationalization Has High Stakes

If, as I have argued, the rationalization for socioeconomic arrangements, policies and activities that the comparative advantage–driven case for free trade provides in respect of international trade is mistaken, what then is at stake in accepting and acting upon this mistaken rationalization? My claim is that the stakes are high, and the ramifications can be seen as falling into four (interrelated) categories. I shall say a little in relation to each.

Misapprehension of the virtue of particular arrangements, policies or practices

At the most basic level, incorrectly accepting the efficiency rationale of international trade and specialization provided by the case for free trade causes misunderstanding as to the nature and character of particular policies, arrangements and practices, and specifically, of their virtues. Reliance on bad or wrong theory leads to bad or wrong policy. Incorrectly believing that free trade and specialization are efficient and welfare enhancing can lead to the skewing of policy recommendations on the basis of fallacious foundations.

Even more seriously than this, though, is comparative advantage's illusory linkage of individualistic, self-regarding economic behaviour to the overall good of the whole. Again, accepting comparative advantage's rationalization leads to a misestimation of the character and benefits to be garnered from such conduct. In the absence of the robust linkages posited by comparative advantage, preference for those interests becomes unmasked for what it is: nothing but a naked and unjustified decision to prefer those interests over others. Contrary to the mainstream's technical and moral rationalization of free trade, of pursuing self-interest and of preferring the interests of the few, reality can be seen to manifest precisely the opposite situation. Internationally, some countries are enriched at the expense of others. Domestically, some actors are enriched at the expense of others, and sometimes at the expense of the whole. As Blecker points out, in the context of the US economy the interests of international trading corporations are unmoored from those of society as a whole.

> Although the US economy has been running large trade deficits that represent net losses of jobs in tradeables industries, US-based corporations have no such large deficit and have profited immensely from their foreign operations [...][17]

Obscuring of important aspects of these arrangements, policies or practices

Related to these misapprehension effects is the additional fact that the mistaken rationalization 'frames out' of consideration issues relevant to international trade. We have discussed at length above the partial nature of the comparative advantage analysis and the manner that this partiality affects the robustness of the conclusions to which the analysis leads. This partiality has the effect of deemphasizing – and to an extent hiding from view – important issues and considerations relevant to international socioeconomic arrangements and practices. It obscures particular economic arrangements and processes, certain of their outputs, and leaves the horizon of normative and evaluative analysis of these arrangements needlessly stunted. More accurate, appropriate and less impoverished positive and evaluative criteria are rendered 'irrelevant' by the mainstream's faulty partiality.

Bluntly put, the case for free trade screens from view the nature and processes of economic accumulation by differentially (institutionally and legal-institutionally) empowered agents, painting instead a benign economic picture of yeomen producers, Robinson Crusoes and mutually enjoyed gains. The partiality of each element of the comparative advantage analysis works to generate a particular effect: it casts as a matter of efficiency that which is primarily determined by social relations of power and distributional struggle. Static analysis sanitizes the picture of international trade, relegating from consideration issues of power in economic affairs. And yet it is nothing other than power relations that drive the system and shape its outputs; power works its will in the real world of trucking and bartering, even if not in abstract neoclassical models. As Robinson has powerfully argued,

> In neoclassical trade theory there is no path, no process, no movement of any kind. An isolated country in a stationary equilibrium and hey presto! trade puts it in a new equilibrium, with a different composition of output but resources, knowledge and tastes all the same. This has cut off the 'pure theory' from any relation to the trade that takes place in real life and has reduced it to an idle toy.[18]

Thus seen, the case for free trade devolves into a veneer of respectability that masks the ills of maximizing behaviour and obscures more accurate understanding of the economic processes of international trade and specialization. That which drives international trade is precisely that which comparative advantage does not measure, cannot evaluate, and in relation to which leaves us silent.

Misunderstanding the nature of the trade-offs involved in socioeconomic arrangements

Additionally, and in part as a result of the points mentioned above, the comparative advantage rationale casts the nature of the trade-offs involved in international trade in a particular fashion. Specifically, arguments concerning the predicted efficiency gains from international trade invoke the spectre of the efficiency–equity trade-off. That is, as we have seen in the previous chapters, the argument from mainstream economists is that, in respect of international trade, priority should be given to making the international pie as big as possible before (politically) deciding how to divide it. Of course, in light of the failure of comparative advantage to robustly bear out the mechanisms claimed to deliver the gains that maximize the international pie, this framing of the trade-off is less than convincing. Deviating from free trade does not necessarily involve departing from efficient socioeconomic arrangements.

The same applies in relation to the efficiency–morality trade-off, discussed above, that is implied by mainstream economic thought through the separation of these two criteria. The moral excuse or trade-off posited in respect of the direct ills of maximizing behaviour on the basis of the material gains that these bring ceases to have clout with the failure of the efficiency/welfare rationalization of free international trade. It is not the case that one must necessarily trade off (at least in the context of comparative advantage) between the efficient mode of organization and other moral or evaluative considerations, criteria or ends in the manner that mainstream analysis might suggest. If the relevant economic activity fails to generate the efficiency gains promised, it is difficult to ignore its moral character and consequences, at least on the basis argued for.[19]

Now, all of this is sharpened by the fact that even if international trade were efficient in the sense suggested by mainstream economics, this efficiency is 'efficiency *given* particular social and institutional frameworks and environments.' Legal-institutional means construct the bases of trade and the magnitude of efficiency gains thrown up by trade. In this sense, what is efficient is, in important senses, dependent upon, and a product of, sociopolitical choice and factors. This is also the point at which the separation posited by mainstream analysis between – on the one hand – economic arrangements, and – on the other – the sociopolitical, fractures and disintegrates; the point at which problems of welfare economics actually *does* 'dissolve into a study of aesthetics and morals'.[20] The very bases of economic arrangements are social and political. There can be no isolation of the former from the latter two in the manner implied by the mainstream tendency to cast trade and economic arrangements as primarily about efficiency, and resistant to social, political and moral evaluation. Efficiency, in the sense of gains from trade, is a partial effect of sociopolitical decision. Failure to see it as such is a result of accepting comparative advantage's rationalization and creates an incorrect impression as to the nature of what is to be traded off against what.

Limiting of our understanding of the policy resources available to address international trade: False choices and hidden alternatives

Finally, and importantly, the case for free trade and its associated analyses colour – or more accurately fetter – our collective imagination as to the kind of policy and institutional means we have at our disposal to tackle issues of international trade. The comparative advantage rationale would have us believe that the market is the best institution for dealing with these issues. Other than that, we are told, the alternative policy framework that we have at our disposal is protection, either partially or all the way to autarky: if you aren't a free trader, you must be a tariff builder.

However, this dichotomy is premised upon accepting, improperly, the fruit of a poisonous tree. Free trade itself – as we have seen – is at base a policy setting of only illusory and fictitious concreteness. The analysis presented in chapter 4 makes clear that state involvement in the bases and patterns of international trade is not limited to an on/off tariff switch or a simple dichotomy between free trade and protectionism. Rather, there is a range of policy levers available to the state to shape and influence a domestic economy, and how it relates to other economies internationally. Moreover, in chapter 5 we saw that there are any number of effects not cognized by mainstream analysis that are generated by particular configurations of production specialization, and that are normatively and evaluatively relevant in setting the diverse legal-institutional frameworks that impact production and trade.

That is, there are both positive and normative reasons to reject the limited set of resources placed before policy-makers by mainstream economics in respect of international trade. The error that leads to this limitation can again be traced back to mainstream economics' relative neglect of the process of production and focus on exchange. For the mainstream, all that can be done other than allowing free international exchange (trade) is impose a limit, in whole or in part of that trade (protectionism). Of course, this choice is a false one. To put the matter more dramatically, we alienate our social powers when we think that our only means to solve problems relating to international trade is either more or less market.[21]

To be clear, a comprehensive answer to the question 'if not free trade, then what?' is not one we can answer here. And if the answer is expected to be simple or 'general', the problem is not merely one of scope or space. Rather, as I have attempted to impress upon the reader throughout our discussion, questions like this are not susceptible to comprehensive, for-all-times-and-places answers.[22] An important component of my argument has been that the abstract, mechanistic modelling of the economy – and the confident surety of policy prescription that this tends to generate – are fundamentally mistaken. Actual economies in the real world are complex. They are messy. Policy prescriptions that tend to operate in a law-like and general fashion, in all times and in all places, are not comfortable in this real world.

Economics and Expertise – From Analysis to Assertion

Let me be perfectly plain. The case for free trade fails on its own terms to perform *precisely* the task that it is claimed to perform. It emphatically does *not* explain patterns of international trade and specialization. It does *not* establish a clear normative case in favour of free trade. It does *not* give guidance to the policy-maker. It does *not* make sense of, or give reason to, the social world, to particular socioeconomic arrangements or to international trade.

Rather, what the comparative advantage–based case for free trade *does* is offer a comforting fantasy about socioeconomic phenomena and international trade. It *does* offer a flawed technical and moral cover for particular kinds of arrangements, particular kinds of action and behaviour, and to the interests of particular economic and social actors. It *does* frame out of consideration criteria and action that are relevant to devising and evaluating the terms of social life. It *does* misidentify the nature of trade-offs implied by particular socioeconomic orderings. And finally, it *does* leave us collectively without understanding as to the scope of both our ability, and of available resources, to evaluate, author and justify our social and economic world.

Even more than this, the claim of expertise by the economist – the scientist of human decision, counsel to policy-makers, scourge of waste and prophet of efficiency – must also now be seen differently. What justifies the mainstream economist's claim to authority in policy and intellectual discourse is the ability to logically and neutrally solve certain kinds of problems: particularly, the problem of how to effectively use resources in a situation of scarcity. Specifically, the economist claims to match means to ends in an evaluatively neutral fashion – working at the service of a self-evidently desirable end (maximization of material well-being) within the context of existing constraints. And moreover, this claim to authority, as I have argued time and again, is not couched in modest or contingent terms. The arguments for markets, for free trade, and in favour of comparative advantage are confidently presented as facts. This should not be surprising – hard, 'objective', 'scientific' claims rather than 'soft' or 'modest' ones are those that achieve currency in our current public and indeed intellectual discourses. [23]

The manner in which the economist's perceived expertise allows counterevidence to be understood is also instructive. As we have seen repeatedly in the preceding chapters, empirical counter-evidence dogs the various claims of the case for free trade. The economist's belief in her models allows her to read such counterevidence and any counterexamples as exceptional – the freak effect of unpredictable situational considerations. Those comparative advantage models are, however, read as being sound. And for the economist they must be – these models are aimed at the most salient questions of social analysis, and firmly grounded in the most impeccable kind of logic.

But the economist's notion of scarcity is deceiving, and thus the kinds of questions she seeks to answer suspect. Her methodology is skewed and her answers are mistaken. Indeed, on the basis of the analysis contained in the preceding chapters, we have an insight into neoclassicalism's failure. The expertise of the economist fails us for *precisely* the same reason that it claims its authority. That is, the expertise fails because it attempts to understand human behaviour and economic phenomena, which are social, relational and institutional, as though they were individualistic, isolated and mechanistic. The economist's strategy of abstraction, of eschewing focus upon the world as it is and of relying on her models to guide real-world action hides this fact and is fundamentally flawed. The problem lies not so much in the logic of comparative advantage or the economist's models, but rather in the relevance of those models to the phenomena under examination.

That which guides the economic phenomenon of international trade and specialization is not mechanistically or abstractly logical. It is rather concretely and institutionally social. Hence the kind of counterevidence that the economist so easily dismisses is in fact ubiquitous and ultimately devastating to the economist's predictions.

In a sense, in the pages of this book we have chased through several domains the invisible hand – the mechanistic understanding of the economy and economic action. We picked up its scent in the domain of positive economics, pursued it into normative economics, and in between grappled with solidity of the bases which it takes for granted and upon which it is said to work its alchemic magic. But despite our fervent pursuit, we continually emerged from the hunt empty-handed, so to speak. The mechanism posited by economics – the invisible hand, the basis of Ricardo's gauntlet – was nowhere to be found. All that presented itself was the mailed fist of social power. Despite all of the mainstream talk of efficiency and effectiveness in welfare maximization we must ask, as Alasdair MacIntyre has,

> What if effectiveness is part of a masquerade [...] rather than a reality? What if effectiveness were a quality widely imputed [...] but which rarely exists apart from its imputation?[24]

And in so doing we have found a final fiction that we must reject – that of the economist as infallible scientist.

What then becomes of *arguments* for free trade when the *analytic* that supposedly supports it is undermined? Does the advocate of free trade abandon the argument? The ideology is so deep that this is difficult. Does she ignore the challenge? Perhaps.

One last case study is interesting. After writing his article *Where Ricardo and Mill Rebut and Confirm Arguments of Mainstream Economists Supporting Globalization* (mentioned above[25]), Paul Samuelson was roundly criticized by his fellow economists as 'muddling the case for free trade'.[26] His response to this claim (somewhat confusingly expressed in the third person) was illuminating:

> The correct arguments by Paul A. Samuelson in the *JEP* do not (repeat, not) persuade me to advocate abandoning free trade policies by advanced industrial countries like the United States, by successfully developing economies like Japan or India, or by still-floundering basket-economy cases in Africa or the Middle East.

The reason is simple and nonequivocal: *Economic history and best economic theory together* persuade me that leaving or compromising free trade policies will most likely reduce future growth in well-being in both the advanced and less productive regions of the world. Protectionism breeds monopoly, crony capitalism and sloth. It does not achieve a happy and serene egalitarian society.[27]

What is particularly interesting about this passage is that it demonstrates that when elements of economic theory are challenged or troubled, the advocate of free trade policies may shift to some other form of justification – here economic history, and some link to the notion of achievement of a happy, serene and egalitarian society. Samuelson seeks to have his cake and eat it too – he both seeks to reestablish an alternative justification for free trade, while at the same time affirm that the *best theory* support free trade.

The first question that must be asked is, if the *best theory* is damaged (as it was by Samuelson's analysis), in what sense does it matter that it is *best*? If our best theories are partially or completely wrong, it seems this should militate against relying upon them. Or at least, once we have uncovered the possibility of incorrectness, surely a more modest – less certain – view should be taken of the strength of the conclusions and policy implications that emerge from that theory? Wrong theory, even if it is the best we can generate, cannot be compelling once we have discovered its falsity.[28]

More importantly, a chastening of the theoretical case for free trade may cause economists – as it did cause Samuelson – to introduce new criteria into the mix, specifically economic history and the achievement of utopia. These criteria are interesting because of their pervasive and common-sense status among not only economists, but in public discourse writ large. They represent both a discourse of progress and a version of Wilsonian international liberal idealism: free trade and democracy as the recipe for a revised Kantianesque perpetual peace. However, as soon as the justificatory discourse switches away from theory, the neoclassical economist is on very thin ice. Neoclassical economics is not known for its attention to issues of history or sociology. Indeed, that has been the core of the critique that I have been levelling against it in these pages. In fact, on the historical point, the 'free-trade-is-a-myth-never-actually-practiced-by-the-powerful' school has Samuelson dead to rights.[29] In respect of the obscure implied claim that free trade leads to a 'happy and serene egalitarian society', Samuelson would need to do a lot more work in order to make such a claim plausible. That is, robbed of a firm theoretical base, the free trade advocate has to fall back upon peculiar and unjustified tropes – often heard but seldom if ever established. The economist is forced from analysis to assertion, and flimsy assertions at that.

* * *

So now we can see the case for free trade is little more than a fairy tale – a longstanding and pervasive work of fiction that we have mistaken for fact, with dangerous implications for socioeconomic practices, activities and outcomes. Comparative advantage fails on its own terms to provide an explanation, a rationale or a justification for policies of free trade, or for the various socioeconomic arrangements and outputs that they entail. Confident assertions of the efficiency or welfare benefits of free trade are unmoored from proper analytical or normative foundation.

And so what has Ricardo's gauntlet led us to? Rather than cold logic and geometric models, the debater is forced into a pitched battle with a many-headed hydra. In the heat of the battle, the critic of free trade is faced by a beast against which success seems remote – severing one monstrous head merely causes ever more snarling maws to spring forth. While the predicament looks initially dire, one must never forget that the monster is based on, and riddled with, fiction. The one path we have available – the successful strategy whenever make-believe runs away with us – is to look closely at the beast, see through it, and cease believing in it.

Indeed, seeing our social arrangements as being the effect of scarcity and exogenous considerations, seeing comparative advantage as a 'law' external to social decision, and looking intently and exclusively to the economic expert for guidance as to what to do are all avatars of the same beast – the alienation and surrender of our social powers. We must recognize that just as our socioeconomic arrangements are, in very large part, our own creatures, so too are the shackles that bind our imaginations and the blinders that obscure our sight.

This project has been at base a critical one. It has aimed to clear the ground that has been so successfully covered by the intellectual edifice that is comparative advantage, and to make space for other ways of evaluating, devising and justifying alternative socioeconomic arrangements.

But as we have seen, in the world of policy, normative considerations predominate and decisions have to be made. It might be comforting to imagine that – along technical and moral dimensions – we collectively possess the resources, provided to us by reason, to clearly and unambiguously address the question of 'what is to be done' in respect of our international socioeconomic arrangements. However, any comfort that we might be afforded by comparative advantage would be ephemeral and deceiving. The answer to this question is much more fraught – much more complicated – than mainstream analysis would have us believe.

And while together we may have disassembled and watched the dissolution of the fictitious case for free trade, we will invariably be asked (by some as though such a question invalidates all that has come before): What now? Granting, perhaps, our protestations that simple generalities will not suffice, in particular policy contexts we will nonetheless again be challenged by our adversaries – whose arguments now lie in tatters – this time to answer the question: If not free trade, then what?

And thus the next gauntlet is thrown before us.

NOTES

Chapter One   Introduction: Ricardo's Gauntlet and the Case for Free Trade

1 Robinson, 'History Versus Equilibrium', 49–50.
2 Findlay, 'Comparative Advantage', 514.
3 Samuelson, when a member of the Society of Fellows at Harvard University, was challenged by a then leading mathematician to identify one idea emerging from the social sciences that is both true and not trivial. Although he did not answer at the time, Samuelson later stated that the perfect response to that challenge would have been the theory of comparative advantage: see further Samuelson, 'The Way of an Economist'.
4 Krugman, 'Ricardo's Difficult Idea'.
5 Krugman, 'Is Free Trade Passé?', 131.
6 I use the terms 'mainstream' and 'neoclassical' here somewhat loosely and interchangeably. As to finer points of definition and evolution, see Arnsperger and Varoufakis, 'What Is Neoclassical Economics?'; Colander et al., 'The Changing Face of Mainstream Economics'; Davis, 'The Turn in Economics'.
7 Krugman, 'Introduction: New Thinking about Trade Policy', 10.
8 Ricardo, *Principles of Political Economy and Taxation*, 139.
9 Mankiw, *Principles of Economics*, 57.
10 For a smattering of these kinds of counter-attacks and characterizations see Mankiw, ibid., chapter 9; Krugman, 'Ricardo's Difficult Idea'; Dixit and Norman, *Theory of International Trade*, 2.
11 See for specific detail the discussion in note 17 to chapter 2 and note 55 to chapter 3 below, further literatures mentioned therein, and accompanying text.
12 See, for example, notes 28–36 to chapter 2 and notes 22–28 to chapter 5 below, further literatures mentioned therein, and accompanying text.
13 For more on this style of argument, see Chang, *Kicking Away the Ladder* and *Bad Samaritans*. Chang is strongly influenced by the German Historical School, and particularly by Friedrich List: see List, *National System of Political Economy*. See also, though from different perspectives, Robinson, 'Inaugural Lecture'; Amsden, *The Rise of 'The Rest'*.
14 For key (though different) formulations of the principle, see Wilson, 'Substances without Substrata', 532; Davidson, *Inquiries into Truth and Interpretation*, especially chapter 13.

15 See Mandeville, *The Fable of the Bees*.

16 A common simplification utilized by economics – see, for some discussion, von Mises, *Human Action*, chapter 11.

17 Of course, I am not the first to suggest that there is something peculiar about the mode of modern economic analysis and argumentation. Leaving aside the greatest critics of the discipline – which would include Karl Marx, John Maynard Keynes, their followers and their extended families – more recently, thinkers such as Deirdre McClosky have identified the rhetorical and metaphorical nature of economic discourse (McClosky, *The Secret Sins of Economics* and *The Rhetoric of Economics*). Steve Keen has pointed to the multiple myths that seem to permeate modern economics' most basic analytical moves (Keen, *Debunking Economics*). More closely related to our current investigation, Ha-Joon Chang's excellent work has confronted the mythical tale that is so often told that casts free trade's history as at one with the history of how which today's 'developed' capitalist nations became 'developed' (Chang, *Kicking Away the Ladder* and *Bad Samaritans*). Each of these – and many others – provides a critical insight into the operation and use of economic thought, analysis and argumentation.

18 Within this trend, Marglin's 1974 'What Do Bosses Do' stands as exemplar. Marglin claimed that so-called 'technical aspects' of capitalist economic organization were justified not by efficiency but rather explained by distributional struggle between classes of economic actors. Marglin's work was explicitly preliminary in nature and has been subject to critique on the basis that the historical data that he cited in support of his claims was weak and equivocal (see, for example, David Landes, 'What Do Bosses Really Do?'). Criticisms of substance aside, however, Marglin's strategy was both sound and to the point.

A differently focused though thematically related exploration in respect of the international division of labour is contained in Brenner, 'Origins of Capitalist Development'. In that article, historian and social theorist Brenner is particularly focussed on attacking a line of writers that ignore social class relations in capitalist development, mimicking instead the Smithian notion that the development of trade and the resulting division of labour brings about economic development. The core of Brenner's point is that properly understanding the historical development of capitalism demonstrates that social relations, rather than 'efficiency', guide the path of economic development. The analysis that I will present here seeks to make a related point at the level of theory in respect of comparative advantage and the supposed efficiency gains from international trade.

19 Or '*ideologiekritik*'. This is a method that finds its genesis in the critical tradition of which Kant, Hegel and Marx are fathers, and the Frankfurt School inheritors. I will have more to say about the precise senses in which I use the terms 'ideology' and 'ideology critique' in due course. It will be clear from what follows that the particular critical method that I employ here both incorporates but goes beyond what is sometimes termed 'internal critique' – which can be understood as the examination of a system purely on its own terms in order to assess its claimed or asserted coherence and completeness. The method of ideology critique that I employ here includes internal evaluation, but is also open to introducing external evaluative criteria also (such as how a theory measures up to reality or

institutions 'as they are', or perhaps as they appear to be, given current existing epistemic access). As to the need for ideology critique to move beyond purely internal critique, see Geuss, *The Idea of Critical Theory*, 33, 64–65, 78.

20 Hegel, *The Phenomenology of Mind*, 81.

21 See Thompson, *The Poverty of Theory*. In the epigraph Thompson attributes this phrase to Marx.

22 As to the historically contingent roots of the modern ideology of international economic cooperation, see Brenner, *The Boom and the Bubble*, 12.

23 The kernel of this argument – though differently framed and much truncated – is presented in Kishore, 'Sleight of Hand'.

Chapter Two Exploring the Case for Free Trade: Unexpected Twists in a Simple Story

1 Holmes Jr, 'The Path of the Law', 469.

2 This is especially so given the fact that even highly sophisticated economists sometimes seem to misstate or muddle the core of the principle: see, for example, Gomory and Baumol, *Global Trade and Conflicting National Interests*, 3: 'each country ends up producing the goods at which it is naturally *best*, compared to other countries and products' (my emphasis). Though this statement is capable of being unpacked in a way that makes clear the nature of the comparative advantage analytic (and while I have little doubt that both Gomory and Baumol understand the analytic), alone this formulation is liable to cause confusion.

3 The discussion that I present here reflects the basic presentations of the comparative advantage model that one sees in basic economic texts such as Mankiw, *Principles of Economics* (especially chapter 3), and standard international economics texts such as Krugman and Maurice Obstfeld, *International Economics* (especially part 1) or Caves et al., *World Trade and Payments* (again, especially part 1). These presentations tend to be mixes of Ricardian and later developments in the theory concerning comparative advantage. As my goal here is to address the principle as it tends to be understood, rather than each historical instantiation of it, I will follow the approach of these presentations.

4 There is some debate as to the actual originator of the doctrine of comparative advantage. Both Henry Thornton (*Enquiry into the Nature and Effect of the Paper Credit of Great Britain* (1802)) and Robert Torrens (*Essay on the External Corn Trade* (1815)) allude to something akin to the basic idea of comparative advantage. The machinations of comparative advantage's intellectual history is less important here, and while comparative advantage-type arguments might have lurked beneath the surface of the work of earlier political economists, the principle was first clearly and unequivocally stated by Ricardo in his *Principles of Political Economy and Taxation* (1817). It is Ricardo's exposition that has been the focal point for development within economic theory.

5 The notion here is that if a country has an absolute advantage in production, that is, if it can produce goods more cheaply, it will not realize benefits from trade. The less productive country will have an incentive to trade – it can (assumedly) have its goods at a cheaper relative price than it could produce

them domestically (at least for as long as the money does not run out). The more productive country, on the other hand, has no incentive to trade (assuming sufficient demand for goods at home).

6 Which imposed tariffs on grain imported into England with the intention of protecting the price of domestically produced corn.

7 At least in its modern rendering.

8 These can be termed the relative prices of goods – the cost of one good in terms of – relative to – the other.

9 This was Ricardo's example in his *Principles of Political Economy and Taxation*. As a somewhat quirky side note, Ricardo, though born in England, was of Portuguese background.

10 Nostalgia only goes so far – I have reorganized the Ricardian example to hold constant labour inputs and time intervals for the sake of simplicity.

11 It is worth noting that – according to comparative advantage – it is advisable to pursue a policy of free trade even if other countries do not; free trade and specialization on the basis of comparative advantage ensures that as between two methods for securing a good (either by manufacturing at home or securing through trade), the more efficient method is picked. See further Bhagwati and Srinivasan, *Lectures on International Trade*, especially chapter 17.

12 Incomplete specialization may result depending upon

   1. the relative size of each country (as measured by the labour force and its productivity in relation to the production of the relevant goods); and
   2. the extent to which the two goods is favoured by patterns of world demand.

   To be clear, this does no violence to the theory of comparative advantage or to the notion that specialization and trade are mutually beneficial.

13 Ricardo had little to say about the manner in which the terms of trade would be set. It was John Stuart Mill (followed by Marshall, Edgeworth and others) who concluded that the terms of trade and international prices would depend upon the relative strengths of the demand for commodities in the trading nations, thus moving away from a purely supply-side understanding of comparative advantage. For further detail, see Findlay, *Trade and Specialization*, especially chapter 1.

14 Ricardo, *Principles of Political Economy and Taxation*, 131.

15 John Stuart Mill, for example, warned that the protection of infant industries might be necessary and justifiable. I will have more to say about this issue in chapter 5.

16 This point concerns 'retaliatory protection' – the use of protection as a punitive technique in the event that a foreign country erects tariffs or duties against a country's goods. Protection can be used as a means of provoking a shift in relation to such foreign policies. Smith was also alive to this possibility: see Smith, *The Wealth of Nations*, 586–88. See also Bhagwati, *Protectionism*, 25–26.

17 See, for example, the discussion of the New International Economics school, notes 28–36 below and accompanying text. See also Chang, *Bad Samaritans*, especially chapter 3 concerning social cost assumptions and perfect factor mobility; Prasch, 'Reassessing the Theory of Comparative Advantage', concerning (among other things) capital mobility.

18 For example, the role of demand (see discussion in note 13 above); the integration of the interaction of preferences, technology, multimarket interactions and prices in a general equilibrium framework (see Haberler, *The Theory of International Trade*; Leontief, 'The Use of Indifference Curves in the Analysis of Foreign Trade'; Lerner, 'The Diagrammatic Representation of Cost Conditions in International Trade'); the operation of comparative advantage at higher orders (i.e., more commodities and more countries – see Viner, *Studies in the Theory of International Trade*); the question of explaining particular patterns of comparative advantage (particularly relevant here is the so-called Heckscher–Ohlin–Samuelson family of theorems, in relation to which I will have more to say in chapter 4); and questions of domestic distribution and welfare (again, I will return to this in chapter 5).

19 Dixit and Norman, *Theory of International Trade*. Also, although Krugman variously describes comparative advantage as 'difficult', or 'more difficult than it seems', he also claims that to those who understand it, it is 'simple and compelling', and to the extent that it is harder at a deeper level, it is because it refers to a set of linked ideas, the existence of which one does not ordinarily know about unless one is a trained economist. See further, Krugman, 'Ricardo's Difficult Idea'.

20 See notes 21 and 22 below.

21 Chang, *Bad Samaritans*, 47.

22 Hahnel, *ABCs of Political Economy*, 180.

23 Let us assume at this point that it is possible to specify what this means in a policy sense – I will return to this question in chapter 4.

24 I do not claim to be the only one who has made this kind of clarification. Shaikh ('Laws of International Exchange') makes a similar distinction, which he then goes on to interrogate using an orthodox Marxian analysis. However, Shaikh differently articulates, orders and characterizes his 'prescriptive' and 'descriptive' claims. Moreover, the further distinction that I propose in the following paragraph between the positive and normative elements of comparative advantage is not a focus of Shaikh's disaggregation of the principle.

25 Ricardo, *Principles of Political Economy and Taxation*, 139.

26 Mankiw, *Principles of Economics*, 57.

27 Krugman, 'Is Free Trade Passé?', 132.

28 A segment of this school is sometimes called the 'Strategic Trade Theory' school.

29 Krugman, 'Is Free Trade Passé?', 143.

30 See, for example, Krugman, 'Does the New Trade Theory Require a New Trade Policy?'

31 Krugman, 'What do Undergrads Need to Know', 120.

32 Krugman, 'Myths and Realities of U.S. Competitiveness', 102.

33 Krugman, 'Ricardo's Difficult Idea'. See also Milberg, 'Is Absolute Advantage Passé?', 219. And note the following from Krugman, 'Is Free Trade Passé?', 427:

> What the new trade theorists did, in a variety of ways, was to get away from [...] the idea that one had to make an either/or choice between comparative advantage and increasing returns. In particular, the now

classic early models of intraindustry trade generally assumed a hierarchical structure, in which large groups of differentiated products were all produced with identical factor proportions, and could thus be aggregated into 'industries'. Comparative advantage continued to rule at this aggregate level: 'interindustry' trade continued to be determined by Heckscher–Ohlin theory. But 'intraindustry' trade, the result of specialization within industries, was now supposed to be driven by increasing returns. The apparent opposition between comparative advantage and increasing returns was thus eliminated, allowing one to believe in both.

34 Bhagwati, 'Free Trade: What Now?' What Bhagwati says here very much tracks the movement of Krugman's attitude, which can be thought of – as I have argued above, and as I believe Bhagwati thinks (at 4) – as exemplar.

35 Ibid., 6.

36 Ibid., 8.

37 Ibid. See also Krugman, 'Does the New Trade Theory Require a New Trade Policy?', 433–34.

38 Irwin, *Against the Tide*, 223–24.

39 Ibid., 224.

Chapter Three   The Tale of International Trade's Invisible Hand

1 MacIntyre, *After Virtue*, 70.

2 As to this kind of move being common in economics, see McCloskey, *Secret Sins of Economics*. Empirical testing of the Ricardian comparative advantage model has been extremely limited. Indeed, such testing really only began in 1951 with the publication of MacDougall, 'British and American Exports'. Other key studies are Stern, 'British and American Productivity and Comparative Costs' and Balassa, 'An Empirical Demonstration of Classical Comparative Cost Theory'. Although the stated and claimed conclusion of these studies was, at base, that international trade would indeed follow comparative rather than absolute advantage, they have been described as 'theoretically fuzzy' and standing for something weaker than the Ricardian prediction: see Leamer and Levinsohn, 'International Trade Theory and Evidence', 1339, 1344; Deardorff, 'Testing Trade Theories'. For a critique of the methodology and conclusions of these studies see Bhagwati, 'The Pure Theory of International Trade'. In the intervening forty-five plus years, there has been little empirical work done to bear out the notion that international trade will follow comparative advantage: see also Leamer and Levinsohn, above; Perdikis and Kerr, *Trade Theory and Empirical Evidence*. Indeed, Krugman and Obstfeld concede that 'recent evidence on the Ricardian model has been less clear cut, in part because of the difficulties in securing information about potential productivity in industries that do not exist in a country: see *International Economics*, 44.

3 Though usually associated with Smith, something akin to the invisible hand plays a starring role in Mandeville's *The Fable of the Bees*, though differently described and evaluated.

4 Elster, *Explaining Technical Change*; Elster, 'A Plea for Mechanisms'; Elster, *Explaining Social Behavior*.

5 See, particularly, Elster, *Explaining Technical Change*. Elster also – more confusingly and less relevantly for present purposes – talks about providing a mechanism involving offering something less than a general law-like explanation for social phenomena, but something more than mere description. Such an intermediate form of explanation would focus upon frequently occurring and easily recognizable causal patterns that are triggered under generally unknown conditions or with indeterminate consequences. Again, this definition is less relevant for our exploration here.

6 And particularly given economics' reticence to consider empirically the question of whether trade follows comparative advantage, discussed above.

7 Elster himself seems to hint at this evaluative use of a mechanism, although this is less clear in some of the examples that he offers: Elster, 'A Plea for Mechanisms', 46–47.

8 See further, Davidson, *John Maynard Keynes*, especially chapter 9; Blecker, 'International Economics'.

9 Krugman, 'Ricardo's Difficult Idea' (emphasis added).

10 Krugman and Obstfeld, *International Economics*, 45.

11 Mankiw, *Principles of Economics*, 54.

12 See also Hayek, 'The Use of Knowledge in Society', in which Hayek rejects the reduction of economic problems to ones of pure logic.

13 See McCloskey, *Secret Sins of Economics*, 9–16; Krugman, 'Ricardo's Difficult Idea'; Keen, *Debunking Economics*, chapter 12.

14 See, for example, Krugman and Obstfeld, *International Economics*, 45; Findlay, 'Comparative Advantage', 515. See also the presentation of comparative advantage and international trade in Mankiw, *Principles of Economics*, chapters 3 and 9.

15 Musgrave, '"Unreal Assumptions" in Economic Theory'.

16 See notes 18–22 below and accompanying text.

17 See notes 23–28 below and accompanying text. Heterodox and radical voices that call for the provision of such a mechanism (or something similar) include Anwar Shaikh (orthodox Marxism) – see Shaikh, 'Laws of International Exchange', 205–06; William Milberg (post-Keynesian) – see Milberg, 'Is Absolute Advantage Passé?'; 'Say's Law in the Open Economy'; and Robert Blecker (again, post-Keynesian) – see Blecker, 'Financial Globalization, Exchange Rates and International Trade'.

18 Set out in chapter 7 of his *Principles of Political Economy and Taxation*.

19 Hume, 'Of the Balance of Trade'.

20 The adjustment mechanism might be usefully understood as involving a relationship between four key variables – prices, the wage rate, the profit rate and the price of gold (or under contemporary international monetary arrangements, the price of foreign currency). In the Ricardian framework, changes in the wage rate are reflected by corresponding (inverse) changes in the profit rate. Given that (for Ricardo) real wages are fixed at the subsistence level, and the mobility of capital is foreclosed, adjustment must occur elsewhere – through the price of gold, via the specie-flow mechanism.

21 As Foley rightly points out, the quantity-of-money theory of prices that Ricardo uses to close the argument in relation to comparative advantage and the attractiveness of free trade is not consistent with his labour theory of value, articulated and used elsewhere in his conceptual scheme. See Foley, *Adam's Fallacy*, 68.

22 For a more technical discussion of how this operates, refer to ibid., 66–67 and Appendix (especially 240–41) or Eichengreen, *Globalizing Capital*, 24–25.

23 At least in relation to countries with flexible exchange rates: see Krugman, 'Myths and Realities of U.S. Competitiveness', 90. As Blecker notes, 'For countries with fixed exchange rates, economists often cite an automatic balance-of-payments adjustment such as the Hume specie-flow mechanism or modern update thereof'. See further Blecker, 'Financial Globalisation, Exchange Rates and International Trade', 186.

24 Krugman, 'Myths and Realities of U.S. Competitiveness', 90. Similarly, Keynes noted, allowing wages to do the adjusting might aid balance of trade issues, but noted a drastic reduction of money wages would lead to 'social injustice and violent resistance since it would greatly benefit some classes of income at the expense of others' (Keynes, *Collected Writings Vol. IX*, 235–36, see also Milberg, 'Is Absolute Advantage Passé?', 226–27; Milberg, 'Say's Law in the Open Economy', 241–42), and therefore would not be the most desirable social policy.

25 See Krugman, 'Myths and Realities of U.S. Competitiveness', 90; Krugman, 'Ricardo's Difficult Idea', 8; Blecker, 'Financial Globalization, Exchange Rates and International Trade', 176; Dernburg, *Global Macroeconomics*.

It should be noted that in supposing that the exchange rate will adjust and balance trade, models usually make the assumption that domestic output prices are rigid (at least in the short term), but that the domestic currency price of foreign imports will vary in line with an exchange rate adjustment. This conclusion is complicated by the phenomenon of limited exchange rate pass-through – the observation of rigidity in the prices foreign goods, notwithstanding exchange rate fluctuations: see, generally, Arestis and Milberg, 'Degree of Monopoly, Pricing, and Flexible exchange rates'. For current purposes, rather than delving into this literature, however, I accept the assumption of foreign good price responsiveness to exchange rate fluctuations and instead probe the mainstream theory for its coherence and closure in isolation from this issue.

26 Krugman, 'What do Undergrads Need to Know', 125. Somewhat peculiarly, notwithstanding his clear acknowledgement that the Humean–Ricardian mechanism is insufficient to explain balances in the modern economy (see note 23 above), Krugman makes the claim that the most important things to teach undergraduates in relation to trade – in addition to the self-correction of trade imbalances – are the Humean and Ricardian classical models.

27 Blecker, 'Financial Globalization, Exchange Rates and International Trade', 191.

28 See ibid.; MacDonald, 'Long-Run Exchange Rate Modelling', 482; Harvey, 'Exchange Rate Theory'; Driskill, 'Flexible Exchange Rates', 393; Krugman, 'Myths and Realities of U.S. Competitiveness', 90; Krugman, 'The Persistent US Trade Deficit'.

29 Harvey, *Currencies, Capital Flows and Crises*, 1.

30 The mainstream models are usefully set out in a number of texts and articles including Sarno and Taylor, *The Economics of Exchange Rates*; Harvey, 'Orthodox Approaches to Exchange Rate Determination'; Copeland, *Exchange Rates and International Finance*; Hallwood and MacDonald, *International Money and Finance*. For excellent and accessible systematizations and critiques of these models, see Blecker, 'Financial Globalization, Exchange Rates and International Trade'; Harvey, *Currencies, Capital Flows and Crises*, especially chapter 2; Taylor, *Reconstructing Macroeconomics*.

31 Harvey, ibid., 16; Blecker, ibid., 192.

32 See also Blecker, ibid.; Harvey, ibid., 16–17.

33 As to possible historical reasons for the model's persistence in the face of this poor fit, see Blecker, ibid., 194.

34 Harvey, *Currencies, Capital Flows and Crises*, 19.

35 Specifically, it represents an attempt to extend the Keynesian IS-LM analysis into the open-economy setting.

36 See further, Taylor, *Reconstructing Macroeconomics*, 315.

37 See also Taylor, 'Exchange Rate indeterminacy'.

38 See further, Taylor, *Reconstructing Macroeconomics*, 315, 330.

39 This model tends to focus more upon explaining short- rather than long-run exchange rate fluctuations (see Sarno and Taylor, *The Economics of Exchange Rates*, 115 onwards), and is therefore perhaps less relevant to our current enquiry (in that it is well acknowledged by mainstream economists that in the short run, exchange rates tend not to adjust to trade-balancing levels). Nonetheless, this approach tends to be invoked from time to time in the literature, and for the sake of completeness, I will sketch its contours here.

40 See Harvey, 'Orthodox Approaches to Exchange Rate Determination', 572; Sarno and Taylor, ibid., 115 (who possibly think they are saying the opposite, but end up saying the same thing).

41 See further Harvey, *Currencies, Capital flows and Crises*.

42 Dornbusch, 'Expectations and Exchange Rate Dynamics'. In a sense, this model might be termed a 'sticky-price monetary model': see Sarno and Taylor, *The Economics of Exchange Rates*, 104.

43 Harvey, *Currencies, Capital Flows and Crises*, 21. See also Taylor, *Reconstructing Macroeconomics*, 339.

44 Harvey, ibid.

45 Blecker, 'Financial Globalization, Exchange Rates and International Trade', 190.

46 See further, the excellent discussion in Harvey, 'Exchange Rate Theory' concerning the definition of the 'fundamentals' and their role in international finance economics.

47 Taylor, *Reconstructing Macroeconomics*, 339.

48 Harvey, *Currencies, Capital Flows and Crises*, 2.

49 Blecker, 'Financial Globalization, Exchange Rates and International Trade', 191. See also, Aliber, 'Exchange Rates'; Harvey, ibid., especially chapter 3.

50 See further Bank for International Settlements, *Triennial Central Bank Survey – Preliminary global results – Turnover (September 2010)*.

51 Harvey, *Currencies, Capital Flows and Crises*, 2.

52 World Trade Organization, *International Trade Statistics 2012*.

53 By identity, the balance of payment *account* as a whole must balance. This does not mean, however, that its various components (current account, capital account and financial account) cannot each individually be in positive or negative territory. The exchange rate will be determined by the total supply and demand for currency, but total supply and demand will not necessarily equilibrate to a trade-balancing exchange rate.

54 See *Principles of Political Economy and Taxation*, 143.

55 As to the debate concerning the implications for comparative advantage of capital mobility, and mainstream attempts to develop ancillary analyses to debase critique, see: Mundell, 'International Trade and Factor Mobility'; Prasch, 'Reassessing the Theory of Comparative Advantage'; Ferguson, 'International Capital Mobility and Comparative Advantage'; Boudreaux, 'Does Increased International Mobility of Factors of Production Weaken the Case for Free Trade?'.

56 I have been surprised – although I should not be – to find, after a first attempt at drafting this list, that Joan Robinson, that most under-appreciated of economists, identified a similar set of points in 1937. The fourth point is hers: see Robinson, *Essays in the Theory of Employment*, 134.

57 Milberg, 'Say's Law in the Open Economy', 242.

58 Harvey, *Currencies, Capital Flows and Crises*, 64.

59 Ibid., 3.

60 See Blecker, 'Financial Globalization, Exchange Rates and International Trade', 194–45; Aliber, 'Exchange Rates', 212; Frankel and Rose, 'Empirical Research on Nominal Exchange Rates' 1339, 1344; Frankel and Froot, 'Chartists, Fundamentalists, and the Demand for Dollars'; Taylor, *'Exchange Rate Indeterminacy'*; Harvey, ibid., chapter 3.

61 Blecker, 'International Capital Mobility', 127.

62 For an excellent attempt to model some of these considerations, see Harvey, *Currencies, Capital Flows and Crises*, especially chapter 5.

63 For a similar argument concerning the operation of the stock market, see Brenner, *The Boom and the Bubble*, 229.

64 Harvey, *Currencies, Capital Flows and Crises*, 100–2.

65 See Harvey, 'Exchange Rate Theory', for a similar argument at a different but associated level concerning the manner in which mainstream theory imbues the term 'fundamentals' with whatever content is required to demonstrate the efficient functioning of finance markets.

66 Davidson, *John Maynard Keynes*, 139.

67 Ibid., 140–41.

68 See also, Blecker, 'International Economics', 202.

69 Krugman and Obstfeld, *International Economics*, 434; Davidson, *John Maynard Keynes*, 139.

70 Mainstream economists acknowledge that this might last for several years. See discussion in Davidson, ibid., 140–42.

71 The obvious example of this would be the United Sates: see ibid., 141–4; Milberg, 'Is Absolute Advantage Passé?', 224–26.

72 See Chrystal, 'International Monetary Arrangements', 50; Blecker, 'International Economics after Robinson', 325.

73 Robinson, 'The Need for a Reconsideration', 17.

74 See Meese and Rogoff, 'Empirical Exchange Rate Models'; Rogoff, 'The Failure of Empirical Exchange Rate Models'.

75 Indeed, it is well established that in the short run, models fail to outperform a random-walk forecast (i.e., forecasting that predicts using a trajectory derived by taking one random step after another): see Meese and Rogoff, and Rogoff, ibid.

76 Mark, 'Exchange Rates and Fundamentals'; Sarno and Taylor, *The Economics of Exchange Rates*, 96; Krugman, 'Myths and Realities of U.S. Competitiveness', 90–91.

77 Eatwell and Taylor, *Global Finance at Risk*; see generally the essays collected in Eatwell and Taylor (eds.). *International Capital Markets in Transition*; Blecker, 'International Economics after Robinson', 327. Eichengreen helpfully sketches both the historical development of this trend, its interaction with the system of flexible international exchange rates that became increasingly dominant and co-emerged at this time, and the manner in which this has led to increased exchange rate and monetary instability and volatility: see Eichengreen, *Globalizing Capital*, especially chapters 5–7.

78 See, for example, UNCTAD, *Trade and Development Report 2009*, chapter 1, 12:

> The most visible evidence of imbalances was the large current-account deficits in the United States, the United Kingdom, Spain and several East European economies, on the one hand, and large surpluses in China, Japan, Germany and the oil-exporting countries, on the other.

Krugman, 'Myths and Realities of U.S. Competitiveness' looks at the twenty-nine-year period from 1960 until 1980 and claims that this demonstrates that trade balances. However, things look significantly different after that point – with the US balance, for example, not having balanced since the mid-1970s – see Milberg, 'Is Absolute Advantage Passé?', 225; Blecker, 'International Capital Mobility', 137. See also Alonso and Garcimartin, 'A New Approach to the Balance-of-Payments Constraint'; Blecker, 'Financial Globalization, Exchange Rates and International Trade', 192.

79 Although, it must be remarked, that given the incredible volatility and repetition of crisis in recent times (e.g., the Latin American debt crises of the 1970s and 1980s, the East Asian Crisis of 1997, and the 'dot-com' crash of 2000), the insistence remains incredulous even absent the recent/current crisis. Heterodox and radical voices have been pointing to financial volatility and successive crises for decades. See, for example, Brenner, *The Boom and The Bubble*; Brenner, *Economics of Global Turbulence*; Strange, *Mad Money*; Hahnel, *Panic Rules!*; Harvey, *Limits to Capital*; Arrighi and Silver, *Chaos and Governance*.

80 See UNCTAD, *Trade and Development Report 2009*, chapter 4, 116, 127 (references omitted).

81 Krugman, 'Ricardo's Difficult Idea'.

82 See note 26 and accompanying text.

83 Mill, *Principles of Political Economy*, III.18.2. Ricardo essentially makes much the same point, see *Principles of Political Economy and Taxation*, 143–44.

84 Although as to the origin of the phrase 'veil of money', see the debate encapsulated in: Patinkin and Steiger, 'In Search of the "Veil of Money"'; Klausinger, 'The Early Use of the Term 'Veil of Money'''.

85 See also Epstein, 'Introduction: Financialization and the World Economy', 8.

86 And it tends to be the case that international finance scholars seem to outstrip their trade colleagues in generating such results and models. For example, Frankel and Rose, 'Empirical Research on Nominal Exchange Rates.', 1707–8: 'no model based on such standard fundamentals like [...] current account balances will ever succeed in explaining or predicting a high percentage of the variation in the exchange rate [...]'.

87 Robinson, 'History Versus Equilibrium', 53.

88 Marglin, *The Dismal Science*, 278.

89 It is worth noting that this fictional model of trade – of goods being exchanged for other goods on the basis of relative prices, of money being a veil, and of actors being fundamentally the same – is an importation to the international level of an old idea in political economy. That idea is Say's Law: simplistically, the notion that supply creates its own demand and that systemic overproduction is not a risk in a market society. A detailed discussion and examination of Say's Law itself is unnecessary to my current argument, the discussion above being enough to lay bare its problematic application in free trade and comparative advantage analysis. For a discussion and thoroughgoing critiques of Say's Law, my reader should refer to Say, *Letters to Mr Malthus*; Sowell, *Say's Law: An Historical Analysis* and 'Say's Law'; Sardoni, 'Say's Law' and 'Marx and Keynes'; Shoul, 'Karl Marx and Say's Law'; Lapavitsas, 'Marx's Analysis of Money Hoarding'; Milberg, 'Say's Law in the Open Economy'.

The theoretical inadequacies of Say's Law are bolstered by recent empirical history of the global economy. Specifically, Brenner's social theoretically rich account of the history of the post-World War II global economy bears out well the problem of overcapacity in the global economy, contradicting standard Say's Law implications and results. Brenner presents evidence of and seeks to explain a pattern of systemic overproduction and overcapitalization (which lead to flagging profitability). Specifically, he traces these to the interrelationship of horizontal, interfirm competition at the international level, speculation and financialization: see Brenner, *Economics of Global Turbulence*, especially chapter 1.

90 Such searches are not unheard of in economics. This is a phrase used by Harcourt to describe the search for a distribution- and price-independent measure for a quantity of capital (of which I will say more in the coming chapter): see Harcourt, 'Capital Theory Controversies', 31.

91 See Shaikh, 'Laws of International Exchange', 226. See generally note 79 above and references mentioned therein.

Chapter Four   Clockwork Production and the Origin-Myths of Specialization

1 Marx, *The Poverty of Philosophy*, 225–56.

2 See notes 20–22 to chapter 2 and accompanying text.

3 The challenge that I levied against this aspect of the comparative advantage analytic in chapter 3 was as not being – alone – meaningful as a matter of *social analysis* or *explanation.*

4 In the sense of the productivity of labour in generating the relevant goods.

5 Findlay points out that a more complex analysis is contained in Ricardo's *An Essay on Profits*, in which he explores the relationship between the size of the 'wage fund' in relation to the supply of land, the consumption pattern of landowners *as well as* technology. See Findlay, 'Relative Prices, Growth and Trade'.

6 The reading that I am arguing against here is a bizarre but common mistake. See, for example, Paul in 'Free Trade, Regulatory Competition' in which it is claimed, 'Ricardo assumed that comparative advantage was immutable based on the available labor and capital' (34). This is completely incorrect. Firstly, technology plays a key role in the Ricardian determination of comparative costs story. Moreover, there is nothing, for Ricardo, immutable about comparative advantage. Ricardo expressly contemplates the notion that changes in technology might occur, and would alter the pattern of comparative advantage as between two trading counties (see *Principles of Political Economy and Taxation*, 144).

7 See further, Findlay, 'Comparative Advantage', 516, and also for a discussion of the manner in which Ricardo, though a classical economist and therefore predating the general equilibrium analysis of neoclassical economics, in other work evinces precursors to that analysis. See also discussion in note 5 above.

8 Specifically:

1. Heckscher–Ohlin theorem: Nations will export that commodity which is produced with relatively large amounts of its relatively (either physically or price-defined) abundant factor.

2. Factor price equalization theorem: Two or more countries sharing the same technology will find that free trade equalizes factor returns if their endowments are sufficiently similar and they produce in common a significant number of commodities.

3. Stopler–Samuelson theorem: A rise in the relative price of a good will lead to a rise in the return to that factor which is used most intensively in the production of the good, and conversely, to a fall in the return to the other factor.

4. Rybczynski theorem: At constant relative goods prices, a rise in the endowment or supply of one factor will lead to a more than proportional expansion of the output in the sector which uses that factor intensively, and an absolute decline of the output of the other good.

9 There is a question, though not one immediately relevant here, concerning what is meant by the term 'abundance' – see Perdikas and Kerr, *Trade Theory and Empirical Evidence*, 23; Chipman, 'International Trade'.

10 See Robinson, *Reflections on the Theory of International Trade*, 18–19; Blecker, 'International Economics after Robinson', 331.

11 For a deep, sophisticated and yet witty examination of this debate, its various positions and its relationship to economic theory more broadly, see Harcourt, *Some Cambridge Controversies*. For a more recent treatment, see also Cohen and Harcourt, 'Whatever Happened to the Cambridge Capital Theory Controversies?'

12 Cohen and Harcourt, ibid., 206; Samuelson, 'A Summing Up'.

13 Cohen and Harcourt, ibid.

14 Much of this debate is highly technical and mathematical. However, the key issues can be rendered through relatively simple description. My summary here leans heavily on Harcourt, *Some Cambridge Controversies*; Cohen and Harcourt ibid.; Hunt, *History of Economic Thought*, 434–44, and to a lesser extent Keen, *Debunking Economics*, chapter 6.

15 See Samuelson, 'Parable and Realism in Capital Theory'.

16 In the neoclassical scheme, rate of profit and rate of interest can be and are used interchangeably. These two variables are, in the neoclassical scheme, drawn to equality through the equilibrating mechanism in the market for loans in the financial market. See also Pasinetti and Scazzieri, 'Capital Theory: Paradoxes'.

17 Incidentally, Veblen also pointed to this issue, some half a century prior to the formal explosion of the Cambridge–Cambridge Capital Controversy: see Veblen, 'Professor Clark's Economics', 161–169. See also Marx, *Capital: Volume III*, 953.

18 Which involves the consideration of time, and 'dated labour' – the value of a machine produced in 2014 can be treated as the aggregate of the labour and commodities required to produce it in 2013 multiplied by the profit rate, those commodity inputs could further be decomposed into the labour and commodity inputs required to produce them in 2012 multiplied by the rate of profit and so on. That is, it is possible to sum the direct and indirect labour required to produce a commodity as if they were produced today. See further Bose, 'The "Labour Approach" and the "Commodity Approach"'.

19 This model follows Samuelson's adoption of the distinctively Austrian rendition (à la Böhm-Bawerk and Hayek) of 'capital as time'. That is, in this illustration, capital is represented by the productivity of a period of time: see Samuelson, 'A Summing Up'.

20 See further Cohen and Harcourt, 'Whatever Happened to the Cambridge Capital Theory Controversies?', 202–4; Hunt, *History of Economic Thought*, 237–38.

21 The effect of the Cambridge Capital Critique is less severe in respect of the Stopler–Samuelson theorem (concerning the distributional effect of trade as between factor owners): see Blecker, 'Stolper-Samuelson after Kalecki'. However, the predictions as to patterns of comparative advantage made by the Heckscher–Ohlin–Samuelson approach are not so immune. See also Blecker, 'International Economics after Robinson', 332–33.

22 But see Bliss, 'Heterogeneous Capital', in which he claims that the Heckscher–Ohlin–Samuelson theorems failed due to Wicksell effects only: intermediate goods are produced, and those intermediate goods might be used as capital goods, a shift in the wage rate or profit might have the effect of changing the price of an intermediate capital good, and that change of cost might have an effect on the attractiveness of a given technique that could end up dominating the effect of the wage/profit range change itself. This is true to an extent. But the Cambridge Radicals also pointed to reswitching and capital reversing as a result of Wicksell effects. These two cumulate to cause irresolvable difficulties for the Heckscher–Ohlin–Samuelson approach.

23 For a working out of the technical argument in the context of the Heckscher–Ohlin–Samuelson theorems, see Metcalfe and Steedman, 'Heterogeneous capital'. See also the collected essays in Steedman (ed.), *Fundamental Issues in Trade Theory*.

24 See further Jones, 'Heckscher–Ohlin Trade Theory', 621.

25 See Leontief, 'Domestic Production and Foreign Trade'.

26 Other paradoxical results include (at the time of survey) labour-rich Japan (1959) and India (1962) exporting capital-intensive goods. For more detail of these and results that test the predictions of Heckscher–Ohlin–Samuelson theory, see Perdikis and Kerr, *Trade Theory and Empirical Evidence*, especially chapter 3, and references therein.

27 Cohen and Harcourt, 'Whatever Happened to the Cambridge Capital Theory Controversies?', 208.

28 For a critique of this, see Roosevelt, 'Cambridge Economics as Commodity Fetishism'.

29 Via an Edgeworth–Bowley box diagram. My reader will be correct to intuit that the inclusion of capital in a production function raises Cambridge Capital Critique–style issues.

30 The convexivity of the production possibility frontier to the origin reflects (*contra* a purely Ricardian model) the assumption of diminishing marginal rates of substitution.

31 Indeed, such frontiers are sometimes termed 'deterministic': see, for example, Fandel, *Theory of Production and Cost*, especially chapters 2 and 5.

32 See also Samuels and Schmid, 'The Concept of Cost in Economics', 222.

33 I will return to certain caveats that sophisticated economists make in respect of certain limited instances of 'constructed' rather than exogenous or 'given' comparative advantages. See notes 76–80 below and accompanying text.

34 In a sense, scarcity defines a relationship between means and ends – specifically, a relationship marked by the insufficiency of the former to achieve the latter. As such, if one is interested to explore the implications of scarcity for contemporary economics and society more broadly, one could investigate either side of the dynamic – considering either the ends that are sought to be achieved or the means to do so. Mainstream economics deals with this dialectic by suppressing one half of it – ends – which are taken to be both infinite and given. For present purposes, it is not necessary for me to investigate the effects of so doing. For the moment, I will merely address the aspect of scarcity upon which mainstream economics focuses – limited means.

35 A similar distinction is termed by Samuels and Schmid, somewhat opaquely in my view, as one between 'physical scarcity' and 'interest scarcity': Samuels and Schmid, 'The Concept of Cost in Economics', 228.

36 Marx, *Capital: Volume III*, 969.

37 Understanding the importance of the latter in economic processes and theory might be understood, as Commons suggested, as 'political economy': see Commons, *Legal Foundations of Capitalism*, 3.

38 See ibid., 3 as to the need for economic theory to recognize its nonmechanistic and social subject matter.

39 See Schmid, 'Law and Economics'.

40 See Commons, *Legal Foundations of Capitalism*, especially chapter 1.

41 Robinson, 'History Versus Equilibrium', 58.

42 See generally Hodgson, *Economics and Institutions* and *The Evolution of Institutional Economics*.

43 I have touched on the above problems – identified in the context of the Cambridge Capital Controversy – involved in attempting to specify a meaning for 'capital' as a factor of production. Accordingly, here I attempt an articulation that does not involve these problems.

44 As it is not strictly relevant to the point that I seek to demonstrate here, I can avoid some of the interesting but fraught questions as to what, at the penumbra, should be delineated as factors or outputs. For example, are worker motivations and work ethics 'factors' or 'outputs' of a production process? I will have more to say about some of these issues in chapter 5 of this book. For present purposes, however, I assume, to some extent with the mainstream, that we can understand both the inputs and outputs of a production process as commodified.

45 The discussion here owes much to Cohen's careful discussion of the forces of production in Cohen, *Karl Marx's Theory of History*, chapter 2. Cohen's is an expressly Marxian discussion, relying on traditional Marxian categories, and pursuing analytical Marxian aims. The discussion here is not so geared, and as I have a different goal in mind (showing a distinction between physical and social aspects of production), I am able to be somewhat more expansive in relation to what is categorized as a factor of production, and under what subheading. The account here differs from Cohen's most obviously in relation to making broad enough the third category to take into account the productive coordination role, which more traditional Marxian analysis would not include in a discussion of the forces (or factors) of production. This highlights the difficulties of such (although certainly not all) Marxian analysis to grapple with and render intelligible the 'labour' involved in the capitalist entrepreneurial function of the capitalist and the subsequent delegation of much of that function in the age of the large corporate form, to a (wage labouring) managerial class. See generally Baran and Sweezy, *Monopoly Capitalism*.

46 Spaces for Cohen belong to a different category of forces of production than 'instruments of production' (see Cohen, ibid., 50–52). Given, however, the fact that spaces are closely associated with premises, and premises are helpfully classified as instruments of production, I think no violence is done by grouping spaces under the same heading.

47 Coase, 'The Problem of Social Cost'.

48 Ibid., 43–44.

49 Coase and I are essentially taking different routes to the same destination. The point is, at base, that what it means to be able to own and use a factor of production is the product of legal-institutional rules and regimes that provide rights as between people, rather than self-evident or inherent properties of the factors in question.

50 Langille claims that governmental regulatory policy is a factor of production, albeit a created one (see Langille, 'General Reflections', 236. I am not sure that this is a helpful categorization. Thinking of legal and regulatory considerations as factors requires significantly expanding what is meant by a 'factor', risks

inaccuracy (they are not used, or used up, in production) and is apt to cause confusion. It is far more correct to say that the regulatory regime conditions and constitutes the rights to use, control, develop, etc., factors of production.

51 Bator, 'Simple Analytics of Welfare Maximization', 34.

52 See also Kennedy, 'Role of Law in Economic Thought', 960. Kennedy interestingly points out that, in spite of key differences between neoclassical and classical economic schemes, the implicit assumptions of each concerning law are, in the main, held in common.

53 See also Kennedy, 'Law-and-Economics'.

54 See generally Bentham, *Principles of the Civil Code*, chapter 8.

55 Cohen, 'Property and Sovereignty', 45 (the emphasis and addition are mine).

56 Kennedy, 'Law-and-Economics', 466.

57 Holmes Jr., 'Privilege, Malice, and Intent'.

58 Ibid., 3.

59 See Coase, 'The Problem of Social Cost'.

60 See also Cohen, 'The Basis of Contract'.

61 There is often posited a distinction between the rules that establish the market and the rules that regulate the market. The former are posited as creating the baseline for the market and economic activity, while the latter distort or regulate that baseline operation. It is not necessary for me to deal exhaustively with the erroneous nature of that distinction here. It is enough to note, as the discussion above demonstrates, that each of the body of private law rules that are supposed to establish the baseline of the market (by reference to master concepts of freedom, efficiency or whatever) do not so establish it in any kind of apolitical or neutral way. Rather, the line between regulating and constructing the market is not a bright one. See further: Kennedy, 'Law-and-Economics'.

62 This characterization of the economy is Samuels' reading of Hale: see Samuels, 'The Economy as a System of Power'.

63 See Hohfeld. 'Some Fundamental Legal Conceptions'.

64 See Hale, 'Bargaining, Duress, and Economic Liberty', 603.

65 Ibid., 606, 626, 627–28.

66 Ibid., 628; Hale, 'Coercion and Distribution', 474, 478–79.

67 I adapt Hale's phrase 'coercive weapons': see Hale, 'Coercion and Distribution', 478.

68 This insight essentially involves and makes possible a 'bottom-up' establishing, in fine-grained legal-institutional and social-relational relief, the kind of disproportionate social power to which Marx pointed through his structural analysis of capitalism. For a similar focus on social relations (although unsurprisingly for a social theoretically inclined historian less 'legally rigorous' or focused), see the structural institutionalism obvious in Brenner, 'The social basis for economic development'.

69 Hunt, 'Radical Critique of Welfare Economics', 244.

70 The interconnectedness of economic actors at the level of legal and cost interactions mirrors the Cambridge Radicals' point concerning the material interconnectedness of the economy, and the manner in which fluctuations in, say, output prices for capital goods, will have ricochet effects throughout the system in terms of costs structures, valuation, distribution of income and so forth: see Sraffa, *The Production of Commodities* (which is well 'translated' into

intelligible terms by Steedman, *Marx after Sraffa*). More broadly, the UK side of the Cambridge Capital Controversy conceived of the economy as driven by the profit-making decisions of capitalistic firms, rather than the utility-maximizing savings and consumption decisions of fundamentally similar economic actors (as in neoclassical economics): see further, Cohen and Harcourt, 'Whatever Happened to the Cambridge Capital Theory Controversies?', 208.

It is precisely where the Cambridge Radicals left off that legal realist/ institutional analysis in the sense discussed here becomes useful. The latter provides the microfoundational basis for rejecting the neoclassical abstractions for understanding the economy. However, the thematic and methodological similarities should not surprise. Indeed, in later work, Joan Robinson noted that Veblen (a leading political economist of the institutional school) had, several decades before she and her Cambridge colleagues, pointed to the incoherence of the marginalize notion of capital, and to the institutional basis of capitalist socioeconomic power. See also discussion in note 17 above.

The preoccupations and postures of each of these schools were fundamentally the same – the critique of scarcity-based explanations for distributive shares between capital and labour in favour of introducing explicitly the role of power in economics (Cohen and Harcourt, 'Whatever Happened to the Cambridge Capital Theory Controversies?', 208), the rejection of monadic individualism in modeling modern economies in favour of more integrated and interconnected modeling, the importance placed on economic evolution in real time rather than marginal/equilibrium analysis, and indeed, a near-paranoid anxiety of influence in respect of Marx (although less so with Robinson than anyone else).

71 Hale, 'Coercion and Distribution', 473 (though in a different context).

72 Samuels and Schmid, 'The Concept of Cost in Economics', 277.

73 Ibid., 221.

74 Marglin, 'What Do Bosses Do?', 65.

75 Of course, as mentioned above (see discussion in note 6 and associated text), Ricardo was clear that comparative advantage might change when technology changes. The role of legal-institutional factors in the construction of comparative advantages only underscores this mutability over time.

76 Krugman, 'Myths and Realities of U.S. Competitiveness', 96.

77 It is not entirely clear what Krugman means, especially in light of these examples, by differences in 'society' as driving international trade.

78 Krugman, 'Myths and Realities of U.S. Competitiveness', 96.

79 Ibid., 97.

80 Ibid., 98.

81 I shall say more in the coming chapter concerning whether patterns of state-made comparative advantage can be justified as welfare maximising: see chapter 5, section C^3.

82 See Cohen, *Karl Marx's Theory of History*, 115. While the term does have a history that dates back to the study of religion, it is not correct to suggest that to fetishize something is merely to worship it. In this sense, Kennedy is correct in his rejection of understanding commodity fetishism as the worship of commodities or some form of hypermaterialism: see Kennedy, 'Role of Law in Economic Thought', 968–69.

83 Though not – as mentioned in the previous footnote – materialism run wild, commodity fetishism *is* (to use Kennedy's direct phrase) 'one of the mind-fucks of capitalism': see Kennedy, ibid., 969.

84 Tarullo has advanced a related argument in the context of state action in the form of 'market corrective strategies' to correct for impermissible/unfair/distortive action by other states, specifically antidumping laws and countervailing duty legislation. He argues, rightly, that both of these kinds of trade laws rest impliedly or explicitly on a normal conception of governmental nonintervention. Tarullo claims that the economic norms established by these norms are not consonant with the efficiency gains on which the supposedly stand, and that no satisfactory efficiency analysis can be embodied in a coherent and workable system of US international trade regulation. See Tarullo, 'Beyond Normalcy'. See also Langille, 'General Reflections', 50, in which Langille extends Tarullo's argument to the context of free trade writ large, and to suggest that in an internationalized market that lacks a coherent means of drawing an economic baseline, regulatory competition has been the result. Given that trade is always and everywhere regulated, political and controversial, for Langille, fair trade is free trade's destiny. Once we realize that all governmental action is in some sense a subsidy, we can no longer rely on stylized ideas about the relationship between the state and the market, and rather, instead, have to engage in a debate about the appropriate scope of market regulation. This is right, but I am less sure that 'fair' trade is necessarily the direction of policy travel.

85 Langille, ibid.

86 Even where sophisticated economists do see the constructed nature of comparative advantage, what remains to be recognized is its relational aspect.

Chapter Five   'And They Lived Happily Ever After...': Fictions of Being Better Off and Stories of What 'Should' Be

1 Cohen, 'Property and Sovereignty', 68.

2 Indeed, modern welfare economic analysis can be seen as the intellectual outgrowth of the great debates between Smith and the Mercantilists, between Ricardo and supporters of the Corn Laws – fundamentally, between those who point to the beneficence, efficiency or welfare enhancing aspects of (in modern times appropriately – but minimally – tinkered with) markets, and those who doubt such claims.

3 Ricardo, *Principles of Political Economy and Taxation*, 131.

4 Krugman and Obstfeld, *International Economics*, 210.

5 As to such benefits see Smith, *The Wealth of Nations*, 10–12.

6 For a fulsome (though optimistic) discussion of the various gains (economic and otherwise) from trade, see Irwin, *Free Trade under Fire*, chapter 2. Interestingly, in Irwin's rendering, there is basically no benefit that free trade cannot bring – prosperity, freedom from war, democracy, human rights, environmental protection. The list is impressive. But it is also far more expansive than the list of gains promised by the case for free trade.

7 Ibid., 40. It is interesting that while Irwin is at first tentative about overclaiming about the ability to demonstrate the gains from trade, in subsequent pages, his language quickly, and for no apparent reason, becomes much more robust.

8 Leamer and Levinsohn, 'International Trade Theory and Evidence', 1344.

9 For a similar point, see Hahnel, *ABCs of Political Economy*, 184; Baker, 'Trade and Inequality: The Role of Economists'.

10 See Mankiw, *Principles of Economics*, chapter 3; Krugman, 'What Do Undergrads Need to Know', 120, 123.

11 I am not alone in my suspicion and diagnosis of mainstream presentations as implying this more simplistic understanding of the gains from trade: see also Prasch, 'Reassessing Comparative Advantage', 429–30.

12 See note 13 to chapter 2.

13 See, for example, Caves et al., *World Trade and Payments*. For Krugman and Obstfeld, *International Trade* the qualification comes in chapter 9 and the argument is given a few more pages – five, in fact.

14 These were later collated and published in Torrens, *The Budget*.

15 See further, Irwin, *Against the Tide*, chapter 7; Robbins, *Robert Torrens*; Corry, 'Robert Torrens'.

16 Irwin, ibid., 101.

17 See also note 16 to chapter 2.

18 In recent history, think of the US–EC trade war that grew out of disputes concerning banana subsidies offered to former European colonies, expanded to restrictions on beef injected with growth hormones, and generated various other retaliations and counter-retaliations. For a useful tabular summary of much of the history of the dispute, see Dunoff et al., *International Law*, 843–44.

19 Mill, *Essays on Some Unsettled Questions*, I.55.

20 See Krugman, 'Introduction: New Thinking about Trade Policy', 10.

21 To be clear, when mainstream international economists consider the prospect of 'exploitation', their consideration tends to be based around what can be characterized as an 'emotional' or 'bleeding heart' argument – specifically, that Third World producers are often paid lower wages than those in the First World, and are therefore exploited in some sense. The mainstream answers to such arguments are predictable and point to the consumptive efficiency gains and real income rises that free trade brings to such workers. See, for example, Krugman and Obstfeld, *International Economics*, 39–40. Of course, the possibility that I am raising here is different. It concerns the sharing of gains between countries.

22 Work in relation to theories of unequal exchange began to emerge in earnest in the 1950s. Key early works were Prebisch, *The Economic Development of Latin America*; Singer, 'The Distribution of Gains' which noted declining terms of trade for raw materials as opposed to manufactures (eventually becoming known as the Prebisch-Singer thesis). Later works include Emmanuel, *Unequal Exchange*, which emphasized the role of wage differentials in effecting surplus transfers from peripheral countries to core ones using Marxian metrics. The analysis in Amin, *Accumulation on a World Scale* was similar to Emmanuel's approach but emphasized the disarticulation of capitalist and other modes of production in peripheral areas: see also, Amin, *Unequal Development*. Other approaches that

could also fairly be termed 'unequal exchange' analyses with an avowedly Marxian flavour would include Weeks, *Capital and Exploitation*; Shaikh, 'Laws of International Exchange'; and Mandel, *Late Capitalism*. For a helpful mapping and critique of the unequal exchange debate, see Janvery and Kramer, 'The limits of unequal exchange'.

23 Kymlicka makes a strong, largely accessible, although not altogether charitable assault on some of these points of controversy in the subject–object renderings of exploitation: Kymlicka, *Contemporary Political Philosophy*, 177–87. See also Wertheimer, *Exploitation*. Taken together, these (and references therein) provide an adequate starting point for further reading.

24 In some, but certainly not all, Marxian renderings, 'value'.

25 See generally Cohen, *History, Labour, and Freedom*, especially chapter 11.

26 The question of Marx's views on the justice or injustice of capitalism and its particular arrangements has been the subject of much debate; for an excellent review of much of that literature, see Geras, 'The Controversy About Marx and Justice' and the follow-up piece 'Bringing Marx to Justice'.

27 See further Kymlicka, *Contemporary Political Philosophy*.

28 Moreover, during the last commodity price and energy price boom, the terms of trade of many (commodity exporting) developing countries *improved* while East Asia (with strong export volume of manufactured goods) suffered deteriorating terms of trade: see UNCTAD, *Trade and Development Report 2008*, chapter 2.

29 See Roemer, *A General Theory*; *Free to Lose*; and 'Unequal Exchange, Labor Migration and International Capital Flows'.

30 Clear connections will be seen between this and the (admittedly more nuanced and crisp) approach of Hale discussed in the previous chapter. The approaches might usefully be grouped under the heading of 'rent analyses'.

31 See Hahnel, *ABCs of Political Economy*, 185–87; Hahnel, *Panic Rules!*, Appendix B. See also, Hahnel, 'Exploitation: A Modern Approach'.

32 Baiman, 'Unequal Exchange'.

33 As I seek to provide the contours of this exploitation here, I will present a composite of the two approaches.

34 That is, the only difference between Southern and Northern countries is a differential capital endowment.

35 For that, see particularly Baiman, 'Unequal Exchange' who corrects for some of the deficiencies of Hahnel's approach (see references mentioned in note 31 above).

36 Hahnel, *ABCs of Political Economy*, 186.

37 See Baiman, 'Unequal Exchange', 78.

38 As to market norms, see Anderson, *Value in Ethics and Economics*, chapter 7.

39 Even Robert Nozick – the intellectual high-water mark of libertarian political philosophy, with its lauding of the justice of market-based freedoms – cleaves to this position: see Nozick, *Anarchy, State, and Utopia*, 150–182. This is an enquiry, however, that lies, characteristically, outside the scope of the economic literature.

40 As was discussed in chapter 4.

41 For a similar argument, though in the context of a proposed Rawlsianesque international justice framework, see Beitz, 'Justice and International Relations', 367–68.

42 A helpful collation, typologizing and cataloguing of some of the related literature, is presented in Fisher and Syed, 'Global Justice in Healthcare', 591–601. See also note 22 above and references mentioned therein.

43 This is a recurrent theme in the relevant literature. See Beitz, 'Justice and International Relations'; Beitz, 'Bounded Morality'; Pogge, 'Egalitarian Law of Peoples' and *Realizing Rawls*; Barry, 'Humanity and Justice'.

44 Chang, *Bad Samaritans*, 73.

45 Robinson, *Reflections on the Theory of International Trade*, 134–35.

46 Chang, *Bad Samaritans*, 74.

47 For the intellectual history of this argument, see Irwin, *Against the Tide*, chapter 8. For the economic analytics, see Cypher and Dietz, *The Process of Economic Development*, chapter 9.

48 See discussion in Milberg, 'Say's Law in the Open Economy', 232. See also, references mentioned in note 53 below.

49 Mankiw, *Principles of Economics*, 191.

50 Ibid., 190–91. See also Irwin, *Free Trade under Fire*, especially chapter 5.

51 Irwin, ibid., 42.

52 Mankiw, *Principles of Economics*, 191.

53 See particularly Chang, *Bad Samaritans*, especially chapters 2 and 3; Chang, *Kicking Away the Ladder*; Amsden, *The Rise of "The Rest"*; Dosi, 'Institutions and Markets'; Dosi and Soete, 'Technical Change and International Trade'.

54 See Mankiw, *Principles of Economics*, 191.

55 As to the plausibility of the Stolper–Samuelson theorem in light of the Cambridge Capital Critique, see note 21 to chapter 4 and references mentioned therein.

56 Unlike neoclassical economics, Ricardo's concern (as was common among the classical economists) was much less efficiency and much more the appropriate distribution of income to generate economic *growth*.

57 See, for example, note 14 to chapter 2 and accompanying text. See further Irwin, *Against the Tide*, 181–82.

58 For classic statements see Robbins, *Nature and Significance of Economic Science*, chapter 6 and 'Interpersonal Comparisons of Utility'.

59 That is, the analysis of the New Welfare Economics *itself* is hoped or claimed to be devoid of value content – it aims merely at the maximally efficient provision of economic goods to people, according to people's relative desires for those goods: see Hahnel and Albert, *Quiet Revolution in Welfare Economics*, 15. As Little has famously said, the approach of this welfare economics is that 'It is a good thing that individuals should have what they want, and they themselves know best what they want': see further, Little, *Critique of Welfare Economics*, 258.

60 Kaldor, 'Welfare Propositions in Economics'.

61 Hicks, 'Foundations of Welfare Economics'; Hicks, 'The Valuation of Social Income'.

62 Mill, 'The Corn Laws'.

63 See also Irwin, *Against the Tide*, 183.

64 See also note 9 above and references therein.

65 See the debate that occurred in the pages of the Journal of Economic Perspectives in 2004–2005: Samuelson, 'Ricardo and Mill'; Dixit and Grossman, 'Comment: The Limits of Free Trade'; and Samuelson, 'Response from Paul A. Samuelson'.

66 The inclusion of economists 'John or Jane Doe' is Samuelson's. I take him to be suggesting that the view that he sets out is pervasive and forms a kind of 'common sense' throughout the economic community.

67 Samuelson, 'Ricardo and Mill', 135. For a similar paraphrasing of the mainstream position, see Chang, *Bad Samaritans*, 72.

68 Samuelson, ibid., 136. See also, Samuelson, 'Little Nobel Lecture of 1972'; Johnson and Stafford, 'International Competition and Real Wages'; Gomory and Baumol, *Global Trade and Conflicting National Interests*; Chang, ibid.

69 See Scitovsky, 'Welfare Propositions in Economics'.

70 See generally, Little, *Critique of Welfare Economics*, chapter 6. See for discussion Feldman, 'Welfare Economics', 892.

71 See also Irwin, *Against the Tide*, 188.

72 Kaldor, 'Welfare Propositions in Economics', 550.

73 Sen hints at this point in Sen, *On Ethics and Economics*, 33, although it is surprising that this be considered a controversial question to ask. As to the failures of the New Welfare Economics more generally, see Chipman and Moore, 'The New Welfare Economics'.

74 For a clear and helpful summary of the methodology of welfare economics in respect of normative policy (particularly legal policy) analysis, see Kaplow and Shavell, *Fairness Versus Welfare*, especially chapter 2.

75 For Arrow, these criteria were universality, Pareto consistency, independence and nondictatorship. See Arrow, *Social Choice and Individual Values*; Blau, 'Direct Proof of Arrow's Theorem'; Sen, 'Personal Utilities and Public Judgements' and literatures mentioned therein; Hunt, 'The Mathematics of Behavior', chapter 6.

76 See Arrow, ibid.

77 J. de V. Graaff, Theoretical Welfare Economics (1957). For discussion see Feldman, ibid., 893.

78 That is, not just the degree of equality or not of income, but also the appropriate rules for inclusion, the relevant time horizons, attitudes towards uncertainty, etc.

79 See Feldman, 'Welfare Economics', 894. For a similar point, see Hahnel and Albert, *Quiet Revolution in Welfare Economics*, 25–26.

80 See Hahnel and Albert, *Quiet Revolution in Welfare Economics*, 26.

81 Irwin, *Against the Tide*, 188; Findlay, *Trade and Specialization*, chapter 6; Bhagwati, *Pure Theory of International Trade*, 54–55.

82 Bhagwati, ibid., 58. Bhagwati is here speaking about policy recommendations made under 'second best' assumptions; however, his comments in relation to overlooking the difficulties involves in the conceptual apparatus of welfare economic generally as it applies to international trade appear to be motivated by similar/identical considerations. See also 72–73.

83 See also Kennedy, 'Role of Law in Economic Thought', 958–60.

84 Hunt, *supra* note 14, *History of Economic Thought*, 375.

85 Ibid., 381–82.

86 Ibid., 383.

87 Other critiques can be made (with varying degrees of strength and coherence) of welfare economics. My purpose here is not to fully map and evaluate all proper critiques of welfare economics. Rather, I seek to present one style of (radical institutionalist-minded) critique that holds particular relevance for the question of the normative persuasiveness of a policy of comparative advantage-based international trade.

88 As opposed to classical economists such as Smith and Ricardo and their loudest critic, Marx, who were much more aware of or focused upon the production process, as evinced by their various labour/cost theories of value.

89 Hunt, *History of Economic Thought*, 373.

90 This discussion draws heavily on the excellent and lucid presentation ibid., 379–81 and the more technical but nonetheless clear presentation in Bator, 'Simple Analytics of Welfare Maximization'.

91 See also Hunt, *History of Economic Thought*, 391. As Kennedy notes, a more technical, post-Coasian definition of an externality might be along the following lines (see Kennedy, 'Cost–Benefit Analysis of Entitlement Problems', 398:

> An externality is a cost [that is, disutility], associated with an activity that is not reflected in the activity's price because transaction costs prevent those on whom the loss falls from making a contract with whoever might prevent it.

92 See also Kennedy, ibid., 398–400; Kennedy, 'Law-and-Economics', 466–67; Hunt, 'Radical Critique of Welfare Economics', 244; Hahnel and Albert, *Quiet Revolution in Welfare Economics*, 62.

93 It is important to note that a market failure should not be thought of – from a mainstream perspective – as a 'failure of markets' as much as a 'failure of markets to properly establish themselves'. This failure to establish a market creates a legitimate role for the state to intervene and establish the preconditions, in one way or another, to achieve market efficiency.

94 See Coase, 'The Problem of Social Cost'.

95 Kennedy, 'Cost–Benefit Analysis of Entitlement Problems', 398-400 and 'Law-And-Economics', 467.

96 Hunt, 'Radical Critique of Welfare Economics', 244. Arrow has also acknowledged the problem that interconnected utility functions poses for the limited and 'exceptional' conception of externalities incorporated mainstream welfare economic analysis: see Arrow, 'Political and Economic Evaluation'.

97 It might be wondered, 'does the Coasean solution to externalities offer a way out of this situation for welfare economics?' That is, can we not just commodify (give legal rights in respect of) all of the effects of socioeconomic ordering and let markets figure out the most efficient outcome. It is not necessary for me to deal with this musing in detail here. Suffice it to say, there are good reasons to be dubious of this. The Coasian solution to externalities is a solution in the event that externalities are exceptional. Where they are not, the task of granting rights becomes incredibly complex and difficult. This task is only complicated further by the fact that the decision to allocate rights to one rather than another party in the event of an external effect is inevitably 'political',

and amounts to making a decision between actors as to whose interests will become a cost to whom. Further, it cannot be settled by reference to 'physical' causation or efficiency (any efficient outcome depending upon the allocation of the right in the first place) (see also, Kennedy, 'Cost–Benefit Analysis of Entitlement Problems'). Finally, there are good reasons to think that many of the most important human or social noncommodity outputs of production and trade are not capable of being properly treated or valued (for ethical and social reasons) through the mechanism of the market or through market logics: see further, Anderson, *Value in Ethics and Economics*, especially chapters 7 and 9; Radin, *Contested Commodities*, 'Market Inalienability' and 'Property and Personhood'.

98 For an excellent summary of the literature, see Bowles, 'Endogenous Preferences'. See also Hahnel and Albert, *Quiet Revolution in Welfare Economics*, chapter 4.

99 To be clear, there is certainly a degree of overlap between these two.

100 Smith, *The Wealth of Nations, 987*.

101 See Scanlon, 'Moral Basis of Interpersonal Comparisons'; Harsanyi, 'Utilities, Preferences, and Substantive Goods'.

102 It has sometimes been thought by critics of economics that the demonstration of the malleability of preferences for that reason alone in some way invalidates economic analysis. That is not my claim here. Indeed, the issue has probably never really been 'do preferences change over time?' Economists would agree or concede that they do. The issue is more 'should economists (rather than say psychologists) concern themselves with the nature and sources of such changes?' See also Hahnel and Albert, *Quiet Revolution in Welfare Economics*, 76.

103 A mathematical proof that traditional welfare theory will misestimate welfare effects of economic policies if preferences are endogenous can be found in Gintis, *Alienation and Power*, and is further developed and elaborated upon in ibid., chapter 6. See also, a discussion of the (few) mainstream treatments of this issue, ibid., 81–90.

104 Gintis, ibid., 118.

105 See also Hahnel and Albert, 'Quiet Revolution in Welfare Economics', 230.

106 See notes 78–81 to chapter 4 and accompanying text.

107 To be clear, the mainstream economists would tend to accept this point as it relates to international trade and comparative advantage: see, for example, Mankiw, *Principles of Economics*, 190, although they would hasten to add that such arguments tend to be abused in calling arguments about trade policy (that is, with national security or related arguments might be reasonable reasons to restrict free trade, such arguments in the real world of policy discourse tend merely to hide the protectionist agendas of one interest group or another).

108 Hunt, *History of Economic Thought*, 393.

109 Coase, 'The Problem of Social Cost', 43.

110 Even J. S. Mill, who went further than most in recognizing the endogeneity of human development to social arrangements, confined endogeneity to cultural and political institutions/context but not economic environments: see Mill, *On Liberty*, chapter 3. For discussion see Gintis, *Alienation and Power*, 184–87; Hahnel and Albert, *Quiet Revolution in Welfare Economics*, 79.

111 Krugman, 'What Do Undergrads Need to Know', 123.

112 See Tiebout, 'Pure Theory of Local Expenditures'.

113 See Trachtman, 'International Regulatory Competition'. It should be noted, however, that even if correct (and I will suggest that it is not), applying the Tiebout model in the fashion suggested here to justify comparative advantages as efficient requires (problematically for those seeking to do so) disturbing base assumptions of the comparative advantage model, specifically the possibility of factor mobility across countries.

114 See Hahnel and Albert, *Quiet Revolution in Welfare Economics*, 240; and literatures referred to in Bratton and McCahery, 'New Economics of Jurisdictional Competition'.

115 Bratton and McCahery, ibid., 230. Contesting the notion that private law rules are efficient was a theme of the small cadre of academics from the Critical Legal Studies movement who engaged with claims to the contrary made by (some) Law and Economics scholars. See for example Kennedy and Michelman, 'Are Property and Contract Efficient?'; Kelman, *Guide to Critical Legal Studies*, chapter 5.

116 Bratton and McCahery, ibid., 222–25.

117 Ibid., 225–30.

118 See ibid., 209. See also notes 80–82 above and associated text.

Chapter Six   Conclusion by Way of *Ideologiekritik*: Fiction and Rationalization

1 Samuelson, 'Foreword', ix–x.

2 Although ideology and its critique in their contemporary guises are importantly related to the tradition of Marx and those who followed him, it will be clear that my use of ideology – and the critique that I advance here – is more modest than is often the case in Marxian strains of the same. Here I diagnose and critique the ideology of which comparative advantage is a part, and its resultant effects. I do not attempt to provide the additional argumentation required to establish purposive 'functional' claims concerning that ideology and those effects (for example, to establish the claim that the 'purpose' of comparative advantage is to generate the effects that I identify, or even that the deployment of comparative advantage has such a purpose). As to the necessary (though often omitted) steps to establish such arguments see Elster, 'Marxism, Functionalism, and Game Theory', and related debate in Cohen, 'A Reply to Elster'; Van Parijs, 'Functionalist Marxism Rehabilitated'; Jon Elster, 'Reply to Comments'. For helpful treatments of ideology in various forms and incarnations, and for various uses, see Geuss, *The Idea of Critical Theory*; Larrain, *The Concept of Ideology* and *Marxism and Ideology*; Eagleton, *Ideology: An Introduction*; Plamenatz, *Ideology*; Žižek (ed.), *Mapping Ideology* and essays collected therein; Kennedy, *A Critique of Adjudication*, especially parts 3 and 4.

3 As mentioned in the opening chapter to this work, economics is a knowledge that explains, and by implication justifies, aspects of the social world. The task of giving meaning to the social world and the criteria and terms used in doing so has obviously changed and evolved over time. Theistic or religious accounts

of meaning were replaced by naturalizing explanations (or vice versa, in some cases), and so on. Sometimes elements of one method of giving meaning might coexist with elements from others. For the time being, I leave these issues to the side. For present purposes, I concern myself only with the effect of rationalization, which, in our disenchanted Weberian modernity, remains the dominant explanatory relation that we use to examine the social world.

4 See note 13 to chapter 1 and references mentioned therein. See also Heilbroner, *Nature and Logic of Capitalism*, 107.

5 Mankiw, *Principles of Economics*, 188.

6 See further, Langholm, *Legacy of Scholasticism in Economic Thought* and *Price and Value*; Landreth and Colander, *History of Economic Thought*, 34–39.

7 Foley, *Adam's Fallacy*, 3.

8 This is, as I have discussed on several occasions, precisely the structure of criticism of arguments for protectionism.

9 But see discussion in note 3 to chapter 3.

10 See note 100 to chapter 5 and accompanying text.

11 See also, Heilbroner, *Nature and Logic of Capitalism*, 114.

12 For interesting analogous discussions within the field of moral philosophy, see MacIntyre, *After Virtue*, especially chapter 6.

13 See note 110 to chapter 5 and discussion therein.

14 See note 111 to chapter 5 and accompanying text.

15 See also Landreth and Colander, *History of Economic Thought*, 44.

16 I take some inspiration from the related (though different) point being made in Blecker, 'International Economics after Robinson', 341.

17 Ibid.

18 Robinson, *Reflections on the Theory of International Trade*, 141.

19 This is, of course, all the more salient given the incompleteness of the evaluative considerations that mainstream economic analysis is willing to countenance.

20 See note 109 to chapter 5 and accompanying text.

21 See also Brenner, 'Origins of Capitalist Development', 91; Kennedy, 'Role of Law in Economic Thought', 964 (albeit in a different context). Kennedy has pointed out the manner in which mainstream economic thought frames the question of the economy as one of choosing between the free market and regulation, and particularly, between efficiency (understood to be enshrined in the outcomes of markets) and equitable distribution. This diagnosis is – in my view – entirely correct.

22 See also and generally, Chang and Grabel, *Reclaiming Development*.

23 David Kennedy has written extensively – though in quite a different way, and from quite a different (sociologically/quasi-sociologically informed) perspective – about the expertise and role of experts. See for example Kennedy, 'Challenging Expert Rule'; *Dark Sides of Virtue*; 'Laws and Developments'; 'International Style in Postwar Law and Policy'.

24 MacIntyre, *After Virtue*, 77.

25 See note 65 to chapter 5 and accompanying text.

26 Samuelson, 'Response from Paul A. Samuelson', 242. For example, see Dixit and Grossman, 'Comment: The Limits of Free Trade'.

27 Ibid., emphasis added.

28 To be clear, Samuelson cast only limited doubt on the theory of international
    trade and its conclusions. Accordingly, I am not claiming that he should
    necessarily have abandoned these entirely. However, a somewhat chastened
    attitude to the standard economic predictions concerning free trade *does* seem
    to be appropriate on Samuelson's part. What seems less appropriate is his
    claim that the reason to continue to pursue free trade is 'nonequivocal', or the
    justificatory criteria to which he shifts his support of free trade.
29 See, again, note 13 to chapter 1 and references mentioned therein.

BIBLIOGRAPHY

Aliber, Robert Z. 'Exchange Rates'. In *The New Palgrave: A Dictionary of Economics*, edited by Peter Newman, John Eatwell, and Murray Milgate. London: Palgrave Macmillan, 1987.

Alonso, José, and Carlos Garcimartin. 'A New Approach to the Balance-of-Payments Constraint: Some Empirical Evidence'. *Journal of Post Keynesian Economics* 21, no. 2 (1998): 259–82.

Amin, Samir. *Accumulation on a World Scale*. Translated by Brian Pearce. New York: Monthly Review Press, 1974.

———. *Unequal Development: An Essay on the Social Formations of Peripheral Capitalism*. Translated by Brian Pearce. New York: Monthly Review Press, 1976.

Amsden, Alice H. *The Rise of 'The Rest': Challenges to the West from Late-Industrialization Economies*. New York: Oxford University Press, 2001.

Anderson, Elizabeth. *Value in Ethics and Economics*. Cambridge, MA: Harvard University Press, 1995.

Arestis, Philip, and William Milberg. 'Degree of Monopoly, Pricing, and Flexible Exchange Rates'. *Journal of Post Keynesian Economics* 16, no. 2 (1993): 167–88.

Arnsperger, Christian, and Yani Varoufakis. 'What is Neoclassical Economics? The Three Axioms Responsible for its Theoretical Oeuvre, Practical Irrelevance and, thus, Discursive Power'. *Panoeconomicus* 53, no. 1 (2006): 5–18.

Arrighi, Giovanni, and Beverly J. Silver. *Chaos and Governance in the Modern World System* Minneapolis: University of Minnesota Press, 1999.

Arrow, Kenneth J. *Social Choice and Individual Values*. New York: Wiley, 1963.

———. 'Political and Economic Evaluation of Social Effects and Externalities'. In *Frontiers of Quantitative Economics*, edited by Michael D. Intriligator and D. A. Kendrick. Amsterdam: North-Holland, 1974.

Baiman, Ron. 'Unequal Exchange Without a Labor Theory of Prices: On the Need for a Global Marshall Plan and a Solidarity Trading Regime'. *Review of Radical Political Economics* 38, no. 1 (2006): 71–89.

Baker, Dean. 'Trade and Inequality: The Role of Economists'. *Real-World Economics Review* 45 (2003): 23–32.

Balassa, Bela. 'An Empirical Demonstration of Classical Comparative Cost Theory'. *Review of Economics and Statistics* 45, no. 3 (1963): 231–38.

Bank for International Settlements. *Triennial Central Bank Survey – Preliminary global results – Turnover (September 2010)*. http://www.bis.org/publ/rpfx10.htm.

Baran, Paul A., and Paul M. Sweezy. *Monopoly Capitalism: An Essay on the American Social Order*. New York: Monthly Review Press, 1968.

Barry, Brian. 'Humanity and Justice in Global Perspective'. In *NOMOS XXIV, Ethics Economics and the Law*, edited by J. R. Pennock and J. W. Chapman. New York: NYU Press, 1982.

Bator, Francis M. 'The Simple Analytics of Welfare Maximization'. *American Economic Review* 47, no. 1 (1957): 22–59.

Baumol, W. J. 'Say's (at Least) Eight Laws, or What Say and James Mill May Really Have Meant'. *Economica* 44, no. 174 (1977): 145–61.

Beitz, Charles R. 'Justice and International Relations'. *Philosophy and Public Affairs* 4, no. 4 (1975): 360–89.

_____. 'Bounded Morality: Justice and the State in World Politics'. *International Organization* 33, no. 3 (1979): 405–24.

Bentham, Jeremy. *Principles of the Civil Code*. Edinburgh: William Tait, 1843.

Bhagwati, Jagdish. 'The Pure Theory of International Trade: A Survey'. *Economic Journal* 74, no. 293 (1964): 1–84.

_____. *Protectionism*. Cambridge, MA: MIT Press, 1988.

_____. 'Free Trade: What Now?' Keynote Address delivered at the University of St. Gallen, Switzerland, 25 May 1998 on the occasion of the International Management Symposium at which the 1998 Freedom Prize of the Max Schmidheiny Foundation was awarded. http://academiccommons.columbia.edu/catalog/ac:123560.

Bhagwati, Jagdish, and T. N. Srinivasan. *Lectures on International Trade*. Cambridge, MA: MIT Press, 1983.

Blau, H. 'A Direct Proof of Arrow's Theorem'. *Econometrica* 40 (1972): 61–67.

Blecker, Robert A. 'International Capital Mobility, Macroeconomic Imbalances, and the Risk of Global Contraction'. In *International Capital Markets: Systems in Transition*, edited by Lance Taylor and John Eatwell. New York: Oxford University Press, 2002.

_____. 'International Economics'. In *The Elgar Companion to Post Keynesian Economics*, edited by John King. Cheltenham: Edward Elgar Publishing, 2003.

_____. 'Financial Globalization, Exchange Rates and International Trade'. In *Financialization and the World Economy*, edited by A. Epstein. Cheltenham: Edward Elgar Publishing, 2005.

_____. 'International Economics after Robinson'. In *The Economics of Joan Robinson: A Centennial Celebration*, edited by Bill Gibson. Cheltenham: Edward Elgar Publishing, 2005.

_____. 'Stolper–Samuelson after Kalecki: International Trade and Income Distribution with Oligopolistic Mark-Ups and Partial Pass-Through'. 2008. http://nw08.american.edu/~blecker/research/BleckerTradeModel-EEA 2009.pdf

Bliss, C. J. 'Heterogeneous Capital and the Heckscher–Ohlin–Samuelson Theory of Trade: Discussion'. In *Essays in Modern Economics*, edited by Michael Parkin and A. R. Nobay. London: Longman, 1972.

Bose, Arun. 'The "Labour Approach" and the "Commodity Approach" in Mr. Sraffa's Price Theory'. *Economic Journal* 74, no. 295 (1964): 722–26.

_____. *Marx on Exploitation and Inequality*. Oxford: Oxford University Press, 1980.

Boudreaux, Donald J. 'Does Increased International Mobility of Factors of Production Weaken the Case for Free Trade?' *Cato Journal* 23, no. 3 (2004): 373–79.

Bowles, Samuel. 'Endogenous Preferences: The Cultural Consequences of Markets and other Economic Institutions'. *Journal of Economic Literature* 36, no. 1 (1998): 75–111.

Bratton, William W., and Joseph A. McCahery. 'The New Economics of Jurisdictional Competition: Devolutionary Federalism in a Second-Best World'. *Georgetown Law Journal* 86, no. 2 (1997): 201–78.

Brenner, Robert. 'The Origins of Capitalist Development: A Critique of Neo-Smithian Marxism'. *New Left Review* 104, no. 1 (1977): 25–92.

———. 'The Social Basis for Economic Development'. In *Analytical Marxism: Studies in Marxism and Social Theory*, edited by John Roemer. Cambridge: Cambridge University Press, 1986.

———. *The Boom and the Bubble: The US in the Global Economy*. London: Verso, 2002.

———. *The Economics of Global Turbulence*. London: Verso, 2006.

Caves, Richard E., Jeffrey A. Frankel, and Ronald W. Jones. *World Trade and Payments: An Introduction*, 10th edition. Boston: Pearson, 2006.

Chang, Ha-Joon. *Kicking away the Ladder*. London: Anthem Press, 2002.

———. *Bad Samaritans*. New York: Bloomsbury Press, 2007.

Chang, Ha-Joon, and Irene Grabel. *Reclaiming Development*. London: Zed Books, 2004.

Chipman, John S. 'International Trade'. In *The New Palgrave: A Dictionary of Economics*, edited by Peter Newman, John Eatwell, and Murray Milgate. London: Palgrave Macmillan, 1987.

Chipman, John S., and J. C. Moore. 'The New Welfare Economics 1939–1974'. *International Economic Review* 19, no. 3 (1978): 547–84.

Chrystal, K. Alec. 'International Monetary Arrangements and International Trade'. In *International Capital Markets: Systems in Transition*, edited by Lance Taylor and John Eatwell. New York: Oxford University Press, 2002.

Coase, Ronald H. 'The Problem of Social Cost'. *Journal of Law and Economics* 3 (1960): 1–44.

Cohen, Avi J., and G. C. Harcourt. 'Retrospectives: Whatever Happened to the Cambridge Capital Theory Controversies?' *Journal of Economic Perspectives* 17, no. 1 (2003): 199–214.

Cohen, G. A. *Karl Marx's Theory of History: A Defence*. Princeton: Princeton University Press, 1978.

———. 'A Reply to Elster on "Marxism, Functionalism, and Game Theory"'. *Theory and Society* 11, no. 4 (1982): 483–95.

———. *History, Labour, and Freedom: Themes from Marx*. New York: Oxford University Press, 1988.

Cohen, Morris R. 'Property and Sovereignty'. *Law and the Social Order: Essays in Legal Philosophy*. New Brunswick: Transaction Books, 1933.

———. 'The Basis of Contract'. *Harvard Law Review* 46, no. 4 (1933): 553–92.

Colander, David C., Richard P. F. Holt, and J. Barkley Rosser Jr. 'The Changing Face of Mainstream Economics'. *Review of Political Economy* 16, no. 4 (2004): 485–99.

Commons, John R. *The Legal Foundations of Capitalism*. New York: Macmillan, 1924.

Copeland, Laurence S. *Exchange Rates and International Finance*. Harlow: Pearson, 2005.

Corry, B. A. 'Robert Torrens'. In *The New Palgrave: A Dictionary of Economics*, edited by Peter Newman, John Eatwell, and Murray Milgate. London: Palgrave Macmillan, 1987.

Cypher, James and Dietz, James. *The Process of Economic Development*. Oxford: Routledge, 2004.

Davidson, Donald. *Inquiries into Truth and Interpretation*. Oxford: Clarendon Press, 1984.

Davidson, Paul. *John Maynard Keynes*. London: Palgrave Macmillan, 2009.

Davis, John B. 'The Turn in Economics: Neoclassical Dominance to Mainstream Pluralism?'. *Journal of Institutional Economics* 2, no. 1 (2006): 1–20.

Deardorff, A. 'Testing Trade Theories and Predicting Trade Flows'. In *Handbook of International Economics, Volume 1*, edited by R. W. Kenen, and R. B. Jones. Amsterdam: North-Holland, 1984.

de Janvery, Alain, and Frank Kramer. 'The Limits of Unequal Exchange'. *Review of Radical Political Economics* 11, no. 4 (1979): 3–15.

Dernburg, Thomas F. *Global Macroeconomics*. London: Harper Collins, 1989.

Dixit, Avinash, Gene Grossman, and Paul A. Samuelson. 'The Limits of Free Trade'. *Journal of Economic Perspectives* 19, no. 3 (2005): 241–44.

Dixit, Avinash K., and Victor D. Norman. *Theory of International Trade*. Cambridge: Cambridge University Press, 1980.

Dornbusch, Rudiger. 'Expectations and Exchange Rate Dynamics'. *Journal of Political Economy* 84, no. 6 (1976): 1161–76.

Dosi, Giovanni. 'Institutions and Markets in a Dynamic World'. *The Manchester School* 56, no. 2 (1988): 119–46.

Dosi, Giovanni, and Luc Soete. 'Technical Change and International Trade'. in *Technical Change and Economic Theory*, edited by Giovanni Dosi, Christopher Freeman, Richard Nelson, Gerald Silverberg, and Luc L. Soete.. London: Pinter Publishers, 1990.

Driskill, R. 'Flexible Exchange Rates'. In *The New Palgrave: A Dictionary of Economics*, edited by Peter Newman, John Eatwell, and Murray Milgate. London: Palgrave Macmillan, 1987.

Dunoff, Jeffrey, Steven R. Ratner, and David Wippman. *International Law: Norms, Actors, Process*. New York: Aspen Publishers, 2006.

Eagleton, Terry. *Ideology: An Introduction*. London: Verso, 1991.

Eatwell, John, and Lance Taylor. *Global Finance at Risk: The Case for International Regulation*. New York: New Press, 2000.

Eatwell, John, and Lance Taylor (eds.). *International Capital Markets: Systems in Transition*. New York: Oxford University Press, 2002.

Eichengreen, Barry. *Globalizing Capital: A History of the International Monetary System*. 2nd edition. Princeton: Princeton University Press, 2008.

Elster, Jon. 'Marxism, Functionalism, and Game Theory: The Case for Methodological Individualism'. *Theory and Society* 11, no. 4 (1982): 453–82.

_____. *Explaining Technical Change*. Cambridge: Cambridge University Press, 1983.

_____. 'Reply to Comments'. *Theory and Society* 12, no. 1 (1983): 111–20.

_____. 'A Plea for Mechanisms'. In *Social Mechanisms: An Analytical Approach to Social Theory*, edited by Peter Hedström and Richard Swedberg. Cambridge: Cambridge University Press, 1998.

_____. *Explaining Social Behavior: More Nuts and Bolts for the Social Sciences*. Cambridge: Cambridge University Press, 2007.

Emmanuel, Arghiri. *Unequal Exchange: A Study of Imperialism in Trade*. New York: Monthly Review Press, 1972.

Epstein, Gerald A. 'Introduction: Financialization and the World Economy'. In *Financialization and the World Economy*, edited by Epstein, A. Gerald. Cheltenham: Edward Elgar Publishing, 2005.

Fandel, Günter. *Theory of Production and Cost*. London: Springer, 1991.

Feldman, Allan M. 'Welfare Economics'. In *The New Palgrave: A Dictionary of Economics*, edited by Peter Newman, John Eatwell, and Murray Milgate. London: Palgrave Macmillan, 1987.

Ferguson, D. G. 'International Capital Mobility and Comparative Advantage: The Two-Country, Two-Factor Case'. *Journal of International Economics* 8, no. 3 (1978): 373–96.

Findlay, Ronald. *Trade and Specialization*. Hamondsworth: Penguin, 1970.

_____. 'Relative Prices, Growth and Trade in a Simple Ricardian System'. *Econometrica* 41, no. 161 (1974): 1–13.

_____. 'Comparative'. In *The New Palgrave: A Dictionary of Economics*, edited by Peter Newman, John Eatwell, and Murray Milgate. London: Palgrave Macmillan, 1987.

Fisher, William W. and Syed, Talha. 'Global Justice in Healthcare: Developing Drugs for the Developing World'. *University of California Davis Law Review* 40 (2007): 581–678.

Fleischacker, Samuel. *A Short History of Distributive Justice*. Cambridge, MA: Harvard University Press, 2004.

Foley, Duncan K. *Adam's Fallacy*. Cambridge, MA: Belknap Harvard, 2006.

Forbath, William E. *Law and the Shaping of the American Labor Movement*. Cambridge, MA: Harvard University Press, 1991.

Frankel, Jeffrey A., and Kenneth Froot. 'Chartists, Fundamentalists, and the Demand for Dollars'. In *Private Behaviour and Government Policy in Interdependent Economies*, edited by A. S. Courakis and M. P. Taylor. Oxford: Clarendon Press, 1990.

Frankel, Jeffrey A., and Rose, K. Andrew. 'Empirical Research on Nominal Exchange Rates'. In *Handbook of International Economics, Volume 3*, edited by G. Grossman and K. Rogoff. Amsterdam: North-Holland, 1995.

Fried, Barbara. *The Progressive Assault on Laissez-Faire: Robert Hale and the First Law and Economics Movement*. Cambridge, MA: Harvard University Press, 1998.

Geras, Norman. 'The Controversy about Marx and Justice'. In *Marxist Theory*, edited by Alex Callinicos. New York: Oxford University Press, 1989.

_____. 'Bringing Marx to Justice: An Addendum and Rejoinder'. *New Left Review* 195 (1992): 37–69.

Geuss, Raymond. *The Idea of Critical Theory: Habermas and the Frankfurt School*. Cambridge: Cambridge University Press, 1981.

Gintis, Herbert M. 'Alienation and Power: Towards a Radical Welfare Economics'. PhD dissertation, Harvard University, 1969.

Gomory, Ralph E., and William J. Baumol *Global Trade and Conflicting National Interests.* Cambridge, MA: MIT Press, 2000.

Graaff, J. de V. *Theoretical Welfare Economics.* Vol. 446 of Cambridge University Press Archive, 1967.

Haberler, Gottfried. *The Theory of International Trade.* New York: Augustus M. Kelley, 1936.

Hahnel, Robin. *Panic Rules!* Cambridge: South End Press, 1999.

———. *The ABCs of Political Economy: A Modern Approach.* London: Pluto Press, 2002.

———. 'Exploitation: A Modern Approach'. *Review of Radical Political Economics* 38, no. 2 (2006): 175–92.

Hahnel, Robin, and Michael Albert. *Quiet Revolution in Welfare Economics.* Princeton: Princeton University Press, 1990.

Hale, Robert L. 'Coercion and Distribution in a Supposedly Non-Coercive State'. *Political Science Quarterly* 38, no. 3 (1923): 470–94.

———. 'Bargaining, Duress, and Economic Liberty'. *Columbia Law Review* 43 (1943): 603–28.

Hallwood, Paul C., and Ronald MacDonald. *International Money and Finance.* 3rd edition. Oxford: Blackwell, 2000.

Harcourt, G. C. *Some Cambridge Controversies in the Theory of Capital.* Cambridge: Cambridge University Press, 1972.

———. 'Capital Theory Controversies'. In *The Elgar Companion to Radical Political Economy*, edited by Philip Arestis and Malcolm Sawyer. Aldershot: Edward Elgar Publishing, 1994.

Harsanyi, John C. 'Utilities, Preferences, and Substantive Goods'. *Social Choice and Welfare* 14, no. 1 (1997): 129.

Harvey, David. *The Limits to Capital.* London: Verso, 2007.

Harvey, John T. 'Orthodox Approaches to Exchange Rate Determination: A Survey'. *Journal of Post Keynesian Economics* 18, no. 4 (1996): 567–83.

———. 'Exchange Rate Theory and "The Fundamentals"'. *Journal of Post Keynesian Economics* 24, no. 1 (2001): 3–15.

———. *Currencies, Capital Flows and Crises.* Oxford: Routledge, 2009.

Hayek, Friedrich A. 'The Use of Knowledge in Society' in Hayek, Friedrich A. *Individualism and Economic Order.* Chicago: University of Chicago Press, 1957.

Hegel, Georg Wilhelm Friedrich. *The Phenomenology of Mind: Volume 1*, translated by J. B. Baillie. New York: Cosimo Classics, 2006.

Heilbroner, Robert L. *The Nature and Logic of Capitalism.* New York: Norton, 1985.

Hicks, John R. 'The Foundations of Welfare Economics'. *The Economic Journal* 49, no. 196 (1939): 696–712.

———. 'The Valuation of Social Income'. *Economica* 7, no. 26 (1940): 105–24.

Hodgson, Geoffrey M. *Economics and Institutions.* Cambridge: Polity Press, 1988.

———. *The Evolution of Institutional Economics.* London: Routledge, 2004.

Hohfeld, Wesley N. 'Some Fundamental Legal Conceptions as Applied in Judicial Reasoning'. *Yale Law Journal* 23, no. 1 (1913): 16–59.

Holmes Jr, Oliver Wendell. 'Privilege, Malice, and Intent' *Harvard Law Review* 8, no. 1 (1894): 1–14.

———. 'The Path of the Law'. *Harvard Law Review* 10, no. 8 (1897): 457–78.

Hume, David. 'Of the Balance of Trade'. *Writings on Economics*. Madison: University of Wisconsin Press, 1955.

Hunt, Earl B. *The Mathematics of Behavior*. Cambridge: Cambridge University Press, 2007.

Hunt, E. K. 'A Radical Critique of Welfare Economics'. In *Growth, Profits and Property*, edited by Edward J. Nell. Cambridge: Cambridge University Press, 1980.

_____. *History of Economic Thought: A Critical Perspective*. 2nd edition. New York: ME Sharpe, 2002.

Ingham, Geoffrey. 'On the Underdevelopment of the "Sociology of Money"'. *Acta Sociologica* 41, no. 1 (1999): 3–18.

_____. *The Nature of Money*. Cambridge: Polity Press, 2004.

Irwin, Douglas. *Against the Tide: An Intellectual History of Free Trade*. Princeton: Princeton University Press, 1996.

_____. *Free Trade under Fire*. 3rd ed. Princeton: Princeton University Press, 2009.

Johnson, George E., and Frank P. Stafford. 'International Competition and Real Wages'. *American Economic Review* 82, no. 2 (1993): 127–30.

Jones, Ronald W. 'Heckscher–Ohlin trade. In *The New Palgrave: A Dictionary of Economics*, edited by Peter Newman, John Eatwell, and Murray Milgate. London: Palgrave Macmillan, 1987.

Kaldor, Nicholas. 'Welfare Propositions in Economics and Interpersonal Comparisons of Utility'. *Economic Journal* 49, no. 195 (1939): 549–52.

Kaplow, Louis, and Steven Shavell. *Fairness versus Welfare*. Cambridge, MA: Harvard University Press, 2002.

Keen, Steve. *Debunking Economics*. Annandale: Pluto Press Australia, 2002.

Kelman, Mark. 'Consumption Theory, Production Theory, and Ideology in the Coase Theorem'. *Southern California Law Review* 52 (1979): 669–98.

_____. 'Misunderstanding Social Life: A Critique of the Core Premises of Law and Economics'. *Journal of Legal Education* 33 (1983): 274–84.

_____. *A Guide to Critical Legal Studies*. Cambridge, MA: Harvard University Press, 1987.

_____. 'Could Lawyers Stop Recessions? Speculations on Law and Macroeconomics'. *Stanford Law Review* 45 (1993): 1215–1310.

Kennedy, David. 'The International Style in Postwar Law and Policy'. *Utah Law Review* 1 (1994): 7–103.

_____. 'Laws and Developments'. In *Law and Development: Facing Complexity in the 21st Century*, edited by Amanda Perry-Kessaris and John Hatchard. London: Cavendish Publishing, 2003.

_____. *The Dark Sides of Virtue: Reassessing International Humanitarianism*. Princeton: Princeton University Press, 2004.

_____. 'Challenging Expert Rule: The Politics of Global Governance'. *Sydney Law Review* 27 (2005): 5–28.

Kennedy, Duncan. 'Cost-Benefit Analysis of Entitlement Problems: A Critique'. *Stanford Law Review* 33 (1981): 387–445.

_____. 'The Role of Law in Economic Thought: Essays on the Fetishism of Commodities'. *American University Law Review* 34 (1985): 939–1001.

_____. *A Critique of Adjudication [fin de siècle]*. Cambridge, MA: Harvard University Press, 1997.

_____. 'Law-and-Economics from the Perspective of Critical Legal Studies'. In *The New Palgrave Dictionary of Economics and the Law*, edited by Peter Newman. London: Macmillan, 1998.

Kennedy, Duncan, and Frank Michelman. 'Are Property and Contract Efficient?' *Hofstra Law Review* 8 (1980): 711–70.

Keynes, John Maynard. *The General Theory of Employment, Interest and Money*. Orlando: Harcourt, 1964.

_____. *The Collected Writings of John Maynard Keynes, Volume XXIX*. London: Macmillan Press, 1971.

_____. *The Collected Writings of John Maynard Keynes Volume XIV*. London: Macmillan Press, 1971.

_____. *The Collected Writings of John Maynard Keynes Volume IX*. London: Macmillan Press, 1972.

Kishore, Vishaal. 'Free Trade and Comparative Advantage: A Study in Economic Sleight of Hand'. In *The Elgar Handbook of Political Economy and the Law* (forthcoming 2014).

Klausinger, Hansjorg. 'The Early Use of the Term "Veil of Money", in Schumpeter's Monetary Writings: A Comment on Patinkin and Steiger'. *Scandinavian Journal of Economics* 92, no. 4 (1990): 617–21.

Paul R. Krugman, 'Myths and Realities of U.S. Competitiveness'. *Pop Internationalism*. Cambridge, MA: MIT Press, 1996.

_____. *What Do Undergrads Need to Know about Trade? Pop Internationalism*. Cambridge, MA: MIT Press, 1996.

_____. 'Introduction: New Thinking about Trade Policy'. In *Strategic Trade Policy and the New International Economics*, edited by Paul R. Krugman. Cambridge, MA: MIT Press, 1986.

_____. 'Is Free Trade Passé?' *Journal of Economic Perspectives* 1, no. 2 (1987): 131–44.

_____. 'The Persistent US Trade Deficit'. *Australian Economic Papers* 27, no. 51 (1988): 149–58.

_____. 'Does the New Trade Theory Require a New Trade Policy?' *World Economy* 15, no. 4 (1992): 423–42.

_____. 'Ricardo's Difficult Idea'. Paper for Manchester Conference on Free Trade, March, 1996. http://web.mit.edu/krugman/www/ricardo.htm.

Krugman, Paul R., and Maurice Obstfeld. *International Economics: Theory and Policy*. 7th edition. Boston, MA: Pearson Addison-Wesley, 2006.

Kymlicka, Will. *Contemporary Political Philosophy: An Introduction*. 2nd edition. Oxford: Oxford University Press, 2001.

Landes, David. 'What Do Bosses Really Do?' *Journal of Economic History* 46, no. 3 (1986): 585–623.

Landreth, Harry and Colander, David C. *History of Economic Thought*. 4th edition. Boston: Houghton Mifflin, 2004.

Langholm, Odd. *Price and Value in the Aristotelian Tradition: A Study in Scholastic Economic Sources*. Oxford: Oxford University Press, 1979.

_____. *The Legacy of Scholasticism in Economic Thought*. Cambridge: Cambridge University Press, 1998.

Langille, Brian. 'General Reflections on the Relationship of Trade and Labor (Or: Fair Trade Is Free Trade's Destiny)'. In *Fair Trade and Harmonization*,

Volume 2: Legal Analysis edited by Jagdish Bhagwati and Robert E. Hudec. Cambridge, MA: MIT Press, 1996.

Lapavitsas, Costas. 'On Marx's Analysis of Money Hoarding in the Turnover of Capital'. *Review of Political Economy* 12, no. 2 (2000): 219–35.

Larrain, Jorge. *The Concept of Ideology*. Athens: University of Georgia Press, 1979.

———. *Marxism and Ideology*. Atlantic Highlands: Humanities Press, 1983.

Leamer, E. E., and J. Levinsohn. 'International Trade Theory and Evidence'. In *Handbook of International Economics, Volume 3*, edited by G. Grossman and K. Rogoff. Amsterdam: North-Holland, 1995.

Leontief, Wassily W. 'The Use of Indifference Curves in the Analysis of Foreign Trade'. *Quarterly Journal of Economics* 47, no. 3 (1933): 493–503.

———. 'Domestic Production and Foreign Trade: The American Capital Position Re-Examined'. *Proceedings of the American Philosophical Society* 97, no. 4 (1953): 332–49.

Lerner, A. P. 'The Diagrammatic Representation of Cost Conditions in International Trade'. *Economica* 37 (1932): 345–56.

List, Friedrich. *The National System of Political Economy*, Translated by G. A Matile. Philadelphia: JB Lippincott & Co, 1856.

Little, I. M. D. *A Critique of Welfare Economics*. 2nd ed. Oxford: Clarendon Press, 1957.

MacDonald, Ronald. 'Long-Run Exchange Rate Modelling: A Survey of the Recent Evidence'. *IMF Staff Papers* 42, no. 3 (1995): 437–89.

MacDougall, G. D. A. 'British and American exports'. *Economic Journal* 61, no. 244 (1951): 697–724.

MacIntyre, Alasdair. *After Virtue*. 3rd edition. Notre Dame: University of Notre Dame Press, 2007.

Mandel, Ernest. *Late Capitalism*. London: New Left Books, 1975.

Mandeville, Bernard. *The Fable of the Bees: or, Private Vices, Publick Benefits*. London: Penguin Classics, 1970.

Mankiw, N. Gregory. *Principles of Economics*. 5th edition. Mason: Thompson, 2008.

Marglin, Stephen A. 'What Do Bosses Do? The Origins and Functions of Hierarchy in Capitalist Production, Part I'. *Review of Radical Political Economics* 6, no. 2 (1974): 60–112.

———. *The Dismal Science: How Thinking Like an Economist Undermines Community*. Cambridge, MA: Harvard University Press, 2008.

Mark, Nelson C. 'Exchange Rates and Fundamentals: Evidence on Long-Horizon Predictability'. *American Economic Review* 85, no. 1 (1995): 201–18.

Marx, Karl. *The Poverty of Philosophy*. Chicago: Charles H. Kerr & Company, 1920.

———. *Capital: Volume I*. London: Penguin Classics, 1990.

———. *Capital: Volume III*. London: Penguin Classics, 1991.

McCloskey, Deirdre N. *The Rhetoric of Economics*. 2nd edition. Madison: University of Wisconsin Press, 1998.

———. *The Secret Sins of Economics*. Chicago: Prickly Paradigm Press, 2002.

McPherson, Michael. 'Efficiency and Liberty in the Productive Enterprise: Recent Work in the Economics of Work Organization'. *Philosophy and Public Affairs* 12, no. 4 (1983): 354–68.

Meese, Richard and Kenneth Rogoff. 'Empirical Exchange Rate Models of the Seventies: Do They Fit Out of Sample?' *Journal of International Economics* 14, no. 1 (1983): 3–24.

Metcalfe, J. C., and Ian Steedman. 'Heterogeneous Capital and the Heckcher–Ohlin–Samuelson Theory of Trade'. In *Essays in Modern Economics*, edited by Michael Parkin and A. R. Nobay. London: Longman, 1972.

Milberg, William. 'Say's Law in the Open Economy: Keynes's Rejection of the Theory of Comparative Advantage'. In *Keynes, Uncertainty and the Global Economy*, edited by Sheila C. Dow and John H. Hillard. Cheltenham: Edward Elgar Publishing, 2002.

_____. 'Is Absolute Advantage Passé? Towards a Post-Keynesian/Marxian Theory of International Trade'. In *Competition, Technology and Money*, edited by Mark A. Glick. Cheltenham: Edward Elgar Publishing, 1994.

Mill, James. *Commerce Defended*. London: C & R Baldwin, 1803.

Mill, John Stuart. 'The Corn Laws'. *Westminster Review* 3, no. 4 (1825): 394–420.

_____. *On Liberty*. 4th edition. London: Longmans, Green and Co, 1869.

_____. *Essays on Some Unsettled Questions of Political Economy*. 2nd edition. London: Longmans, Green and Co, 1874.

_____. *The Principles of Political Economy*. 7th edition. London: Longmans, Green and Co, 1909.

Miller, Richard W. *Analyzing Marx: Morality, Power and History*. Princeton: Princeton University Press, 1984.

Mundell, Robert A. 'International Trade and Factor Mobility'. *American Economic Review* 47, no. 3 (1957): 321–35.

Musgrave, Alan. '"Unreal Assumptions" in Economic Theory': The F-Twist Untwisted'. *Kyklos* 34, no. 3 (1981): 377–87.

Nozick, Robert. *Anarchy, State, and Utopia*. New York: Basic Books, 1974.

Ollman, Bertell. *Alienation: Marx's Concept of Man in Capitalist Society*. Cambridge: Cambridge University Press, 1971.

Pasinetti, Luigi L. and Scazzieri, Robert. 'Capital Theory: Paradoxes'. In *The New Palgrave: A Dictionary of Economics*, edited by Peter Newman, John Eatwell, and Murray Milgate. London: Palgrave Macmillan, 1987.

Patinkin, Don and Steiger, Otto. 'In Search of the "Veil of Money" and the "Neutrality of Money": A Note on the Origin of Terms'. *Scandinavian Journal of Economics* 91, no. 1 (1989): 131–46.

Pogge, Thomas W. *Realizing Rawls*. Ithaca: Cornell University Press, 1989.

_____. 'An Egalitarian Law of Peoples'. *Philosophy and Public Affairs* 23, no. 3 (1994): 195–224.

Polanyi, Karl. *The Great Transformation: The Political and Economic Origins of Our Time*. Boston: Beacon Press, 1944.

Prebisch, Raúl. *The Economic Development of Latin America and Its Principal Problems*. New York: United Nations, 1950.

Parkin, Michael, and A. R. Nobay (eds.). *Essays in Modern Economics*. London: Longman, 1972.

Paul, Joel. 'Free Trade, Regulatory Competition and the Autonomous Market Fallacy'. *Columbia Journal of European Law* 1 (1994): 31–62.

_____. 'Do International Trade Institutions Contribute to Economic Growth and Development'. *Virginia Journal of International Law* 44 (2003): 285–340.

Perdikis, Nicholas, and William A. Kerr. *Trade Theory and Empirical Evidence*. Manchester: Manchester University Press, 1998.

Plamenatz, John. *Ideology*. New York: Praeger, 1970.

Prasch, Robert E. 'Reassessing Comparative Advantage: the Impact of Capital Flows on the Argument for Laissez-Faire'. *Journal of Economic Issues* 29, no. 2 (1995): 427–33.

———. 'Reassessing the Theory of Comparative Advantage'. *Review of Political Economy* 8, no. 1 (1996): 37–56.

Radin, Margaret Jane. 'Property and Personhood'. *Stanford Law Review* 34 (1982): 957–1015.

———. 'Market Inalienability'. *Harvard Law Review* 100 (1986): 1849–1937.

———. *Contested Commodities*. Cambridge, MA: Harvard University Press, 2001.

Ricardo, David. *Principles of Political Economy and Taxation*. 3rd edition. London: John Murray, 1821.

Robbins, Lionel. *An Essay on the Nature and Significance of Economic Science*. London: Macmillan, 1932.

———. 'Interpersonal Comparisons of Utility: A Comment'. *Economic Journal* 43, no. 4 (1938): 635–41.

———. *Robert Torrens and the Evolution of Classical Economics*. London: Macmillan, 1958.

Robinson, Joan. *Essays in the Theory of Employment*. 2nd edition. Oxford: Blackwell, 1947.

———. 'Inaugural Lecture (Cambridge October 15, 1965)'. *Collected Economic Papers Volume IV*. New York: Humanities Press, 1973.

———. 'The Need for a Reconsideration of the Theory of International Trade'. *Collected Economic Papers Volume IV*. New York: Humanities Press, 1973.

———. *Reflections on the Theory of International Trade*. Manchester: Manchester University Press, 1974.

———. 'History versus Equilibrium'. *Collected Economic Papers Volume V*. Oxford: Basil Blackwell, 1979.

———. 'Kalecki and Keynes'. *Collected Economic Papers Volume III*. Oxford: Basil Blackwell, 1975.

Roemer, John. *A General Theory of Exploitation and Class*. Cambridge, MA: Harvard University Press, 1982.

———. 'Unequal Exchange, Labor Migration and International Capital Flows: A Theoretical Synthesis'. In *Marxism, Central Planning, and the Soviet Economy*, edited by Padma Desai. Cambridge, MA: MIT Press, 1983.

———. *Free to Lose*. Cambridge, MA: Harvard University Press, 1986.

Rogoff, Kenneth. 'The Failure of Empirical Exchange Rate Models: No Longer New, but Still True'. Economic Policy Web Essay, 2001. http://www.economic-policy.org/pdfs/responses/Kenneth-Rogoff.pdf.

Roosevelt, Frank. 'Cambridge Economics as Commodity Fetishism'. In *Growth, Profits and Property*, edited by Edward J. Nell. Cambridge: Cambridge University Press, 1980.

Samuels, Warren J. 'The Economy as a System of Power and its Legal Bases: The Legal Economics of Robert Lee Hale'. *University of Miami Law Review* 27 (1973): 261–371.

Samuels, Warren J., Steven G. Medema, and A. Allan Schmid. 'The Concept of Cost in Economics'. *The Economy as a Process of Valuation*. Cheltenham: Edward Elgar Publishing, 1997.

Samuelson, Paul A. 'Parable and Realism in Capital Theory: The Surrogate Production Function'. *Review of Economic Studies* 29, no. 3 (1962): 193–206.

_____. 'A Summing Up'. *Quarterly Journal of Economics* 80, no. 4 (1966): 568–83.

_____. 'The Way of an Economist'. *International Economic Relations: Proceedings of the Third Congress of the International Economic Association.* London: MacMillan, 1969.

_____. 'Little Nobel Lecture of 1972'. *The Collected Scientific Papers of Paul A. Samuelson Volume 4.* Cambridge, MA: MIT Press, 1979.

_____. Foreword. *The Principles of Economics Course: A Handbook for Instructors.* By Phillip Saunders and William B. Walstad. New York: McGraw-Hill, 1990.

_____. 'Where Ricardo and Mill Rebut and Confirm Arguments of Mainstream Economists Supporting Globalization'. *Journal of Economics Perspectives* 18, no. 3 (2004): 135–46.

_____. 'Response from Paul A. Samuelson'. *Journal of Economics Perspectives* 19, no. 3 (2005): 242–44.

Sardoni, Claudio. 'Marx and Keynes: The Critique of Say's Law'. In *Marx and Modern Economic Analysis Volume II*, edited by G. A. Caravale. Aldershot: Elgar, 1991.

_____. 'Say's Law'. In *The Elgar Companion to Post Keynesian Economics*, edited by John King. Cheltenham: Edward Elgar Publishing, 2003.

Sarno, Lucio, and Mark P. Taylor. *The Economics of Exchange Rates.* Cambridge: Cambridge University Press, 2002.

Scanlon, Thomas M. 'The Moral Basis of Interpersonal Comparisons'. In *Interpersonal Comparison of Well-being*, edited by Jon Elster and John Roemer. Cambridge: Cambridge University Press, 1991.

Schlag, Pierre. 'An Appreciative Comment on Coase's *The Problem of Social Cost*: A View from the Left'. *Wisconsin Law Review* (1986): 919–62.

_____. 'The Problem of Transaction Costs'. *Southern California Law Review* 62 (1989): 1661–1700.

Schmid, Allan A. 'Law and Economics: An Institutional Perspective', In *Law and Economics*, edited by Nicholas Mecuro. Boston: Kluwer Academic, 1989.

Scitovsky, Tibor. 'A Note on Welfare Propositions in Economics'. *Review of Economic Studies* 9, no. 1 (1941): 77–88.

Sen, Amartya K. 'Personal Utilities and Public Judgements: Or What's Wrong with Welfare Economics'. *Economic Journal* 89 (1979): 537–58.

_____. *On Ethics and Economics.* Oxford: Blackwell, 1992.

Shaikh, Anwar. 'On the Laws of International Exchange'. In *Growth, Profits and Property*, edited by Edward J. Nell. Cambridge: Cambridge University Press, 1980.

Shoul, B. 'Karl Marx and Say's Law'. *Quarterly Journal of Economics* 71, no, 4 (1957): 611–29.

Singer, Hans. 'The Distribution of Gains between Investing and Borrowing Countries'. *American Economics Review* 40, no. 2 (1950): 473–85.

Smith, Adam. *The Wealth of Nations.* New York: Bantham Classics, 2003.

_____. *The Theory of Moral Sentiments.* Amherst: Prometheus Books, 2000.

Sowell, Thomas. *Say's Law: An Historical Analysis.* Princeton: Princeton University Press, 1972.

_____. 'Say's Law'. In *The New Palgrave: A Dictionary of Economics*, edited by Peter Newman, John Eatwell, and Murray Milgate. London: Palgrave Macmillan, 1987.

Sraffa, Piero. *The Production of Commodities by Means of Commodities.* Cambridge: Cambridge University Press, 1960.

Steedman, Ian. *Marx after Sraffa.* London: Verso, 1977.

———, ed. *Fundamental Issues in Trade Theory.* New York: St Martin's Press, 1979.

Stern, Robert M. 'British and American Productivity and Comparative Costs in International Trade'. *Oxford Economic Papers* 14, no. 3 (1962): 275–96.

Strange, Susan. *Mad Money.* Manchester: Manchester University Press, 1998.

Tarullo, Daniel. 'Beyond Normalcy in the Regulation of International Trade'. *Harvard Law Review* 100 (1987): 546–628.

Taylor, Lance. *Reconstructing Macroeconomics.* Cambridge, MA: Harvard University Press, 2004.

———. 'Exchange Rate Indeterminacy in Portfolio Balance, Mundell-Fleming and Uncovered Interest Rate Parity Models'. *Cambridge Journal of Economics* 28, no. 2 (2004): 205–27.

Thompson, E. P. *The Poverty of Theory and Other Essays.* London: Merlin Press, 1978.

Thornton, Henry. *An Enquiry into the Nature and Effect of the Paper Credit of Great Britain.* London: J. Hatchard et al., 1802.

Tiebout, Charles M. 'A Pure Theory of Local Expenditures'. *Journal of Political Economy* 64, no. 5 (1956): 416–24.

Torrens, Robert. *An Essay on the External Corn Trade.* London: J. Hatchard, 1815.

———. *The Budget: On Commercial and Colonial Policy.* London: Smith, Elder, 1844.

Trachtman, Joel P. 'International Regulatory Competition Externalization, and Jurisdiction'. *Harvard International Law Journal* 34 (1993): 47–104.

UNCTAD. *Trade and Development Report 2009,* http://unctad.org/en/Pages/PublicationArchive.aspx?publicationid=2167.

———. *Trade and Development Report 2008,* http://www.unctad.org/en/docs/tdr2008_en.pdf.

Unger, Roberto Mangabeira. *Free Trade Reimagined.* Princeton: Princeton University Press, 2008.

van Parijs, Philippe. 'Functionalist Marxism Rehabilitated'. *Theory and Society* 11, no. 4 (1982): 497–511.

Veblen, Thorstein. 'Professor Clark's Economics'. *Quarterly Journal of Economics* 22, no. 2 (1908): 147–95.

Viner, Jacob. *Studies in the Theory of International Trade.* New York: Harper and Brothers, 1937.

von Mises, Ludwig. *Human Action: A Treatise on Economics.* 4th edition. San Francisco: Fox & Wilkes, 1963.

Weeks, John. *Capital and Exploitation.* Princeton: Princeton University Press, 1982.

Wertheimer, Alan. *Exploitation.* Princeton: Princeton University Press, 1996.

Wilson, Neil L. 'Substances Without Substrata'. *Review of Metaphysics* 12, no. 4 (1959): 521–39.

World Trade Organization. *International Trade Statistics 2012,* http://www.wto.org/english/res_e/statis_e/its2012_e/its2012_e.pdf.

Žižek, Slavoj, ed. *Mapping Ideology.* London: Verso, 1995.

INDEX

Numbers in bold refer to tables and figures.

Printed in the USA
CPSIA information can be obtained
at www.ICGtesting.com
JSHW082202140824
68134JS00014B/387